THE DRAGON HAS TWO TONGUES

THE DRAGON HAS TWO TONGUES

Essays on
Anglo-Welsh Writers and Writing
by
Glyn Jones

Revised edition

Edited with an introduction and notes
by
Tony Brown

UNIVERSITY OF WALES PRESS
CARDIFF
2001

British Library Cataloguing-in-Publication Data.
A catalogue record for this book is available from the British Library.

ISBN 0–7083–1693–X

THE ASSOCIATION FOR
WELSH WRITING IN ENGLISH
CYMDEITHAS LLÊN SAESNEG CYMRU

Typeset at University of Wales Press
Printed in Great Britain by Dinefwr Press, Llandybïe

Er cof am
Doreen

CONTENTS

PREFACE TO REVISED EDITION

DURING the closing years of his long life, Glyn Jones expressed the wish that *The Dragon has Two Tongues*, the first book-length study of the English-language literature of Wales, be republished. Discussion ensued, with my colleague Dr John Pikoulis and then with myself, as to quite what form this should take, given that some quarter of a century had ensued since its original publication, years in which, of course, much new writing, both creative and critical, had appeared. Glyn himself went through the text of *The Dragon*, identifying what would need updating and drafting some revisions to passages in the early chapters. He also drafted a Preface to the new edition, which indicated his intentions:

> *The Dragon has Two Tongues* was first published in 1968. I had intended in writing it that it should deal with a certain group of writers of our country and with certain events and literary developments during the previous thirty years or so in which these writers had been involved.
>
> I think it would be a mistake for someone with my experience to try to bring up to date here what I had to say in 1968. Far too much has changed in Wales for me to attempt to do this adequately. The events of the last quarter of a century surely deserve treatment in a book by a different hand.

Glyn Jones felt, however, that clearly some revisions had to be undertaken − the insertion of dates of the deaths of those writers who had died since 1968, the correction, in his words, of 'some errors of fact' and the removal of 'a few infelicities of expression'. He also wanted to incorporate as many as possible of the footnotes in the original edition into the text.

I have attempted as closely as possible to follow Glyn Jones's wishes in editing this new text, including consulting his own copy of the book which contains his marginal queries. The death of some authors whom he discussed has of course necessitated some alteration of tenses, and some passages which deal with factual and statistical matters now well out of date have been revised or removed. Some explanatory notes have been added. The attempt has been, in other words, to produce a text which has few obvious signs of datedness and and to allow Glyn Jones's account of the evolution of Wales's English-language literature and his reflections on that first generation of writers, the writers whom he knew personally, to speak to the reader as freshly and directly as ever.

Glyn Jones dedicated the original edition of *The Dragon has Two Tongues* to his wife, Doreen. This edition is dedicated to her memory.

ACKNOWLEDGEMENTS

I should like to express my indebtedness and gratitude to the following: Cyngor Llyfrau Cymraeg (the Welsh Books Council) for their kindness in answering my questions; the Town Clerk of Merthyr Tydfil and the Director of Education for Glamorgan for a similar courtesy; Mr Brynmor Jones of the National Library of Wales for undertaking to read my book in manuscript and for allowing me to see his unpublished bibliography of Anglo-Welsh writers.

EDITOR'S ACKNOWLEDGEMENTS FOR THE REVISED EDITION

My greatest debt is, of course, to Glyn Jones himself, for many fascinating and happy hours of discussion about his writing, including the present volume. I am also much indebted to the preliminary textual work on *The Dragon has Two Tongues* which was undertaken by my colleague Dr John Pikoulis; Dr Pikoulis's sharp eye identified many of the textual issues which I needed to consider and resolve, including some that I might otherwise have missed. I am also extremely grateful to Mrs Linda Jones, Research Administrator in the Department of English, University of Wales, Bangor, both for her detailed work in transferring the text into an electronic form and for her constantly reassuring assistance with proofs. My thanks are due to Dr Meic Stephens for supplying me with bibliographical information on Glyn Jones and Gwyn Thomas. As ever I am deeply grateful to Sara and Alys (who remember Glyn Jones fondly as the first 'real writer' they met) and Nancy for all their support – and their tolerance.

INTRODUCTION

I was a boy with a romantic spirit and, like my father, a great reader.
I would consume so many books that Mam would sometimes turn
to me and say: 'For goodness' sake take your nose out of that old book
for a change'.[1]

THIS is Glyn Jones at the age of fourteen. What was he reading, this
imaginative, romantic young boy, brought up in a Welsh-speaking
family in Merthyr Tydfil in the early years of the twentieth century? Glyn
Jones lists some of them in the same memoir: Captain Marryat's *Children
of the New Forest* and *Mr Midshipman Easy*, Sir Walter Scott's *Ivanhoe*,
Quentin Durward and *Kenilworth*, the novels of Robert Louis Stevenson,
Tom Brown's Schooldays, and the novels of G. A. Henty. Not only are these
books in English, of course, but they include books whose essential
ideology was that of the English middle classes: the public school and its
ethics, the Empire, the achievement of personal honour and integrity in
defence of the Crown. These are works which were being read not only
by boys across England but by English-speaking boys across the Empire.

As Glyn Jones emphasizes in the autobiographical chapter of *The
Dragon has Two Tongues*, while Education Acts passed at the Westminster
Parliament from the 1870s onwards had made state secondary education available to all, the Act of 1889 establishing state secondary
education in Wales had laid down that the medium of that education
was to be English, regardless of the child's native language. Obviously
there were other factors which were causing English to become the
language of the streets and homes of Merthyr in this period, mainly the
massive incursion of English-speaking workers in the late nineteenth
century to develop the coal and iron industries of south Wales. But it
was above all the government's determination that Wales should be
educated in English that brought about for the first time, in Glyn Jones's
generation, a significant body of literature expressing the distinctive

experience of Welsh life not in Welsh but in English. Glyn Jones argues in *The Dragon has Two Tongues*:

> It seems to me that the language which captures [a writer's] heart and imagination during the emotional and intellectual upheavals of adolescence, the language of his awakening, the language in which ideas – political, religious, aesthetic – and an understanding of personal and social relationships first dawn upon his mind, is the language likely to be the one of his creative work.[2]

And so it was, not only for Glyn Jones but for the generation of writers whom he discusses in *The Dragon*, for Gwyn Thomas in the Rhondda, for Idris Davies in Rhymney and for Dylan Thomas in Swansea (though perhaps Thomas was a special case, given the fact that his father, as a teacher of English, was part of the education system). While Glyn Jones continued to hear Welsh spoken by older relatives and neighbours, his teenage imagination, as he became 'obsessed by poetry' (*DTT* 25), was fired by the richness of English poetry, by the vividness and sensuality of Keats and the other Romantics, of Morris, Rossetti and Tennyson, contained in the copy of Palgrave's *Golden Treasury* which he was given at the age of fifteen.[3] Later, as he relates in *The Dragon*, he discovered the poetry of D. H. Lawrence and Gerard Manley Hopkins and again he responds to the poetry's rich verbal texture and sensual immediacy.

Perhaps surprisingly, it was to be some years before Glyn Jones began himself to write. As he indicates in his 'Autobiography' chapter in *The Dragon,* these were years of acute loneliness, teaching in a school in the slums of Cardiff with few if any close friends. His interest in literature and contemporary writing was sustained by his contact with the literary group run by Catherine Maclean, a member of the University's English Department, and then by various extramural classes. Jones seems to have begun to write during a period of ill health in 1929–30, his early poems being, as is the case with many young poets, imitations of the writers he had been reading, including the poets who had attracted him in the *Golden Treasury*, especially Browning and Morris.[4] At the same time, even as he began to write in English, he was making friends, at the Welsh-speaking chapel in Cardiff which he attended with his parents, with young Welsh-speaking students studying at the nearby university. Through them he began to study Welsh-language poetry and he was especially drawn to the vivid imagery and intricate aural patterning of the medieval *cywyddwyr*. He began to study the intricacies of *cynghanedd* and also to translate Welsh poetry into English.[5] Thus Glyn

Jones's poetic career begins during the period in which he also begins to discover Welsh literature and to reorientate himself towards the Welsh-language culture which he had gradually lost as a boy. From the outset, we might argue, Glyn Jones's writing in English is written within earshot of the Welsh language.

Glyn Jones's early poems were published in the 1930s in *The Dublin Magazine*, in *Poetry* (Chicago) and in London journals such as Middleton Murry's *The Adelphi* and Robert Herring's *Life and Letters To-day*. There were no literary magazines in Wales itself in which to publish English-language writing until the launch of Keidrych Rhys's *Wales* in 1937, with the planning of which Glyn Jones became actively involved, and Gwyn Jones's *The Welsh Review* in 1939. Glyn Jones wrote regularly for both journals over the years.

Glyn Jones's *Poems* appeared from the London-based Fortune Press in 1939, two years after the publication of his first collection of short stories, *The Blue Bed* (Cape). The latter received an outstandingly positive reception; at Cape itself Rupert Hart Davis commented that 'it is one of the most remarkable first books I have ever read', while Cape's own reader, the distinguished editor and writer Edward Garnett, had written that 'Glyn Jones is a genius . . . his stories have a strange imaginative quality about them unlike anything else'.[6] Press reaction must have been equally gratifying to the young Welsh writer: H. E. Bates wrote of the author's 'uncommon talent', while Humbert Wolfe compared Jones's work to that of D. H. Lawrence.[7] Jones's second collection, *The Water Music* (1944) was also well received. The volume in part continued the enigmatic, dream-like, occasionally surrealist style of the stories in *The Blue Bed* but also contained, in stories like 'Explosion', 'An Afternoon at Ewa Shad's' and 'Bowen, Morgan and Williams', narratives in which events were seen through the eyes of boys not unlike his childhood self, in an urban setting not unlike Merthyr.

Although he appears to have begun writing it in the 1940s, Glyn Jones's first novel, *The Valley, The City, The Village* appeared from Dent in 1956.[8] It is a *Bildungsroman* which follows the life of an artistic young boy from his upbringing in the south Wales valleys to a Welsh university college and on to a village based on Llansteffan in Carmarthenshire (with which Jones had close family ties and where he spent summer holidays throughout his life). Its somewhat episodic structure has been criticized as being too evidently the work of a writer whose natural talent was for the short story. In fact, and especially compared with the novels of provincial realism being produced in the same period in

England, the book is at times genuinely experimental in its narrative techniques, which include devices which Jones had learned from his reading of Welsh-language literature.

Jones's day-to-day career as a school-teacher in Cardiff resulted in his writing a verse-play for radio, commissioned by Aneirin Talfan Davies at the BBC, entitled *The Dream of Jake Hopkins* (1953). The play, which manifests something of Jones's frustration at his life in the classroom and at the bureaucratic educational system in which he felt trapped, became the title poem of his second volume of poems (1954). What he had seen of the education system in south Wales, and in particular the corrupt canvassing of local councillors by teachers seeking promotion, became the subject of his second novel, *The Learning Lark* (Dent, 1960). Although essentially comic in tone, the book's subject-matter caused it to become for a while the centre of controversy and debate in the press, both in Wales and in London. In many respects the controversy obscured consideration of the book's literary qualities, although Alan Sillitoe, reviewing it in *The Bookman*, compared it favourably with Kingsley Amis's *Lucky Jim* (1954).[9]

Glyn Jones's third and final novel, *The Island of Apples* (Dent, 1965), is undoubtedly his fictional masterpiece. Again rooted in the scruffy streets of a town not unlike Merthyr in the early years of the century and in the sun-filled landscape of rural west Wales, the novel employs the child's point of view used in the later stories to explore the potency, and the dangers, of adolescent romantic imagination, as the narrator, Dewi Davies, becomes involved with the mysterious and exotic stranger, Karl. Though set in south Wales, the novel engages universal themes; it is about the departure of youth and the pain of its loss, and, as Jones himself summed up his journal, about 'How beautiful is the ideal world, how completely enchanting, and how brittle'.[10]

By the 1960s, Glyn Jones was one of Wales's most eminent men of letters. When the Academi Gymreig set up an English-language section in 1968, he was elected its first chairman. In touch with many of the leading English-language writers of Wales, some of whom he had known since the 1930s, and fully involved in the literary scene for some thirty years, Glyn Jones was uniquely placed to undertake the first book-length study of Welsh writing in English in the twentieth century.

Glyn Jones seems to have begun work on the book which became *The Dragon has Two Tongues* early in 1965. He was due to retire from his post as Head of English at Glantaf Secondary Modern School, Cardiff, in June, after forty years as a teacher. There would at last be uninterrupted time, and energy, to devote to his study of 'Anglo-Welsh' writing ('a term . . . I know you dislike as much as I do', he wrote to Keidrych Rhys). He began by listing, in an unused diary for 1964, those articles and essays which had been published in the Welsh literary magazines and in journals outside Wales, like *Life and Letters To-day*, which might provide source material for his study. At the back of the diary he jotted down various brief *aides-memoires*: ' "Fifty Years of Anglo-Welsh" for a title?', 'Look up Dorothy Edwards' work'.[11] He probably began his first draft in the summer of 1965, at the same time continuing to jot down other notes and anecdotes about writers in a series of school exercise books.

He also drew on his written recollections of the writers whom he was considering for inclusion in his book; a number of the episodes noted in these recollections arose from visits and conversations Glyn Jones had with writers when he was preparing a series of broadcast radio interviews in about 1949–50, and a substantial portion of the material in these notes was to be incorporated into the chapters on individual writers in *The Dragon*. Some passages are tactfully altered or omitted. The account of Huw Menai's concern with his appearance, for instance, is slightly different from the published version: 'When Gwyn [Thomas] and Lyn come, I am in the room with Huw. He arranges his bubblecut (hair like Miss Ingrid Bergman) and stands on my hearth ready to receive them'. Rhys Davies, when Jones visits him, is 'rather posh in a smooth tweed suit . . . green flannel shirt and woollen apricot tie. He looked pink, like a made-up actor.'

At this stage Jones had not finally decided which writers would be discussed at length in his book and his sketched recollections include a visit to Richard Hughes and notes about Vernon Watkins – apparently written originally in the early 1950s – including his impressions of a reading by Watkins, which Jones had chaired. He notes that, as he listened to the poetry, 'I had a feeling . . . of its remoteness, its lack of body. Isn't it rather *too* refined, not robust enough'.[12] This sense of remoteness seems to have coloured Jones's feelings towards Watkins on a personal level: 'And yet I rather liked him. But I felt no flow between us as I always do with Dylan'. Jones has inserted later, perhaps when returning to these notes when preparing his book: 'I don't think I "like" Vernon but my God I admire him. I didn't admire Dylan at all, the silly bugger, but every time I saw him loved him'. It was perhaps his sense of a lack of a genuine emotional response to Watkins's work which caused

Glyn Jones finally to decide against including a chapter on him in the book. For Jones clearly admires Watkins's poetry; a draft of Chapter VI, 'Introduction to Poetry' includes the following:

> Vernon's grave, musical and transparent poetry, apart from one exception which I shall mention presently, sometimes arouses in me wonder and admiration rather than any deeper poetic response. But I admire enormously his tremendous dedication to poetry, his steady unswerving devotion throughout his life, ignoring the temptations of ambition and the cheap reputation to be made in other and easier kinds of writing. To me his first volume, 'The Ballad of the Mari Lwyd', is unquestionably his best, partly because the long title poem has an element lacking it seems to me in a good deal of Vernon's work, a sort of vitality, a warmth, a feeling of gusto and rude health. Debility and diffuseness to a person of my no doubt home spun and unregenerate temperament, seem inevitably the besetting faults of this fine poet's work; but he has superb craftsmanship and a sort of Shelleyan purity which I always find attractive in the extreme.

It is a passage which shows a number of the characteristics of Glyn Jones as a critic, especially in *The Dragon*. It is typically self-deprecating about his own critical judgements, judgements which are consciously subjective, and yet beneath the unassuming tone the critical evaluation is nevertheless clear and firm. At the same time there is a concern not to be merely negative; there is admiration for Watkins's qualities both as a poet and as a man – typically the poetry and the person are perceived together. But there is also a clear awareness of the qualities which he finds lacking in Watkins's work, qualities which he almost unfailingly finds in the authors about whom he writes in *The Dragon*: a sense of human warmth and vitality, of the physical and the sensual and, crucially for Glyn Jones, a sense of the communal rather than of the solitary.

By the end of the summer Jones had written a substantial portion of what became Chapter VII and sent this to Michael Geare, an editor at Dent; Geare's response, though ultimately encouraging, seems to have been less than wholly enthusiastic, to judge from Jones's reply (3 September 1965):

> Thank you very much for your kind letter. It was terribly nice of you to write to me directly and in such terms of encouragement. I feel a certain disappointment, of course, that my first 25,000 words didn't make a more favourable impression on you. Never mind. I think I'll

go ahead and try to finish the book and ask Laurence [Pollinger, Jones's literary agent] to let you see the typescript then if he's agreeable. The plan for the whole book is something like this.

Chapter 1. The Welsh society. Welsh and English in Wales – pre C20th Anglo-Welsh writers (Dyer, Vaughan, etc – briefly). Background social, political, religious of Welsh and Anglo-Welsh writers compared. Contrast between modern Welsh language and Anglo-Welsh literatures.

Chapter 2. A literary autobiography illustrating in my own person much of the argument of the previous chapter.

Chapter 3. Anglo-Welsh poetry – Vernon Watkins, R.S. Thomas, Alun Lewis, etc. etc.

[This is the piece I sent to you]
Three Anglo-Welsh poets – Idris Davies, Huw Menai, Dylan Thomas.

Chapter 4. Anglo-Welsh prose – Geraint Goodwin, Rhys Davies, Emyr Humphreys, Richard Hughes.
Three Anglo-Welsh prose writers – Jack Jones, Caradoc Evans, Gwyn Thomas.

Chapter 5. Achievement, future.

I've written a good bit of all this already but I don't know whether I'll be able to sustain this. Perhaps I haven't got the whole thing to the end. I don't know.

Thus, by this point the main structure of the book, which he referred to as 'Notes on the Anglo-Welsh', was clear in Jones's mind and, free from the pressures of teaching, he kept writing. A year later, in September 1966, Laurence Pollinger was writing to him, 'I am delighted to know that you have finished the actual writing of the book about Welsh writers but have still to do some checking of quotations and figures' (23 September 1966); Pollinger also relayed the perhaps not unwelcome news that Michael Geare had been replaced at Dent by T. R. Nicholson. Jones's methodical checking and revising of his manuscript, prior to sending it to a typist, took him until the end of the year; illness held things up but the typescript finally arrived at Pollinger's office in April 1967. He immediately sent the book, at this point entitled *Anglo-Welsh (Background with Figures)*, to Dent. In August, after some prompting from Pollinger over the time that Dent's readers were taking with their decision, T. R. Nicholson wrote to Pollinger to say that Dent 'would like to take the book on the understanding that the author change the title, which is too obscure' (Pollinger to Jones, 1 August 1967); a £200 advance followed, the accompanying letter again emphasizing – with characteristic metropolitan lack of understanding – the fact that 'We should avoid altogether the use of "Anglo-Welsh" and simply set the book down as a work of [sic] Welsh Literature'. Glyn Jones wrote to Pollinger (3 August 1967) saying he was happy to change the title; in September he suggested to Pollinger, perhaps with an eye on the sale of American rights which were under negotiation, 'Guide to Dylan Country'. This still seems not to have been agreeable to Dent, since when the contract for the book was signed in October, it was for a book 'provisionally entitled "Welsh Literature"'. Just before Christmas Pollinger wrote to Jones: 'I note that Dent will probably be calling your book *The Dragon has Two Tongues* and, frankly, I am not very keen about it' (20 December 1967). Jones, however, seems to have been more happy with this rather ingenious title, dreamed up presumably by a Dent editor, and production went ahead. *The Dragon has Two Tongues* was published in November 1968, the book being formally launched at a reception at the Queen's Hotel, Cardiff.

In 1968, of course, reviews in *The Times Literary Supplement* were still, notoriously, anonymous; the author of the substantial review which appeared in the *TLS* on 14 November 1968 was in fact Gwyn Jones, then a regular reviewer of Welsh books for that journal.[13] The review notes the 'explosion' of literary talent which had occurred in Wales during the 1930s and 1940s, and lists over a dozen of the more distinguished writers, before noting that 'Surprisingly, we have had no book till now in English to record the colours of this dawn and assess the brightness of the day it heralded; but *The Dragon has Two Tongues* was worth waiting for'.[14] The review goes on to refer to the complexity of the cultural tensions in Wales:

> The language division, which means a cultural division with all that flows from it, is the most painful in Welsh life today and is one of the issues Mr Glyn Jones handles with a sympathy, common sense, and good temper which have eluded some other contributors to the long debate.

Noting the way in which many of the writers discussed had their imaginative worlds shaped by the poverty of the inter-war years – 'They inhaled poverty and injustice, and breathed out political not national revolt' – the review shrewdly and precisely points to one of the factors which distinguished several of the writers about whom Glyn Jones wrote, and which drew him to them: 'Their early loyalties, always deep, sometimes fierce, have kept most of them rooted in their communities, and warm and nourishing, if sometimes confining, these proved to be'. Gwyn Jones underlines the fact that, within their communities, the writers he had listed at the outset of the review 'felt an active friendship and regard' for each other, knew each other's work in 'a warm and alert . . . fashion': 'Mr Glyn Jones rightly stresses the difficulty of defining them as a group, but they may easily be accepted as a family'. At the end of an astute discussion of the book which also displays the reviewer's familiarity with the book's subjects in vivid terms – Jack Jones is 'now a bearded kestrel of eighty-four' – Gwyn Jones sums up: 'It is a pity that idiomatic South Wales does not extend its "lovely boy" usage to literature, for this is a lovely book . . . rich in humour, humanity, judgement, and understanding; and it is beautifully written'.

In Wales itself, Roy Thomas, writing in *The Anglo-Welsh Review,* judged that in *The Dragon has Two Tongues* Glyn Jones 'has produced a book that can be read with pleasure and profit by anybody interested in what happens outside London literary circles'.[15] Thomas sees the book as being ultimately about a specific historical 'episode', about how the Anglo-Welsh writer emerged when, to quote Jones, a 'radical nonconformist, Welsh-speaking family begins to speak English'. In Roy Thomas's view, what these writers ultimately have in common, in other words, 'is not style, nor subject matter, nor attitude, but, quite simply, background'. But if Anglo-Welsh writing is the product of a finite cultural moment, what future does it have? Thomas is profoundly sceptical that it has one. He cites Emyr Humphreys at a recent colloquium; Humphreys had developed the thesis that 'a writer in the Wales of today had to make a choice: he could either become Welsh-speaking (even if he wished to continue writing in English), or he could become an "exile" (i.e. look beyond Wales for his material)'. Thomas endorses Humphreys's view, seeing the Anglo-Welsh culture described in Glyn Jones's book as one which will inexorably and inevitably merge with a British, perhaps ultimately a European, culture, as Wales becomes more urbanized, less distinct from similarly urbanized areas of England; to write about a Wales that remains Welsh will 'demand a knowledge of what in the future will be the only thing that can keep it Welsh – namely the Welsh language'.

Harri Pritchard Jones's lengthy review in *Poetry Wales* pushed the implications of Glyn Jones's book and the nature of 'Anglo-Welsh' writing even further. The review is a vigorous, polemical essay, going beyond the book itself to consider the issues it raises about language and identity and, like the lecture by Emyr Humphreys referred to in Roy Thomas's review, those issues are perceived very much in the context of Wales in the spring of 1969. While underlining the fact that 'a notable feature of Glyn Jones's exposition is the way he deals with, is aware of and learned in the Welsh language and its literature' ('Too often we have had people writing about our country as if Welsh and Welsh literature did not exist, or . . . were only of marginal importance'), the review is critical of Glyn Jones's selection of writers for discussion: 'in choosing to write about friends of his, Glyn Jones has only presented portraits of those, Idris Davies excepted, who least represent the new era in Anglo-Welsh literature'; that new era was represented by those English-language writers writing, in the 1960s and particularly in the recently founded *Poetry Wales*, with a greater sense of Welsh identity and awareness of the Welsh language:

> It would have been more accurate to represent the non-Welsh speaking community and communities, and the changes taking place in them, by progressing from Caradoc Evans, say, and Jack Jones to Emyr Humphreys, from Huw Menai through Idris Davies to R. S. Thomas – though finding room for the most fascinating account here of Dylan Thomas, which neither makes him out to be a saint nor a savage.[16]

For Pritchard Jones the Welsh writer in English, unlike the Welsh-language writer, is not a firmly accepted and essential part of the community, but is cut off linguistically from it. There is consequently the danger that he will 'indulge himself in word-play for its own sake'. This can give 'brilliance and colour' to some Anglo-Welsh works but 'also leads to much doggerel'. For this reviewer 'there is little in the work of Huw Menai, or most of Idris Davies even, to compare with the best work of the amateur National Eisteddfod poets . . . I can hardly accredit even that importance to much of Gwyn Thomas's work'. (Presumably Pritchard Jones's unstated reason for dismissing Thomas's work was, ultimately, not so much disapproval of his word-play as Thomas's frequently expressed hostility towards the Welsh language.)

The reviewer's scepticism towards English-language writers in Wales is then turned upon the issue of the writers' audience: 'for whom do they write?' To Harri Pritchard Jones it is clear ('even from this charitable appraisal by Glyn Jones') for whom it was that Caradoc Evans wrote: to 'parody the speech and manners of a community of human beings as Caradoc Evans did borders on blasphemy' and he did this 'because he had a foreign public eager to hear what he said, and to laugh "with foreign jaws" . . . Evans wrote from London but not for Wales'. Pritchard Jones compares the Welsh situation with that in Ireland in the last quarter of the nineteenth century and the first quarter of the twentieth, quoting Daniel Corkery's *Synge and Anglo-Irish Literature*:

> The typical Irish expatriate writer continues to find his matter in Irish life; his choice of it however, and his treatment of it when chosen, are to a greater or lesser extent imposed on him by alien considerations . . . This colonial literature was written to explain the quaintness of the humankind of this land, especially the native humankind, to another humankind that was not quaint, that was standard, normal.

'Did not Corkery', asks Pritchard Jones, 'give us a perfect description of much Anglo-Welsh writing until of late?' Moreover, Glyn Jones's definition of Anglo-Welsh writers – those who are Welsh, writing in English and writing about Wales – indicates the inevitable limitedness of such writing: 'Welsh-language writers would baulk at limiting their territory – as writers – to Wales exclusively'; Pritchard Jones cites John Gwilym Jones's view that if Anglo-Welsh literature must deal with Wales or have some 'local colour' in order to show itself as Welsh then it must inevitably be 'provincial if not parochial'. These writers are using – like Glyn Jones himself – 'the language that captured their imagination', English; to try to force that imagination into moulds and metrical forms derived from Welsh in order to prove their Welshness is inevitably artificial and, again, limiting. 'We', says the reviewer – and the pronoun is of course telling – 'must try to capture their imagination in Welsh'. Moreover,

> To solve the dilemma for future generations in Wales we must teach our children Welsh, that they can be free to choose . . . The wider world must be able to speak to the child in Welsh, through signs and documents and officials . . . Here lies the importance for Welsh of having . . . books and periodicals, radio and television programmes, on all subjects, in Welsh.

This, importantly, gives us a glimpse of the cultural situation into which *The Dragon has Two Tongues* was launched. Wales was experiencing a particularly acute crisis of identity: one Wales was struggling vigorously to achieve legal status for the Welsh language at the very time that another Wales was busy preparing for the investiture of a member of the

English royal family as Prince of Wales. Harri Pritchard Jones ends his review with an assertion of the necessity 'to take political action, and to labour that point is to go outside the scope of both this review and of Glyn Jones's very fine book', a judgement which, given what has been said in the preceding five pages, perhaps comes as something of a surprise.

From elsewhere came letters of appreciation and congratulation. A. G. Prys-Jones, editor of the first anthology of Anglo-Welsh poetry, back in 1917, wrote that 'This is likely to become a standard work in its class'. Bryn Griffiths wrote from London: 'It's four in the morning, can't sleep, and I've just been reading "The Dragon has Two Tongues" again. I think its a superb book, long needed . . .' He is especially appreciative of the essay on Idris Davies, 'and I think the last two lines of that essay are equally applicable to you'. Ron Berry thought the book 'A beautiful accomplishment. True to yourself. Only you could have done it. For me, some of the text was like passing through the shades. My sub-terranean years ticktocking on a clock of names'. A further accolade came in March 1969 when the book was awarded the Welsh Arts Council's Literature Prize. On a more material level *The Dragon* sold over 600 copies between its launch in November 1968 and the end of the year. Sales thereafter were steady but modest; the book sold over 100 further copies in 1969 and Glyn Jones's own careful records show that total sales by the end of 1972 were 1,377. Dent did not reprint it.

Gwyn Jones's point in his *TLS* review that many of the writers discussed in *The Dragon has Two Tongues* were 'rooted in their communities' is a shrewd and important one. The book does indeed emphasize such rootedness; for Glyn Jones the essence of the writer in Wales, especially the poet, is that he is not set apart from the community but a member of it. Moreover, he believes that the community is aware of and responsive to its writers; thus he draws attention to the story of the policeman keeping custody of Saunders Lewis, D. J. Williams and Lewis Valentine in a Caernarfon police station in 1936 being able to complete a quotation from a Welsh sonnet when the memory of one of his prisoners fails, and to the Cardiff coalman whose billhead has a slogan in *cynghanedd groes*: '*Dyma'r boi i dwymo'r byd*'. The Welsh writer, Jones argues, is not a barely heard eccentric on the margins of the society as, it might be argued, the poet in England has been, at least since the Romantic period, giving expression to his/her essentially private feelings and experience; 'in Wales he is not a man apart, a freak, but rather an accepted part of the social fabric with an important function to perform'. It is a function that goes back to the oldest traditions of Welsh-language poetry: to preserve the values of the tribe or community, to express and to protect its identity, to give voice to its values and aspirations. For Glyn Jones the position of the Anglo-Welsh writer is, or should be, firmly within this tradition.

But perhaps one ought to be aware, too, of personal tensions which underlie this insistence on the rootedness of the writer in the community. Like many Anglo-Welsh writers, Glyn Jones grew up in a working-class community – in his case in Merthyr Tydfil – but he was not himself working-class, since his father had a clerical position with the Post Office (ill health and family finances had prevented him becoming a teacher and he continued to have intellectual and literary interests) while Jones's mother was a teacher before she married and was manifestly a woman with a very strong sense of bourgeois respect-ability. Thus, by origin and then by education and profession – as a teacher himself – Glyn Jones was a member of the middle classes. And in thus being brought up alongside working-class families and friends, living *in* a working-class community yet not ultimately being part *of* that class, he shares much with those he is writing about, certainly by their adult years when they were writing: Gwyn Thomas went to Oxford and became a teacher; Dylan Thomas was the son of a teacher; Idris Davies began his working life underground in the colliery, but after 1926 he too trained as a teacher. They belong, like Glyn Jones himself, to the middle, or lower middle, class, the very class that would, a generation or so earlier, have been expressing itself in literature in Welsh.

In Glyn Jones's case, however, it seems likely that this sense of not being part of what he saw as the warmth and intimacy of working-class life was a source of unease, even at times of an alienation from the values of the bourgeois life of which he was a part. This alienation, and his desire for what he seemed to have seen as the more physical, more authentic life of the working class, at times finds expression in his journals as well as in his creative writing. For instance, in 1937, when a teacher in Cardiff, his frustrations burst out:

> Tonight I felt full of anger and hatred, in coming back to this house
> . . . I walked in the middle of the road in order not to feel the
> 'smugness' which was coming out of the houses on every side. I felt
> like throwing the shoe I was carrying though one of the windows.

The desire to escape was strong in me . . . I constantly feel like some kind of Ishmael – excluded from everything. This feeling has become part of my nature, worst luck.[17]

Part of what he was feeling was guilt, born of his awareness of the miserable lives led by many of his pupils in the slums of Cardiff's Temperance Town, in contrast to his own middle-class comfort. He had written in the same year to Rhys Davies: 'My attraction is always towards the lowest and most helpless, the dispossessed. I am getting to hate more and more this comfortable middle-class world which seems to be getting me' (September or October 1937). This guilty sense of the falseness of bourgeois life seems to colour his own frustrations – especially his dislike of his job as a teacher – and his sense that a simpler, fuller life was to be found in the life of the working-class areas of Cardiff, a life (whatever the truth of the matter – and Glyn Jones knew how harsh it could be) which he saw as more simple, more sensual, less constrained and thus more attractive. He writes in his journal, in July 1937: 'I'd like to give up all these things – house, my bourgeois life, and go down to Bute Street to live simply, without bothering with neighbours . . . possessions or anything else'.[18] This same sense of alienation, and the same attraction to the comradeship which he discerned within working-class life, is apparent in the poetry. In 'Hills', for instance, the narrator, standing alone on the hillside, thinks of the miners he has seen making their way home after their shift:

> I have stood aside when they flooded down
> The slope from two pits, the sound of their boots
> Like chattering of tipped hail over roofs;
> I can remember like applause the sound
> Of their speech and laughter, the smell of their pit-clothes.[19]

The narrator can only stand aside; he is not part of this natural and spontaneous life of the working men.

In other words, the recurrent concern with class in *The Dragon has Two Tongues*, however relevant it is to an analysis of the actual situation of the writers under discussion, in part has its roots in Glyn Jones's uneasy awareness of his own social situation (itself, of course, in many ways symptomatic of the writers of his generation). There is, thus, a more serious undertone when he makes the apparently light-hearted comment about seeing himself, 'first as Welsh, and second as upper class, upper working class, of course, and during rare moments of delusions of grandeur even perhaps as lower middle class'. While the argument which Glyn Jones develops at some length in 'Autobiography', that the English concern with social class that we see in writers like Forster or Waugh or Lawrence is not apparent in the work of the Anglo-Welsh writers, is largely true, the concern to portray Wales as a society free from class consciousness, as a *community* 'in which class, like colour in a multi-racial society is not of overwhelming importance', needs to be read in the context of these personal concerns.

It is, one might argue, these personal sensitivities which serve to make Jones particularly alert to, and insistent on, the role of the Anglo-Welsh writer within his community.[20] Thus, in the essay on Gwyn Thomas, it is emphasized that 'The identification of his outlook with that of the workers, in his case the miners, is complete': he 'grew up in a solidly democratic society where the idea of any man "knowing his place" was alien'. Gwyn Thomas's antipathy towards Welsh-language culture – towards the eisteddfod and the chapel, towards Plaid Cymru and of course the language itself – Jones notes and registers as being, in his view, wrong-headed. But at the same time he goes on not only to register Thomas's concern for 'human brotherhood' (his anti-nationalism being born of his Socialist internationalism) but to see him as the '*cyfarwydd* [tribal story-teller] of the working class'. The essay on Jack Jones, albeit registering his erratic political career, sees him as 'essentially a novelist of the working class', his novels embodying 'the variety, the restlessness, the vitality of the valleys they are concerned with'. Idris Davies's seven years as a collier are seen as the beginnings of his 'complete identification of himself with the people of the valleys, with the poor, the exploited and the oppressed', an identification which Jones sees as distinguishing him from Huw Menai as a poet of the mining valleys. Fundamentally, of course, Huw Menai's poetry – his register, his imagery and his emotional stance – looks directly and consciously back to the Romantics and the apartness registered in the poetry was enacted in the life, when he became employed by the colliery management as a weigher, a fact Jones points out. Yet Jones still sees him as 'rooted in his own valleys community . . . a sort of *bardd gwlad* [local poet] of the coalfields', albeit, we might suggest, Huw Menai's recognition came in fact not from that community but from London publishers and editors; one might, indeed, argue that for Huw Menai the working-class life of south Wales was ultimately a commodity to be marketed in England.

Glyn Jones uses the essay on Huw Menai not only to define the nature of the *bardd gwlad* – 'the man usually of not very much *formal* education . . . self-educated, cultured, deeply-versed in Welsh literature rooted in and entirely accepted by the community about which and for which he writes' – but, again, to distinguish such a tradition from the culture of the 'rootless Bohemian poet of Chelsea, or the Left Bank, or Greenwich Village', the poet consciously and exotically outside – indeed in defiance of – the mainstream values of his society. And it is here, in this bohemian world, of course, that we find Dylan Thomas. Thomas was the Anglo-Welsh writer whom Glyn Jones knew longest, having visited him in Swansea in 1934 before Thomas left for London; although they saw each other only occasionally after the war, Jones, as we have seen, always seems to have thought of him with warmth and affection. In his *TLS* review, Gwyn Jones asserts that in *The Dragon has Two Tongues* Glyn Jones 'shows more knowledge and judgement of Dylan Thomas in thirty pages than some others have revealed in three hundred'. But while there is much shrewdness about the poetry, it is evident at the same time that Jones remains puzzled by his friend. The two men, as Jones points out, came from very similar backgrounds, but Thomas rejected all that Jones found reassuring: the chapel, the community, and even (for all Jones's ambivalence) the respectability which went with them; 'I represented all that [Dylan] was trying to get away from', Jones noted in his journal in 1964.

What puzzled Jones was the nature of the alternative life that Thomas created for himself, the romantic, bohemian role of the 'wild and petted man apart', 'petted' (and increasingly commodified) by London and then America. Jones's analysis is perhaps by this point in the book predictable (though nonetheless shrewd, and sad):

> I sometimes wonder if the powerful self-destructive impulse in Dylan's life was not somehow mixed up with . . . his sense of being cut off, with having rejected one community and not having found another one to take its place. One agonizes over many explanations when one sees sweet life being poured down the drain.

Visiting Thomas in London in the 1930s, Glyn Jones seems initially to have been rather fascinated by the seedy bohemian house that Thomas shared with the painters Merfyn Levy and Alfred Janes (Jones's own fiction, of course, often shows the same fascination for seedy, even squalid, houses), though one suspects that his response was rather like that which he attributes to Idris Davies: 'His Bohemianism – if that is the word – included a profound regard for soap, water and clean linen'. But later, and in part perhaps because he associated bohemianism *with* what had happened to Dylan Thomas, his attitude to such a lifestyle is consistently antipathetic; for instance, in a review of Rhys Davies, he refers to Nina Hamnet, a friend of Davies, letting her talent 'atrophy in the perpetual self indulgence of parties, booze, friendships and conversation' in bohemian Fitzrovia.[21]

But while Dylan Thomas might have put himself outside Glyn Jones's perception of the Anglo-Welsh writer as essentially a part of his community, he manifested the same acute concern with verse form as the *cynganeddwyr*, traditional Welsh-language strict-metre poets, and the same fascination with words as Glyn Jones himself – *English* words, to the intriguing possibilities of which perhaps this generation of writers was especially alert, the novelty of these words being thrown into relief by the presence of that other, older language, spoken by neighbours and parents. If the concern with class and community is the warp thread of *The Dragon has Two Tongues*, then the weft is the attention that Jones gives to the writers' engagement with the actual crafting of language. Thus he sees as a significant shortcoming the fact that Jack Jones's prose is 'bare, factual', unadorned by 'those marvellous life-giving graces, quirks, fancies, perceptions, images, embellishments and distortions of language we depressingly lump together under the term of "figures of speech" ': 'Jack saw language – granting that he saw language at all – solely as a vehicle, not as something rich and beautiful in itself which had passed through the hands of thousands of artists.'

The sheer volume of Huw Menai's writing results, in Jones's judgement, in an unevenness of quality; despite the 'isolated striking lines or brilliant phrases . . . the number of successful *poems* Huw wrote is, I think, very small indeed'. A Welsh-language poem, constructed as many of Huw Menai's are around one idea or emotion, might be embellished by *dyfaliad*, the intricate piling up of images, 'the craftsmanship goes into the individual images embedded in the couplets rather than into the overall shape of the poem. Huw never worked like that'. Gwyn Thomas, on the other hand, is seen as having possessed 'something of a bardic quality', not simply because of his immersion in his community but also 'in his concern for language, his brilliant use of jesting metaphor'. The very terms in which Glyn Jones writes of his attraction to Gwyn Thomas's work is a measure of the strength of that attraction: 'the extraordinary vigour of the style, the brilliance, the gusto, the torrential language, the inexhaustible imagery'. Idris Davies, though, is seen as deliberately cultivating plainness and rejecting verbal decoration in order that his social concerns be heard clearly and directly. Yet even here Jones detects an underlying impulse towards a very different sort of writing: 'there was in him also, fiercely suppressed in *Gwalia Deserta* and *The Angry Summer*, a lover of style, and fancy and gorgeous language, who makes an appearance, sometimes fitful, in such poems as "Sonnet", "Defiance", "Interlude", "Ruin", "Renaissance" and perhaps "William Morris"'. That tension between a concern for direct expression of compassion for human suffering and the impulse towards 'gorgeous language' is perhaps one with which Glyn Jones was familiar in his own poetry.

Brynmor Jones, whose comprehensive bibliography of Anglo-Welsh writing was shortly to be published,[22] read *The Dragon has Two Tongues* in typescript and in a letter to Glyn Jones (5 November 1967) drew attention to his comment early in the book that 'I find I can only write at length and with understanding about the books of men with whom I have made personal contact, and for whom I feel, or have felt, friendship or at least sympathy'; Bynmor Jones notes that reviewers might 'take issue with you as to how relevant or important it is to know an author personally to be able to judge his work'. Glyn Jones jotted on the letter 'Not to judge – only to write'. But as he himself observes in *The Dragon*, commenting on the difference between the painter and the writer as portrayers of life in Wales, 'words involve us in judgement and often cannot remain morally neutral as paint is able to do'. And that, clearly, is especially true when writing a critically informed literary history; the danger, manifestly, is that personal acquaintance or friendship will muffle critical judgement. It might indeed be argued that at times Glyn Jones's judgements err on the side of generosity, perhaps especially his estimate of the achievements of Jack Jones and Huw Menai, though even the essays on these two writers are not uncritical. On the other hand Glyn Jones can be remarkably clear-eyed in his reading; his awareness of the hostility in Wales towards Caradoc Evans as well as his sense of the obsessive narrowness of Evans's vision, so different from the generous inclusiveness of his own fiction, does not prevent him looking hard at the texts themselves, seeking to analyse the *nature* of Evans's fiction. Jones's familiarity with these writers on a personal level, their circumstances and idiosyncrasies, of course frequently adds a vividness and an insight to his discussion that still makes *The Dragon has Two Tongues* a valuable source-book. Writing for Glyn Jones was the product of the lives of individual human beings – it is striking, in fact, how many times the words 'human' or 'humanity' are used in the book; writing could not, and should not, be divorced from the texture of everyday human life, from the human capacity for generosity, love and humour as well as pain and suffering. In this sense, in constructing its gallery of the writers who emerged from the unique cultural circumstances that existed in south Wales in the early years of the twentieth century, *The Dragon has Two Tongues* also gives us a portrait of the humane, generous, shrewd mind that wrote it.

TONY BROWN

NOTES

1. Unpublished typescript entitled 'Tyfu'n Gymro' ('Growing into being a Welshman'), 10. This typescript is the text, in Welsh, of an autobiographical talk given at GJ's chapel, Capel yr Annibynnwyr, Minny Street, Cardiff, some time after 1985. The translation is my own.
2. *The Dragon has Two Tongues*, p. 24. References are to the present edition and further references will be given in the text.
3. The gift is recorded in the entry for 18 March 1920 in a pocket diary which GJ kept during 1920 (when he was 15). The diary is in the Glyn Jones Collection, Trinity College Library, Carmarthen.
4. See 'Appendix I: Imitations and early poems (1930–1938)', *The Collected Poems of Glyn Jones*, ed. Meic Stephens (Cardiff: University of Wales Press, 1996), 167–224.
5. See, for example, 'The Wind's Complaint', *Collected Poems*, 188.
6. Rupert Hart Davis to Glyn Jones, 25 November 1936. The letter is in the as yet uncatalogued portion of the Glyn Jones Papers, National Library of Wales, Aberystwyth. Garnett's comment is included in a press release which accompanied the publication of the American edition of the novel, published by Dutton.
7. *Morning Post* (29 January 1937); *Sunday Referee* (February 1937).
8. In a letter to Gwyn Jones, 8 May 1949, GJ expresses his impatience that he had not heard from the publishers, Nicolson and Watson, although they had had the manuscript of his novel for more than two months. See Prof. Gwyn Jones Papers II, 9/2, National Library of Wales.
9. *Bookman* (January–February 1960).
10. Journal entry, late 1964, Glyn Jones Papers, National Library of Wales (uncatalogued).
11. Glyn Jones Papers, National Library of Wales, Aberystwyth, NLW MS 20717C. Unpublished notes, drafts and correspondence relating to *The Dragon has Two Tongues* referred to in this Introduction are to be found in NLW 20717C, 20718C or in the as yet uncatalogued portion of the Glyn Jones papers at the National Library.
12. At one point in his notes, Glyn Jones writes, 'I once saw Vernon standing with a pint of bitter in his hand and I felt then that the big glass and the

large volume of brown liquid were somehow holding him down to the floor; so often his poetry floats, wraithlike, a foot or two above the earth'.

13. The review is identified as being by Gwyn Jones in John Harris, *A Bibliographical Guide to Twenty-Four Modern Anglo-Welsh Writers* (Cardiff: University of Wales Press, 1994), 169. In a postcard from Ireland, where he was on holiday, Gwyn Jones wrote to Glyn Jones (30 November 1968):'I'm glad the *TLS* pleased you'. One notes that the author of the review comments that Glyn Jones is 'one of the two most knowledgeable men in his subject', without identifying the other one . .

14. 'Voices of Wales', *TLS* (14 November 1968), 1267.

15. *Anglo-Welsh Review*, 41 (Summer 1969), 215–17.

16. *Poetry Wales*, 3 (Spring 1969), 45–50.

17. Journal entry, October 1937, Glyn Jones Papers, National Library of Wales. This entry is in Welsh, the language in which GJ wrote his more personal entries; the translation is my own.

18. This entry is also in Welsh. Bute Street is in the dockland area of Cardiff, and was within walking distance of where Glyn Jones was teaching, though on the other side of Cardiff from Whitchurch, where he lived. For a fuller account of these issues, see the Introduction to *The Collected Stories of Glyn Jones*, ed. Tony Brown (Cardiff: University of Wales Press, 1999).

19. See *Collected Poems*, 41. On Glyn Jones's references to the working classes in his poetry, see my essay-review of *Collected Poems*, 'Tones of Loneliness', *New Welsh Review*, 39 (Winter 1997–98), 43–7.

20. The masculine pronouns are intentional. Despite the note to 'Look up Dorothy Edwards' work', her fiction, like that of Menna Gallie, is mentioned only in passing; the six authors discussed at length are all men.

21. 'Dedicated professional', *Planet*, 40 (1997), 53–4. Glyn Jones also shows his attitude to bohemianism in his satiric story 'The Tower of Loss' (*Collected Stories*, 294–312), written in the 1960s but set in the 1930s.

22. Brynmor Jones, *A Bibliography of Anglo-Welsh Literature, 1900–1965* (Cardiff: Wales and Monmouthshire Branch of the Library Association, 1970).

I

LETTER TO KEIDRYCH[1]

DEAR KEIDRYCH,

I address this introduction to you because in a way it was you who started it all. By 'it' I mean this particular book and the general inquiry into Anglo-Welsh, a term, by the way, I know you dislike as much as I do.

The Dragon has Two Tongues is really the outcome of a small incident, which I see no reason for your remembering, which took place one Sunday afternoon early in the Second World War, when I was travelling from our suburb into Cardiff on the bus with you, after you had been spending the week-end with my wife and me. I was on my way to the Welsh Sunday school I attended, and you were going to catch your train back to London. 'I don't suppose', I said, 'that many poets will be going to Sunday school this afternoon'.

'Ah,' you replied, 'not *English* poets. But you are not an English poet. You are a Welsh one'.

This was not, as you well know, the first time I had thought of my literary nationality. Even if I had not considered it before 1937, which I had, often, the founding that year of your sensational Anglo-Welsh magazine, *Wales*, would surely have brought it up sharply for me then. But I began to realize that afternoon that the question was really much bigger than I had thought, and that it was by no means entirely a literary one. It involved somehow my going to a Welsh Sunday school as well as the fact of my being a Welshman who wrote in English. Supposing I was a poet at all, was I really a Welsh poet as you so confidently affirmed? I was deeply conscious, certainly, of being a Welshman, and when I met young English poets of my own generation, sometimes in your company, I was often acutely conscious of the differences between them and myself. But although by the time I am speaking of I was able to speak Welsh, I had, unlike you, written no poems in the Welsh language. Also, I had taken very little part in Welsh literary life, in the *eisteddfodau* and so on. And out of this concern with my own position the question arose of those other writers, several of them our friends, whose situation seemed to be in many ways similar to yours and mine. Was Dylan Thomas a Welsh poet or an English one? And Vernon Watkins and Alun Lewis? I have over the years, like other Anglo-Welsh writers, tried to give answers, not always the same ones, to these questions and those related to them, in written articles, in lectures to adult classes in literature and in radio talks and discussions, some of them with you. The idea for this book is really the result. Some of it you will know about already. The chapter on Huw Menai – I wonder if you remember the marvellous night you and I spent with him and Gwyn Thomas in Cardiff just after the war – first appeared, in a very much shortened form, in the *Western Mail* in 1960. I had completed what I had to say about Dylan for this book before the appearance of Constantine FitzGibbon's admirable biography and his *Selected Letters* but, although these reveal that some of my assumptions about Dylan were mistaken, I decided not to remove or to alter anything I had already written.[2] Part of the material about Idris Davies (also a protégé of yours) was broadcast at the time of the poet's death in 1953, and part appeared in an American publication called the *Poetry and Drama Magazine* in 1957. The basis of the autobiographical section which opens the book is a Welsh apologia I delivered to a meeting of the Academi Gymreig, the Welsh Academy of Letters, in 1964.

Although Anglo-Welsh literature began long before 1900 – it is in fact, as Raymond Garlick has reminded us, older than American literature[3] – I am concerned in this book, as I've suggested above, only with what has been written by Welshmen in English in this century, more especially since the outbreak of the First World War. The two people I am most indebted to in this field, apart from yourself, for information and ideas, are Raymond Garlick and Professor Gwyn Jones. To Raymond Garlick I can be specific, when the time comes, in my acknowledgement of indebtedness. I so often, in the thirties and forties, discussed Anglo-Welsh literature with Gwyn Jones that I have no idea now what I knew about it, or what my standpoint was regarding it, before our discussions began. But he of course is not responsible for any of the shortcomings of this book, including the many questions unasked and unanswered. All the wrong-headedness, all the howlers, inaccuracies, generalizations and distortions, inevitable perhaps in a first and informative statement of this sort, are my own private property.

II

AUTOBIOGRAPHY

In 1944 an anthology of poems was published under the editorship of Keidrych Rhys entitled *Modern Welsh Poetry*. Almost twenty years later *The Oxford Book of Welsh Verse* appeared, selected, introduced and annotated by Dr Thomas Parry. One of the many differences between these two books was of course that the first concerned itself entirely with the work of modern, i.e. twentieth-century, poets, while the second covered a vast period of time, thirteen centuries of poetry, in fact, beginning with the *Gododdin* of the sixth-century poet Aneirin, and closing with the work of Bobi Jones, born in 1929. But there was an even more fundamental and striking difference between the two books because, in spite of its title, all the poems in Keidrych Rhys's anthology were in English, while all those in *The Oxford Book of Welsh Verse* were in Welsh.

Dr Parry's right to the word 'Welsh' in his title was clear and unequivocal, since not only were all his poets Welshmen, but they also, even those still living, wrote their poems in the Welsh language. To many, especially to Welsh-speaking *littérateurs*, Keidrych Rhys's use of the same word in *his* title appeared misleading, even presumptuous, because, although it indicated accurately enough the nationality of the majority of the contributors, it completely misrepresented the language in which the poems appeared, which was English.

At this point I feel I ought not to proceed further without restating an elementary fact arising from the above, one which many people outside Wales, and even some within it, hear for the first time with surprise and even incredulity. It is that Welsh is still the first language of hundreds of

thousands of Welshmen and Welshwomen and that a flourishing literature continues to be produced in it: novels, books of verse, plays, short
stories and criticism, as well as newspapers and magazines, children's
books and works of scholarship in history, biography and theology and so
on. It is against this background of living, written Welsh that I am
attempting at the moment to place Keidrych Rhys's contributors.

To return to our two anthologies. In *The Oxford Book of Welsh Verse* is
to be found the work of such famous Welsh poets as Waldo Williams,
Saunders Lewis, Gwenallt and T. H. Parry-Williams. Names, in the
nature of things, unfamiliar outside their native Wales and, possibly, the
departments of Celtic of a few home and overseas universities. On the
other hand, many of the poets represented in Keidrych Rhys's book –
Dylan Thomas, Vernon Watkins, Alun Lewis, David Jones, R. S. Thomas
– are known wherever English verse is read, and indeed it is they, rather
than Dr Parry's writers, who, to many, represent Welsh poetry. But the
truth is that, although Welsh by birth and upbringing, Keidrych Rhys's
poets write entirely in English. To avoid confusion in such a situation,
an obvious necessity has been the invention of a literary term to denote
writers like those represented in *Modern Welsh Poetry*, i.e. Welshmen
who write, whether poems, stories, novels or plays, in English. I
propose, however reluctantly, to follow custom and call them 'Anglo-
Welsh'. When I have occasion to refer to Dr Parry's writers I shall call
them simply 'Welsh', unqualified and unhyphenated, or, where
ambiguity might arise, 'Welsh-language'.

All the poets of *Modern Welsh Poetry* belong to the twentieth century,
and it is with them, and with their contemporaries who write prose,
that I intend to concern myself in this book. But the modern ones,
contrary to general belief, are not by any means the only Anglo-Welsh
writers. It is perhaps impossible now to decide who the first Welshman
to write a poem in English was, but we may be sure that anglicization
would not have to proceed very far before someone had a shot at it.
Professor Gwyn Williams has suggested[1] that it might have been an
Oxford Welshman called Ieuan ap Hywel Swrdwal, who lived between
1430 and 1480. If this is so it means that those who think Anglo-Welsh
writing began, and perhaps ended, with Dylan Thomas, are inaccurate
to the extent of about five hundred years and at least seventy poets, as I
hope, with the help of Raymond Garlick,[2] to show.

Until the time of the Tudors, a dynasty of partly Welsh descent, the vast
majority of Welshmen must have been monoglot Welsh speakers, although a small number were probably bilingual. Shakespeare's Glendower

swanks to Hotspur about his ability to use posh English, but he was an aristocrat who had spent some time at the Inns of Court and as an officer in the army of the English king. Sir Hugh Evans, although in jealous Falstaff's jibe he 'makes fritters of it', yet speaks English at least copiously – but he lived in Windsor, and the Welsh schoolmaster on whom he was probably modelled earned his living in Stratford, a sort of Elizabethan Slough or Coventry.[3] Raymond Garlick says that from the accession of Henry Tudor in 1485, English began to be one of the languages, in some cases the only language, of an increasing number of Welshmen.[4] This tendency to use English was stimulated by Tudor policy in Wales, by the founding of Jesus College, Oxford, and by the establishment of the Tudor grammar schools in the principality. After over four hundred years of union with England and nearly a hundred years of compulsory English primary education, a policy cheered on by amiable Philistines like Matthew Arnold, the situation at the present day in Wales is that only about a fifth of the population are able to speak Welsh, so that monoglot English speakers outnumber Welsh speakers (monoglots and bilinguals) by about four to one. Let me stress at the outset the incalculable extent and value of the contribution to life in Wales of this Welsh-speaking minority, to the country's politics, religion, culture and native literature. And let me restate the, to me, melancholy fact that by now the over-whelming majority of Welshmen cannot speak, read, write or understand Welsh, and that English is willy-nilly their mother tongue.

I have named Ieuan ap Hywel Swrdwal as Professor Gwyn Williams's candidate for the distinction of being the first Welshman to write a poem in English. The name of that poem was, approximately, 'Hymn to the Virgin', and it opens in this way:

> O meichti ladi owr leding – tw haf
>   at hefn owr abeiding
>   yntw ddy ffest efrlesting
>   i set a braents ws tw bring
>
> I wann ddys wyth blyss ddy blesing – of God
>   ffor iwr gwd abering
>   hwier i bynn ffor iwr wynning
>   syns kwin and iwr swnn ys king

We can assume that the author of these strange stanzas was bilingual and acquainted, as befitted the son of a Welsh scholar, genealogist and poet, with the literature of his own country, since although the poem is in English the spelling is Welsh (*hefn* = heaven, ddys = this, *ffor* = for, etc.) and the stanzas are written in the form of *englynion*, the *englyn* being one of the twenty-four metres of classical Welsh poetry.[5] After Ieuan ap Hywel Swrdwal, between Maurice Kyffin (1555–98) and Alun Lewis (1915–44), Raymond Garlick has discovered sixty-nine Welshmen and Welshwomen who, in varying numbers through the centuries, have written poetry in English. Most of these are now forgotten, like Sir John Scourfield, formerly Philipps (1808–76), Dr David Samwell (1751–98), surgeon on the *Discovery* and witness of Captain Cook's death, and John Thelwall (1764–1834), the friend of Hazlitt and Coleridge; but several will still be known to students of English literature, poets like Henry Vaughan the Silurist, George Herbert, John Dyer, who appears in Johnson's *Lives of the Poets*, Hester Lynch Piozzi (*née* Salusbury, of Bachygraig, Flintshire), George Powell, the eccentric friend of Swinburne, and Sir Lewis Morris, who almost became Poet Laureate after Tennyson. (Morris was usually described, after the name of his Welsh home, as 'of Penbryn'. This, someone unkindly remarked, helped to distinguish him from the other Morris, William, 'of Parnassus'.) Several Welshmen, although they have invariably excelled, if they have excelled at all, in only one language, have written poems in both Welsh and in English, and some poets are thus to be found not only in Garlick's necessarily heterogeneous collection, but also among those who have received the accolade of inclusion in Dr Parry's anthology. These poetic bilinguals include Iolo Morganwg (1747–1826), gifted poet, high-principled literary forger and greatest Welsh scholar of his day, who produced two volumes of English verse, and William Williams Pantycelyn (1717–91), regarded by some as the finest of all Welsh lyric poets, who wrote over sixty English hymns. Others were Morgan Llwyd, Lewis Morris (an ancestor of Morris of Penbryn), Ieuan Fardd, Islwyn, Elfed, T. Gwynn Jones, Sarnicol, Dewi Emrys and Wil Ifan. But the important and abiding work of the last eleven poets I have named has been done in their first language, Welsh, and for this reason I see them completely outside the consideration of this book; although five of them are poets of the twentieth century, their work in English is secondary to their great achievement in Welsh. My original definition of Anglo-Welsh, then, ought to be limited to indicate those Welsh writers whose entire work, or, in one or two instances, whose best work, has been done in English in the twentieth century.

Very few Anglo-Welsh writers have been able in fact to speak Welsh at all, much less make use of it for literary purposes. This is true of

Dylan Thomas, Vernon Watkins, Richard Hughes, Alun Lewis, Gwyn Thomas. But these and other Anglo-Welsh writers are nevertheless much closer to their Welsh-speaking and Welsh-writing compatriots than is generally realized even by Welshmen, as I hope to show. When I examine the traditions – social, religious, political – of my own family, I find them to be in large measure, I believe, characteristic of those of a number, even a majority, of modern Anglo-Welsh writers; and although one man is no other man, a description of my own family background will throw considerable light, it seems to me, on the type of society and the conjunction of social forces and influences which helped to bring many of the better-known Anglo-Welsh writers of the twentieth century into being.

I was born in 1905 in Merthyr Tydfil in Glamorgan, into a Welsh-speaking family, so that my own first language was Welsh. The town took its name from Tydfil, saint and martyr, daughter of Brychan, King of Brecon in the fifth century. She was martyred on the site of the Merthyr parish church, St Tydfil's (*Merthyr* = martyr). Until the eighteenth century Merthyr was an agricultural village, standing at the then beautiful head of the Taff (or Tâf) valley; that is, at the extreme northern edge of what was in the next century to be the South Wales coalfield. Iron, coal and steel were all in time produced in Merthyr, and with the influx of workers from England, Scotland and Ireland, and from other parts of Wales, the town grew rapidly in the last century to be for sixty years the largest in Wales, and picked up in the process such records as the possession of the largest iron works in the world and as the place of origin of the first steel rail ever. In 1801 the population was just over 7,000; by 1901 it had jumped to within a few hundred of 70,000. But geology has arranged that industrialism in South Wales can sometimes form a dramatically abrupt boundary with a vast and un-spoilt rural area, and in Merthyr this happened. The heavy and ruthless industrialism of the town was always to some extent mitigated by its position on the fringe of some of the loveliest scenery in our country, the Brecon Beacons area, now one of the national parks.

It is not necessary, for the purpose in hand, to concern ourselves with the history of Merthyr earlier than, say, 1800. As far as my own family is concerned this would bring me back to the generation of my great-grandparents, whose surnames I believe to be Jones and Anthony, Thomas and Phillips, Williams and Huw, Roberts and Rees. (Much of the information which follows about my relations and ancestors came to me from my mother, who lived to be a great age and who was as it were the family genealogist and herald. Some comes from family Bibles and documents.) William Jones, my paternal great-grandfather, lived not at first in Merthyr but near Llanybri in Carmarthenshire, on a farm situated in a beautiful and romantic spot at the mouth of the Tâf, near where the river enters Carmarthen Bay. On the opposite bank of the wide estuary stands Laugharne, which Dylan Thomas has now made famous as his home, and on the hill behind my great-grandfather's farm is what I take to be the 'sea wet church the size of a snail / With its horns through mist' − Llanybri church, perhaps − about which Dylan wrote in 'Poem in October'.

Like many tenant farmers of his time, William Jones thought that life might be richer, freer and easier in the industrial east of Wales, in Glamorgan, and giving up his farm he brought his wife and baby son to Merthyr. From Tâf Carmarthenshire to Tâf Glamorganshire in fact. The family travelled the eighty or so miles by road, walking, and brought part at least of their farm stock and household goods with them. Some of their possessions − woollen blankets and a few articles of furniture made from oak grown on the farm − still exist; and my parents throughout their long lives perpetuated the link with their relatives in this area of Carmarthenshire by regular visits, gifts and purchases, a side of bacon perhaps, and invariably the Christmas poultry. The immigrant family took a house in what was then a pleasant residential suburb overlooking the town of Merthyr, they kept their cows in the fields near by and they sold milk. Later William Jones began to work underground. He and his wife became members at Soar, a chapel of the Welsh Independents, built in 1803, where William Jones became in time a deacon and the official announcer from the Big Seat on Sunday nights of the church's activities for the coming week. This office gave him the almost inevitable nickname, or designation, in a country of very limited surnames, of Jones y Cyhoeddwr, Jones the Announcer.

William Jones's wife came from a family whose members used to intrigue me during my impressionable boyhood with claims of kinship with armigerous families in Carmarthenshire and Pembrokeshire. How much substance was in these pretensions, by my time pretty remote anyway, I have never tried to find out, but I know that my father, at once a great sceptic and a romantic dreamer, accepted the truth of the stories.

William Jones's son, my grandfather, David William Jones, spent the whole of his life in Merthyr, somewhat against his will, and worked for the Scottish Legal Insurance Company. His intention as a young man had been to become a missionary, and he began learning one of the languages of India, Hindustani I believe, with this aim in mind. But his health – he was a chronic sufferer from asthma – forced him to give up the idea, and what remained of the aspirations of this part of his early life, apart from a continued interest in religion, was the Indian diminutive by which he always addressed my father in childhood.

Merthyr in the nineteenth century was a place of many contrasts and enormous changes. It was the great Welsh boom town, the new industrial area eager for manpower for its iron-works and, later, its pits and steel works. 'Ah me!' said Carlyle, looking down upon it in 1850, 'It is like a vision of Hell'.[6] And Professor Gwyn A. Williams quotes the incident in Trollope of the curate who faints when he hears he has been posted there.[7] Housing conditions in large areas of the rapidly expanding town were deplorable[8] and, as a result of the primitive or non-existent sanitation, severe cholera epidemics swept the town in 1849, 1854 and 1866. The life expectancy of a working-class male there in the eighteen-forties was the almost Asiatic figure of seventeen and a half years, and in the next decade Merthyr had the highest mortality rate of any industrial or manufacturing town in Britain. In 1806 and 1816 there were strikes and riots, and in 1831 the unrest became so serious that the military were called in to preserve order, and Dic Penderyn, an alleged leader of the disturbances, was hanged in Cardiff jail as a result. All this sounds like the uproarious, overcrowded, squalid, drunken, turbulent township of Jack Jones's novels.[9] But there was another aspect, largely unrecorded in fiction, to the life of the town. The frustrated and even oppressed Welsh peasantry who flocked into Merthyr brought with them their own language, their religion, their culture, their social and political aspirations. So that Merthyr was not merely a place of poverty, unrest and industrial squalor, but also one of considerable intellectual ferment and artistic activity, a town in which the chapels, as well as *eisteddfodau* and literary, musical and Welsh cultural societies, flourished. This aspect of the town, I must record in fairness to Jack Jones, is represented more fully by him in his other Merthyr novels, namely *Bidden to the Feast* (1938) and *Off to Philadelphia in the Morning* (1947), in which the chapels and the choral societies play their part. The beginnings of a literary tradition might have been encouraged by the presence of Lady Charlotte Guest, who lived in Dowlais, Merthyr, and published the first translation into English of the *Mabinogion* in 1848. In the same year appeared *The Literature of the Kymry*, an account of Welsh poetry and prose between the twelfth and fourteenth centuries written by a remarkable Merthyr chemist, with at one time an international reputation, called Thomas Stephens. Another local author was Dafydd Morganwg, who wrote among other things *Yr Ysgol Farddol* (*The School of Poetry*), first published in 1869, an attempt by means of question and answer to teach the *cynganeddion*[10] from rule one. These were perhaps the best-known literary figures of the town in the last century, but they were by no means the only ones. Poets and musicians seem to have abounded, people like Rosser Beynon, composer, teacher and conductor; Ieuan Ddu, composer and poet; Taliesin ab Iolo, poet in English and Welsh, son of that great and strange Iolo Morganwg whom I have already mentioned, and himself the ancestor of I. A. Williams, the English poet and critic; Tydfylyn, poet and musician; Nathan Dyfed, poet, and his son, Llywarch Reynolds, poet and collector of Welsh manuscripts. The world of these people, and of those like them, was the one to which my grandfather belonged, the world of the Cymreigyddion, the Welsh literary society, of the poets, the musicians, the supporters of the *eisteddfodau* and the chapels and the choirs.

I still have the blue-and-gold illuminated address presented in 1894 to my grandfather by his colleagues on his retirement from the service of his insurance company, and I suppose we can credit the fulsome and pious Welsh of the address and accept that he did his job with conscientiousness and efficiency. But I doubt whether insurance meant much to him. His life, as I have suggested, was the life of books and poetry, of music and *eisteddfodau*. He was in fact a sort of intellectual, at a time when no one in Wales would perhaps have quite understood the word − a great talker and debater, theologian, politician, philosopher, singer and musician, an indefatigable competitor and frequent winner at *eisteddfodau*, a poet of sufficient reputation to have had delivered safely to him a letter from America addressed merely 'Llwch-Haiarn, Wales'. ('Llwch-Haiarn' was his bardic title.) In addition he was a man of great outspokenness and independence of mind and once for a time was deprived of his chapel membership for persisting in active support of a choir organized by the local Roman Catholic church. Rebelliousness seemed part of his nature and he enjoyed the company of others in revolt against oppression and reaction; one of his great friends was Dr Pan Jones, editor, author and critic of landlordism, whose candour brought him on three occasions before the courts on charges of libel, which cost him in all over £1,200. I never saw my grandfather, or any of my grandparents for that matter, but the oil painting we have of him shows a head, baldish and darkly-bearded, on the face the stare of a man prepared if necessary to be nonconformist to the point of offensiveness or truculence, an expression which as a child I found disagreeable and awesome. In fact, although I have described him as expansive and conversable, he was only so in the company of people who shared his interests. Normally he was a brooding, moody and forbidding man, his humour sometimes caustic and wounding. He died before my father and mother were married, but I have heard my mother say she did not exchange more than half a dozen words with him during the whole period of her engagement.

That a man like my grandfather, with a minimum of formal education, an insurance agent, son of a farmer turned milkman turned collier, should be a poet, a master of both the 'free' Welsh metres and of the *cynganeddion*, would cause not the slightest remark in the Wales of his time. This was quite common. In his day large numbers of poets, one is tempted to say *all* Welsh poets, came from homes and conditions similar to his; they were schoolmasters, colliers, ministers of religion, shopkeepers. These men were of course Welsh in speech, and the great majority would be nonconformist in religion and radical in politics. Almost, one might say, a knowledge of poetry was part of the accomplishment of the people described in the last two sentences as it was of the Elizabethan gentleman. And this conjunction, it seems to me, of Welsh speech, religious nonconformity and political radicalism produced in Wales, in the nineteenth and twentieth centuries, the country's most dynamic class, the great creative section of Welsh society from which have sprung almost all its leaders, whether political, artistic, religious or social. I use the word 'class' to describe this group or stratum; but class, as understood in England, is largely transcended here by the fact of common speech, a common religious faith and common political aspirations. To these factors it owed its social homogeneity, and not to consciousness of belonging to a dominant class, to inherited wealth or to having attended common schools and universities. Many observers have remarked on the lack of class consciousness among the Welsh, and some Welshmen have interpreted this as meaning that in Wales we have a classless society. In spite of what I have said above, this is far from being true.[11] Certainly Wales is without those institutions which seem to an outsider like myself to preserve in England the mystique of class. We have no Court or even a royal residence, no native aristocracy, no wealthy public schools, no Brigade of Guards, no clubland, no rich and ancient universities. We have of course an establishment, but the part played by hereditary wealth and privilege in its composition is small. One never hears a Welshman refer to his prep school, let alone his nanny. But social classes and class conflict nevertheless exist in Wales as they do in every country in Western Europe, and anyone brought up in a Welsh mining valley during this century must know that this is so. Because these valleys have been battlefields where the class war, in its industrial aspect, has been fought out with great savagery. Capital and labour, boss-class and workers – these were the troops of the opposing armies, whose propaganda machines were fiery speeches on the one hand and bitter newspaper editorials on the other, and whose battles were lockouts, riots and strikes. But these often devastating encounters were, in a sense, impersonal. People inevitably suffered in them, often long and severely, but they suffered, it seems to me, less individually and in isolation than as part of the whole community to which they belonged. Their own lack of food and clothing was also the lot of thousands all around them. Idris Davies in his poetry, B. L. Coombes in his fine autobiography, Gwyn Jones, Jack Jones and Gwyn Thomas in their novels, have all described for us the bitterness of being involved in the industrial side of the class struggle. But I cannot think of any Welsh or Anglo-Welsh writer who has made class in its personal aspect the subject of his work. We have no E. M. Forster or Evelyn Waugh or D. H. Lawrence. Class feeling between individual and individual, the personal tensions of class, class snobbery, class exclusiveness, the resentments of class humiliation, common in English novels, are to a large extent outside the experience of Welsh and Anglo-Welsh writers who live in Wales. The fun and malice of U and non-U would be impossible in our country, since the image and prestige of such a U-class as we possess are insufficiently powerful to compel social emulation; the patterns of behaviour of this often public-spirited group seem an anglicized irrelevancy to the thrusting, dynamic section of Welsh society which sees itself as the nation's real leaders. I do not of course think the Welshman is fundamentally less snobbish than the Englishman,[12] but he lives in a society whose climate gives the exercise of snobbery less opportunity. I have noticed that sensitive and aware young Welshmen, leaving this relaxed social atmosphere for England, sometimes seem to awaken to the puzzles and eye-openers of the 'hoary social curse' almost with the bewilderment of an adolescent becoming aware of sex.

A revealing story concerned with what I have been saying is the well-known one told about a visit paid by Kuno Meyer (1858–1919),

the celebrated German professor and Celtic scholar, to his friend, the
principal of one of the university colleges of Wales. On Sunday
afternoon the principal invited his guest to accompany him to the
Sunday school at the chapel of which he was a member. (I ought
perhaps to explain that the Welsh Sunday schools have never, like their
English counterparts, been attended exclusively by children, and that
adult classes for men and women have always been a normal feature of
them.) Another member of the group to which the principal belonged
was the college porter and, to Meyer's considerable surprise it was he,
and not the principal, who was the Sunday school teacher. Obviously
the difference in the incomes of the two men involved in the story
would place one of them in the working class and the other in the
middle class. But social class here, as in much of Welsh life, has, I think,
been transcended by what the two men were conscious of sharing,
namely a common language, Welsh, a common religion, nonconformity, and a common political faith, radicalism. And although I know
nothing further of this particular principal I would guess that his
ancestors, like those of his college porter, were tenant farmers. This
sense of having inherited a common tradition – social, religious,
political – has given the Welshman his sense of belonging to a community, and produced his relative indifference to class distinctions
within that community and, by usage, outside it. Welsh speech has been
a sort of social solvent, almost a badge of equality, which has softened
and even obliterated the sharper and more painful asperities of class.
What we have in Wales is not classlessness but a condition in which
class, like colour in a multi-racial society, is not of overwhelming
importance.

   I doubt, as I mentioned earlier, if the Welshman is by nature any more
democratic than the Englishman. But his history is different, and his
democratic sense has been fortified by the conception of *y werin*.
Modern Wales is to all intents and purposes a country without a native
aristocracy. A current jibe has it that the typical Welsh squire is an
English colonel. When the Tudors acceded to the English throne the
trek from Wales into England seems to have become something of a
flood. Then began in earnest the anglicization of the Welsh ruling
classes, and their separation from the mass of the people. They intermarried with their social counterparts in England, and they gradually
came to differ from the rest of their fellow countrymen in those three
aspects I have already named. They became, as David Williams tells us,
English in speech, Tory in politics and Church of England in religion.[13]

From this situation it seems to me the idea of *y werin*[14] took strength. Anyone in Wales today who speaks Welsh is inclined to be regarded, whatever his own wishes in the matter, as a member of *y werin*. He might possibly be a Tory in politics, but his Toryism would appear to his fellow countrymen as a mild deviation or eccentricity, not really important beside the fact of Welsh upbringing and Welsh speech. Similarly with regard to membership of the Church in Wales. The other factor in Welsh *gweriniaeth* (literally 'democracy') was industrialism, the solidarity which a community achieves through resistance to intolerable economic conditions and the fight for social betterment and for political power to ensure it. In all the industrial valleys of South Wales there were thousands of families whose roots were in the agricultural areas and who had brought their discontent with them along with their language and their religion. They resisted their industrial bosses, who were often Englishmen anyway,[15] as they had shaken off the hold of their rural landlords, and they made common cause with others in the valleys – English, Scots, Irish – who did the same. The democracy of language and religion, plus the democracy produced by the pressures of industry, have resulted in Wales in a situation in which, in the 1906 parliamentary elections, not a single Tory member was returned for the principality. Sixty years on, in 1966, of the thirty-six members of Parliament from Welsh constituencies, thirty-two were Labour. (One of these Labour seats was subsequently captured by the Welsh Nationalists.)[16] It is, or was, possible to see contests in local government elections in Wales in which the candidates are Labour, ILP and Communist.

Will Rogers, the American comedian who claimed Red Indian descent, used to say, 'My family didn't come over with the *Mayflower*. They met it'. My mother's family were in a similar sort of situation. They didn't arrive in the Merthyr valley with the floods of immigrants from the north and west as my father's people had done. They were there already. My great-grandfather, William Roberts, or Robart, was born just over a hundred and fifty years ago on a farm at Ynys Owen, an area a little lower down the valley, four or five miles to the south of the town of Merthyr. 'Born on the farm' was literally true of him, because he made his first appearance in this world when his mother was out working in the fields, and he was carried back to the farmhouse in her apron. The tradition of him in the family is that he was cheated out of his possession of the farm as a boy, and was induced to sign it away in exchange for a good suit of clothing. I sometimes wonder if this story is not really a distortion of what had really happened on another farm and a generation or two earlier. We know that the pioneer English iron-masters in the Merthyr valley sometimes secured valuable mineral rights from the local freeholders in return for quite inadequate compensation, and it seems to me likely that some such deception had been practised earlier, and that the event in a garbled form had then become attached in some way to the person of my great-grandfather. However that may be, what is certain is that he himself did not work on his mother's farm but became a shopkeeper, a grocer with a business in what was then a central position in Merthyr, within a few yards of the manor house and St Tydfil's parish church. With the building of the railway close by, his business prospered and he retired early and built two houses – they are still standing – on the hill behind the growing town, one to live in himself and one to rent. The tenant of the rented house is of interest in an account of Anglo-Welsh; he was a man called Francis, a smith, the father of a very distinguished pioneer Anglo-Welsh writer, J. O. Francis the dramatist, the author of those two small masterpieces *The Poacher* (1914) and *Birds of a Feather* (1927).

William Roberts married the daughter of a wealthy and well-connected Swansea doctor. In spite of her distinguished paternity Maria Rees brought her husband little money or possessions. She was, alas, illegitimate, and, although her father contributed towards her education, little of the money was used for its intended purpose. She was a remarkable woman, thoughtful, original, keenly interested in learning and seeming to inherit something of her father's medical interests and ability. She taught herself to read Welsh and English and she used to study with absorption the text-books her granddaughter, my mother, had bought for her teacher's examinations. She loved geography and history, but her favourite subject was physiology; after an evening studying a chapter on 'The Eye', say, she would discuss with my mother with unending wonder the magical efficiency of this organ and the vulnerable delicacy of its structure.

She and her altogether inferior husband, William Roberts, brought up my mother, when their own daughter died young in childbirth. Their son-in-law, my mother's father, Morgan Williams, was the son of William Morgan Williams of Merthyr, a horse contractor, supplying Welsh cobs and ponies to the coal companies for work in the mines of the valley. This second Morgan Williams, my grandfather, attended a private school in Merthyr, founded, owned and headmastered by Taliesin Williams, Taliesin ab Iolo, to give him his bardic name, the son of that astonishing Iolo Morganwg, scholar and forger, whom I have

mentioned earlier. Taliesin Williams was himself a poet in English and
Welsh, and his school had among its pupils the future first Lord
Merthyr and John Petherick, said, at least by Merthyr people, to be the
discoverer of the source of the White Nile. My grandfather, Morgan
Williams, dandy, poet, calligrapher, worked as a local government clerk
in Merthyr, but on the death at twenty-four of his wife he emigrated to
America, leaving my mother, still a baby, to be brought up by her
grandparents. He returned to Wales only once, to represent Y Drych, the
Welsh-language newspaper published in America, when the Welsh
National Eisteddfod was held in Swansea in 1891. He failed to make a
fortune abroad, and at the time of his death he was in debt and working
in the coal-mines of Scranton. He lies buried in Providence Cemetery,
Pennsylvania.

My mother, brought up by her grandparents on the hill Twynyrodyn
('the hill of the lime-kiln') behind the town, received her qualifying
parchment as a school-teacher in 1900, and before her marriage, and
again during the First World War, she taught in various schools in
Merthyr. My father as a young man also had this profession in mind and
stayed on in school as a sort of apprentice teacher, what was called then
a monitor. But two circumstances put a summary end to his teaching
career. The first was meningitis, the almost always fatal 'brain fever' of
the time, which was thought to rule out for those who had recovered
from it any sort of work requiring a preparation of formal study and
mental discipline. But the clinching reason for his abandoning teaching
and finding a messenger's job in the post office was dire poverty. For
years his parents had been in strained circumstances, enduring in fact
the bitter type of poverty known as respectable.

My father's mother, my grandfather Llwch-Haiarn's second wife, had
come to Merthyr from Goodwick, a beautifully-situated village near
Fishguard on the Pembrokeshire coast. Her widower brother, a ship's
master named Captain Ebenezer Thomas, was a great drunkard, a spree
drinker, and my father remembered being taken by her as a small child
to the various British ports at which Eben Thomas's ship was due to
dock, to get as much of his pay as she could from him before he spent it
all ashore on drink. The money she then passed on to Eben's four
motherless children, being cared for by their grandparents in Goodwick. When these old people, and Eben Thomas himself, died, my
grandmother brought the four orphans, three boys and a girl all still of
school age, to Merthyr, and reared them with her own child, my father,
and a daughter of her husband by a previous marriage. How this was

ever accomplished in the circumstances remains something of a mystery even in the family itself. My grandfather, often ill with asthma and unable to do his insurance job, somehow managed to support a wife and six children, four of them not his own, in circumstances that to the outside world appeared to be always fairly comfortable and unharassed. My mother, who knew about so notable a family long before she married into it, describes the endless hospitality of that strange household, where there was something to eat and drink for all callers, the visiting poets and musicians and the literary-minded doctors and ministers who turned in for a talking session with my often housebound grandfather. But this period of youthful and respectable poverty left a profound and ineradicable impression upon my own father, always a proud and sensitive man, who had to endure the anxiety and bitterness of it day by day. Normally he was completely indifferent to money, but in the last years of his old age, when for long periods senility made him oblivious of the world around him and he lived entirely in the past, he would often weep bitterly, recalling and reliving the torment of the contriving and the struggle to keep up a serene exterior during that penniless time of his boyhood.

I was brought up in a home where books were plentiful. My mother's text-books, annotated by her for her teacher's exams, seemed to be chiefly volumes of poetry, Wordsworth, Matthew Arnold, Shakespeare and so on; and as well there were many books of poetry and sermons, most of them in Welsh, left by my grandfather. My father too was a great reader all his life of English and Welsh books, poetry, economics, history, theology. He attended extra-mural classes of the university at Cardiff in literature, in philosophy and in economics, the darling study of the thirties. He was a subscriber to the Welsh Book Club and a member of the Cardiff Cymrodorion, the Welsh literary and cultural society. But his mind was essentially analytical and critical, not creative, and the discipline of writing he hated, as he hated most disciplines, and when he was bringing himself to sit down to compose even a letter his irritability, although he was normally bland and easygoing, communicated itself like an electric storm to everyone near. His main interests were not literary, in spite of what I have said before, but social, economic and above all political. As a young man he had once spent a night in the lock-up of the Merthyr police station, arrested with a number of his radical friends for tipping over on their sides the parked carriages of some Tory politicians who had come to Merthyr speaking and campaigning. But this was almost the limit of his public participation in politics, although he was for very many years before his death a paid-up member of the Labour Party. His attitude towards practical politics was really one of profound scepticism, and he was at heart I suppose some sort of philosophic anarchist without much faith in human nature. He seemed to me from his analyses of events to possess considerable political nous and knowledge, he was often sceptical of the superficial statements and interpretations of the newspapers, and wondered what the cynical reality was which had been covered up in the clichés and evasions and generalizations which more gullible readers would take at their face value. He sometimes foresaw and forecast with great accuracy in the political field, although some of his prophecies at the time appeared to me likely to be very wide of the mark. He was really a poor party man and admired and despised men regardless of their political colour. The popular hero, a Lloyd George or a Churchill, he was inclined to observe with a very cold eye. The fortunes of Plaid Cymru, the Welsh Nationalist Party, founded in 1925, he watched always with interest, sometimes with admiration at the devotion and idealism of its members, sometimes in its early days with gentle amusement at its political naïveté and ineptitude. He was shrewd, sceptical, humorous, detached, and on occasions he flashed out that rapid masterful wit that comes from lost illusions and a profound understanding of first principles. He had none of the attributes which, at least in the popular mind, are associated with a peasant background – greed, cunning, suspicion, narrowness, insensibility. The contradictions and complexities of his character have always fascinated me, e.g. his intellectual independence and his day-to-day passivity. Highly romantic, nourishing a secret life of fantasy, his common sense yet often blew like a bracing wind through the self-delusions of others; inexpressibly tender to those he felt were hurt, or despised, or cheaply held, he could behave sometimes with clumsy and wounding insensitivity towards those he loved; ultra-democratic and egalitarian, he yet harboured in his nature, unsuspected by most who knew him, a streak of suppressed and romantic snobbery. Unambitious and unworldly, the great and damning fault of his character was his spiritual lethargy, a sort of paralysis of the will. To him most human activities and aspirations were a sort of vanity; his most frequently quoted text was, 'Gwagedd o wagedd, gwagedd yw y cwbwl' – 'Vanity of vanities, all is vanity'. He belonged to various organizations, as I have shown, but in spite of his knowledge and judgment he shunned leadership and office. This reluctance was due, I believe, to his scepticism, since one holding the philosophy quoted above could hardly be expected to achieve much in any direction; and this was reinforced by a certain reserve and diffidence and a powerful desire for non-involvement. As he got older, especially when he took to wearing a black jacket and waistcoat and pin-striped trousers, he bore a strong physical resemblance to Winston Churchill, whom he regarded as a highly gifted but dangerously romantic reactionary; he had the same round and balding skull – both men in their youth had been redheads – the same wide, incurved, padded-looking shoulders, the same thickish body and upward-jutting paunch, the same heavy and encumbered movements in old age. But in place of Churchill's rather small nose, always represented by the cartoonists as *retroussé*, my father had a large and fleshy hook.

My mother's family was notable for a powerful religious and devotional strain, which my mother herself inherited in large measure. But what I remember most clearly about her from my boyhood is less her active piety than her remarkable and rather awesome good looks, the pale unblemished skin of the long face, the abundant red-gold hair, the large imperious grey eyes, the slightly aquiline nose with the flared nostrils. Both my parents were members of the chapel my great-grandfather had joined when he first came to Merthyr, she active, he passive, except in the singing school, which gave him an opportunity of exercising his fine bass voice, and in the Sunday school class he belonged to, where he took delight in provoking the less nimble and thoughtful members and in general intellectual horse-play and mischief-making. My mother as a young woman had been a Sunday school teacher in the local Ragged School, and in her own chapel, Soar, she was faithful in her attendance at the weekly prayer meeting, as well of course as at the three Sunday services, the women's afternoon meetings and so on. She acted for one rather remote and scholarly minister as a sort of honorary curate or unofficial secretary, keeping him informed of illness and difficulty and trouble among his membership. She also ran, with the help of three or four other teachers, an evening meeting for boys and girls in a 'branch' belonging to the church, what would now be called, I suppose, a church youth club. My brother and I, grammar schoolboys at the time, although not expected by my mother to attend these meetings with her, were called upon to supply weekly material for them, unpunctuated passages to be read aloud, words for use in the spelling competitions and so on.

On the walls of our home in Merthyr, apart from the wedding present 'chrystoleums' and the flower pieces framed with velvet, painted by an aunt, I remember four things – a portrait of John Ruskin cut from *Great Thoughts* and another of Henry Richard, a nineteenth-century Liberal Merthyr MP, known as the Apostle of Peace; a large brown text card with these words in silver upon it: 'Christ is the Head of this House, the unseen Guest at every Meal, the silent Listener to every Conversation'; and last, a large picture, three feet by four, called 'Oriel y Beirdd' – 'The Gallery of the Bards'. This, compiled in 1893, was a sort of montage formed of the photographs of over a hundred Welsh and Welsh-American poets and literary men, Welsh-language writers all of course, and amongst them, number ninety, was my grandfather, David William Jones, Llwch-Haiarn.

Reading modern English novels, from which I derive many of my notions of the English class system, I sometimes have the impression that the Englishman is more conscious of his class than of his nationality. I do not, as I have already indicated, think this is true of the Welshman, certainly not of the Welsh-speaking Welshman. But the literature I spoke of above, *viz.* twentieth-century English fiction, induces even the Welshman familiar with it to consider himself with as little levity as possible in relation to class; and here, as with nationality, one belongs I suppose, within limits, to the group one chooses to belong to, the one felt to be most congenial and sympathetic. I think of myself first as Welsh, and second as upper-class, upper-working-class of course, and during rare moments of delusions of grandeur even perhaps as lower-middle-class. But when I read accounts of English working-class life, represented as having its own virtues of warmth and vitality, but without culture or refinement, without concern for religion or politics or any form of art, I am struck by the differences that must exist in this one class, the working class, in Britain. I hesitate to claim that these differences are entirely national, although it is part of my thesis that a large number of homes like that of my parents must have existed in Wales during this century and the last. But I wonder, remembering words like those of Gerald the Welshman, whether one feature of my parents' home might not be characteristically Welsh. This was the attitude of my father and mother to guests. Visitors to our house, and there seemed to be many, were treated with an almost Arab courtesy; I sensed that the aim of my parents was always to please and entertain those who visited us and never to let them feel embarrassed or at a loss or unwelcome. The guest seemed sacred and his wishes overrode those of everyone in the family. The appearance of the minister at the front door was to my mother less a visit than a visitation.

Both my parents, as I have said already, were Welsh-speaking, as were of course all my grandparents and great-grandparents. There were no Welsh schools in Merthyr at the beginning of this century, and it was when I reached school age that I began to speak English regularly. A silent, even taciturn, child, I had, I understand, in fact said little in any language until then. English, by the time I was five, was the language of most of our Merthyr neighbours, and gradually, under pressure, my parents began in time to use the *lingua franca* of the surrounding English, Welsh, Irish and Scots, viz. English, when speaking to each other and to my brother and me. Rapidly, in school and at home, I lost the ability and the desire to speak Welsh, and I remained in this condition more or less for the next twenty years, although at no time during this period was I unable to read everyday Welsh or understand ordinary conversation. At home I often heard Welsh spoken when friends and relatives visited my parents; I listened to a Welsh sermon, sometimes two, on Sundays. I heard the Bible read in Welsh and I joined in singing Welsh hymns. But although Welsh was the official language of our Merthyr chapel, the language, that is, in which the church services were carried on, English had already replaced it in those activities which churches provide for their younger members. The Sunday school by the end of the First World War was almost completely anglicized and so was the weekly Band of Hope meeting, and its successor called the Christian Endeavour Movement. Every summer I heard more Welsh conversation in four or five weeks than I had perhaps heard in the previous twelvemonth, because I spent my summer holidays on the hill farm of my uncle, near Llanstephan in Carmarthenshire. He was a bachelor and carried on the farm with the help of his two unmarried sisters and three servants, one female and two male. None of these six spoke any more than the smallest amount of English, and I was forced to use what Welsh I still had to communicate with them. Speaking their minimal English, they were to me sometimes puzzling and amusing. They confused the Welsh pronoun 'hi', which means 'she', with the English pronoun 'he', which has an identical pronunciation, so that when they were discussing sleeping arrangements the 'hi's' and the 'she's' and the 'he's' produced situations as complicated as those of a French farce.

This, from the language point of view, was the situation in which I grew up. At home I heard Welsh spoken intermittently, but I spoke almost none myself; in the chapel I heard none in circumstances where it was of living concern to me; in the elementary school I heard none at all. What of my grammar school? This, it seems to me, was perhaps the most anglicizing influence of my life. I wonder if it would be true to say that the Education Act of 1889, which established state secondary education in Wales, brought the Anglo-Welsh writers of the twentieth century into being? Later in this book I try to classify the educational backgrounds of Anglo-Welsh short-story writers, and it would appear that more of these writers attended grammar schools than any other type of post-junior-school institution. It would seem to me that the grammar schools in Wales have been on the whole such powerful anglicizing agents because they operate on the mind at a time when it is at its most sensitive and receptive and most open to ideas and intellectual influences. As far as many writers are concerned, this period seems of enormous importance. It is often said that a writer's mother tongue, the language he heard first from his mother, is the one which he will inevitably use for his creative work, his poems, novels, plays and stories. This I question. It seems to me that the language which captures his heart and imagination during the emotional and intellectual upheavals of adolescence, the language of his awakening, the language in which ideas – political, religious, aesthetic – and an understanding of personal and social relationships first dawn upon his mind, is the language likely to be the one of his creative work. This is the period, this adolescence lasting from puberty to twenty-five and perhaps beyond (Melville said, 'Until I was twenty-five I had no development at all'), of new experiences and new emotions and new ideas, and I believe that the language of the imagination then is the one the artist will use even in preference to the potent but perhaps limited mother tongue. For the majority of Welshmen that language is now English.

In my grammar school at Merthyr[17] there was, as far as I know, no one qualified to teach Welsh, although there were three or four Welsh speakers on the staff. One teacher, T. J. Thomas, known throughout Wales by his bardic name of Sarnicol, had gained the highest honour of the National Eisteddfod, the award of the chair, for his winning poem in *cynghanedd*, which meant that he was a poet at least of considerable technical skill. But T. J. Thomas was employed to teach us chemistry. Although many of the school's pupils were the children of Welsh-speaking parents, or came from homes where Welsh was still the first language, or were themselves, even, more at home speaking Welsh than English, yet the school's language of instruction was exclusively English. Indeed the establishment might have been in the middle of the Norfolk Broads or up on the Pennines for all the contact it had with the rich life of the community surrounding it. We had no school eisteddfod, we heard nothing of the turbulent industrial history of the town itself, nothing of its Welsh literary associations, nothing of its religious history. Our only contact with Welsh literature, if it can be called a contact, was our reading during the English lesson of Lady Charlotte Guest's *Mabinogion* (1848), which had been translated into English a few miles from the school. It must be obvious that anyone receiving the sort of education I have described would be far more likely to become some sort of Englishman than a Welshman profoundly aware and proud of his heritage, a writer of English rather than of Welsh. How similar, in their attitude to Welsh, were the other grammar schools in industrial South Wales I do not know with any certainty, but it seems unlikely that only one school in the area should have been of the sort I have described, when all the schools came into being for the same reasons and had a similar social background. I do not know either how many Welsh-language writers are actually the products of the valleys' grammar schools, but the writers of novels, stories and poems in English from these schools include, among many others, Gwyn Thomas, Professor Gwyn Jones, Rhys Davies, George Ewart Evans, Dorothy Edwards, Alun Richards and Menna Gallie.

It would be unfair to my grammar school to leave a totally unfavourable impression of it. I ought to say in mitigation that I was a pupil there during the First World War and its aftermath, and that when that war broke out the school had been in existence only about a twelvemonth. Also, although from a Welsh point of view, the influence of the school seems to me now to have been nugatory, my time there I have always regarded as fruitful and most happy, and I look back with satisfaction upon two revelations which I experienced there. One of these I was acutely aware of at the time, the impact of the other I became conscious of only much later.

It was in my grammar school, naturally enough, that I awoke to the marvel of English romantic poetry. My favourite book became the *Golden Treasury with Additional Poems*, i.e. work by William Morris, Rossetti, Browning, Swinburne, Tennyson and so on. I was completely overwhelmed by the loveliness of this work, and by some which was much older. From many sections of the book I committed poems to memory unprompted, including the sonnets of Shakespeare in Book One and the poems of Browning and Emerson in Additional Poems. At that time I was also greatly moved by the plays of Shakespeare, and I read them with a delight I am no longer capable of experiencing. My mind was obsessed by poetry, by its language and sound and imagery, but since for me it appeared to possess powerful and awe-inspiring elements of magic, it never occurred to me at the time to try to write it. Naturally, with such an intense interest in the subject, my work in English was generally satisfactory to the teachers, and once, when I had composed a rather flowery description of my home town in an essay, the English master wrote alongside in the margin, 'Where did this come from?', thinking I had copied the passage from some book about Merthyr. I was too shy to tell him I had written it myself.

The grammar school building was a large and impressive castle, not an old one but an attractive and picturesque imitation in light grey limestone, towered and crenellated, with large windows instead of arrow slits, and lawns and masses of rhododendrons instead of moat and hornwork. The building, Cyfarthfa Castle, had been put up originally by William Crawshay, the Merthyr millionaire iron king, in 1825 as a home for his family, and he had surrounded it with a woodland park of more than a hundred and fifty acres. At the foot of the grassy slope, falling away from the broad terrace before the castle, lay a large lake for boating and fishing, and another and wilder lake was situated at the most distant point of the park.

The whole of this estate lay to the north of Merthyr and overlooked the valley or dell in which the Crawshays' iron and steel works, before the castle became a grammar school, had flourished. But at Cyfarthfa, industrialism, iron- and steel-making and coal-mining, came geographically to an abrupt termination. Outside the northern walls of the school rural Breconshire began. Every midday break, alone or with my friends, I wandered about the marvellous and still unsubdued woods in the vast park surrounding the school, where the weeds and the wilderness were by no means denied their place, and where there were swans on the lakes and fish in them, where one could see, as well as all sorts of trees and flowers and shrubs, kingfishers and moorhens with their young and the marvellous nests of the wrens in the ivy. During the summer, at midday, my friends and I often left the park, attractive though it was, and cycled out through the school gates directly the bell ended the morning session. In spite of my mother's strong disapproval, I always declined to eat school dinners so that I could enjoy this extra time of freedom. We took the road to the north which led us in the direction of the Brecon Beacons, an area to me then of enchantment, of sunshine and blue lakes and woods, and the vast bareness of the mountains rising from the roadside, green and yellow, with the thin cloud shadows lying transparent upon them in the heat, following every ridge and valley in a perfect fit. Sometimes, leaving our bicycles, we found ourselves on the brink of some sheer limestone bluff and, looking down, we saw below us the tops of the trees growing up towards us out of the valley. All this lovely countryside impressed me and disturbed me profoundly with its grandeur and beauty, although I was not aware at the time how lasting and how powerful the effect of this revelation was to be upon me. The idea of *beauty* has always, ever since this period of my life, been mixed up with the two things I have been discussing, romantic poetry and natural scenery like that of the Beacons.

I was a detached and self-absorbed pupil and so, in general, unsatisfactory. I failed the London Matriculation examination in French, although I felt I was not entirely to blame in this since I had been first taught the language in hilarious but barren lessons by a shady and inefficient character who disappeared from the Merthyr scene overnight when called upon to produce documentary proof of his academic qualifications. I had always shown some aptitude for and much interest in drawing and painting, and in the circumstances it was very much the wish of my mother that I should now go to an art school, a common bolt-hole then for people in my situation, but I opted instead for a teachers' training college, an English one, St Paul's College, Cheltenham. What possessed me to make this choice could only have been the fact that one of my closest school friends was already a student there, but within months I bitterly regretted my decision. Cheltenham, a day's cycling distance from my home, seemed entirely cold and alien; to me it was always a place of *hiraeth* and painful exile.

I began teaching in a school in a long since cleared slum area near the centre of the city of Cardiff.[18] The school population was, as always, mixed. Some children came from unexceptional homes, clean, orderly, responsible, concerned, prepared to make sacrifices. Others, a very large number, perhaps even a majority, were surely among the poorest and most wretched in the city, ill fed, ill cared for, dressed in dirty, handed-on clothes often not much better than rags. Several came to school barefooted even in winter, and many more, I often felt, would have been better off with their feet unshod than wearing the broken, sopping boots and stockings they had on. The parents of many of the children, even the apparently neglected ones, were good people often, who sent their children to school badly-nourished and poorly-dressed through no fault of their own. Other children had feckless and negligent parents, criminally indifferent some, gamblers, heavy drinkers, work-shies, whom I saw regularly in the queue that formed outside the pawnbroker's shop opposite the school every Monday morning. Some children had criminal parents in the legal sense, thieves and housebreakers; one father was a convicted coiner, another operated an illicit still, three at least were brothel-keepers, another was involved in a brutal race-gang knifing near the school which resulted in several murder charges. One family, unable to afford a funeral, buried their dead baby in the back garden. I heard of prostitution, incest, sodomy in our children's homes. One of the boys, from a desperately poor family, was solicited by a wealthy local business man and cruelly assaulted sexually. Poverty I knew about well enough in Merthyr before I came to Cardiff, but direct contact with the conjunction of poverty, vice and crime was new to me and I found the experience deeply shocking and distressing. When a child in my class was ill I would sometimes go to his house or room after school to see how he was progressing, and what I witnessed on these visits, the squalor, the overcrowding, the degradation, the poverty, I have never forgotten.[19]

I was not then, between twenty-one and twenty-five, a writer, and I had as yet no conscious thought of becoming one, so that my visits to my sick pupils were entirely innocent and disinterested, not made with any intention of gathering experience and material for my work. But I read widely at that time, both literature and literary journalism. For three or four years, I remember, I read every review and article every week in *The Times Literary Supplement*, reviews of books I would never see, much less read, books on subjects I did not even know existed. I picked up a good deal of information about books, publishers and authors from this stint of course, as well as a realization of the wisdom, subtlety, learning, crankiness and varying standards of critics and reviewers. I joined, and belonged to for several years, an English literature class at Cardiff University College, the tutor of which was Miss Catherine Macdonald Maclean, the Wordsworth scholar, at that time the college's senior lecturer in English. I became friendly with her and visited her home, and it was a pleasant and new experience for me when she listened to and thought about what I had to say concerning the modern writers that had begun to interest me so profoundly – D. H. Lawrence, Aldous Huxley and Virginia Woolf in particular. Miss Maclean was the first person I had ever spoken to about what excited me most at the time, namely contemporary literature.[20]

Cardiff was for me then an extremely lonely place. Apart from Miss Maclean, whose interests were really academic, and were not primarily in modern literature, I knew almost no one with whom I could talk about the writers who fascinated me, and whose pages constituted my real life. This sort of complaint is common, I suppose, among young provincials with literary interests; only as time went on I saw myself less as a provincial when I thought of London than as a foreigner, as perhaps will become clear later. No literary or artistic life existed in the Welsh city. My literary hero then was D. H. Lawrence, and later Hopkins shared with him my admiration. I also felt tremendous interest in Joyce, Wyndham Lewis and Roy Campbell, as well as in Huxley and Virginia Woolf. But no one I knew or met showed any more than a polite interest in these or any other writers. Yes, one smart young English lecturer was patronizing about Lawrence before a group of university students I had addressed, and his clever flippancy at Lawrence's expense made them laugh. To me this was deeply disenchanting and wounding and seemed at the time, coming from such a person, quite unpardonable.

Lawrence had been a young teacher at one time like myself; he had been brought up in a mining area near a countryside of exceptional natural beauty as I had been, his family were Congregationalists and mine were the Welsh equivalent, namely Independents. It was, of course, because of the brilliance of the imagery in Lawrence, the vividness of his language and the deep feeling in poems like 'Snapdragon' and 'Love on the Farm', and not because of these parallels, that I was buying and reading everything of Lawrence I could lay hands on and afford. I had greatly admired his work, especially his poetry, long before I knew anything at all about him personally. I was only just beginning to learn something of his life and circumstances in fact when I visited Vence in the summer of 1930, a few months after I had heard of his death there. But it was the work of Lawrence, dealing with an environment so like in many ways the one I had been brought up in myself, that first made me think of writing.

The year 1931, in which I bought the two volumes of Lawrence's collected poems, saw my own first poems appearing in print. (I will do no more than mention one question that exercised me a great deal at this time. It was whether I had any right, in the condition of Wales and of the whole world, to devote any time to writing at all.) There was no Anglo-Welsh magazine in existence then, like *Wales* or *The Welsh Review* of a few years later, so I sent three pieces to the *Dublin Magazine*, edited by Seumas O'Sullivan, who accepted them with some enthusiasm, although he explained he was unable to pay for them. (*The Dublin Magazine* also later printed the first published poems of Alun Lewis and R. S. Thomas.)[21] One of the poems, a sixty-five line long piece of blank

verse, was called 'Maelog the Eremite' and described the musings of a
hermit who once occupied a cell in Gelli Faelog, near Merthyr, about
whom nothing is known. I was twenty-six at the time and the year was,
as I say, 1931.

My life during the thirties, that part of it whose relevance makes me
want to speak about it, was of course very greatly influenced by the
Depression and left-wing politics, and also by the pacifist debate and
the fear of war. At this time also I became increasingly aware of my
Welsh heritage, and I began to know other young writers. Before the
thirties ended the Second World War had broken out.

The Depression in South Wales appears to some who lived there
through it a more agonizing experience even than the Second World
War. To me, working in Cardiff, in spite of my absorption in the
problems of my own loneliness and frustration, it was inescapable, and I
had no wish to escape it. During the first seven or eight years of the
thirties I watched Wales becoming shabbier, poorer and more desperate,
the children in school, even the children of good parents, growing paler
and more listless and ill-clad. The remembrance of one boy, cowed and
wan, decently dressed in clothing which, although clean and neatly
darned by his mother, had obviously been originally bought for someone
else, has always represented for me an image of the heartbreak of that
period. This boy's father was an unemployed cinema violinist who
walked endlessly about the district around the school wearing on his face
a terrible distracted expression of suppressed rage, bewilderment and
frustration. It was to me an agony to send the imagination into that good
home, to witness the struggle and the defeat, the frustration of tenderness, the tears, the despair. Not all the suffering was by any means passive.
South Wales seethed with protest, expressed in meetings, demonstrations
and 'hunger marches'. One day, not far from the school, a procession of
the unemployed clashed with the police, who drew their batons and laid
out a few of the demonstrators on the roadway. One of the victims I
knew well, and his account of the fracas, which I had expected to hear
trembling with horror or indignation, was hilarious. When I travelled up
into the valleys I saw empty shops, sometimes a row of them, groups of
unemployed men at the street corners, and everywhere a depressing
shabbiness and hopelessness. What I was experiencing vividly from day to
day was being expressed in books and newspapers by such abstract
phrases as 'The standard of living continues to fall'.

Families receiving unemployment pay were subject to inspection by
the 'means-test man', an official whose scrutiny was bitterly resented in

the proud and independent mining communities, and who was hated in direct proportion to his efficiency and conscientiousness. I remember once, at the home of one of my unemployed friends in Merthyr, the visit of this government snooper. On the kitchen table at his entrance he noticed an Ovaltine tin. 'How can you afford to buy that?' were his first words. My friend could not. The tin was used for holding old pieces of string.[22]

But overshadowing the agony of South Wales was the fear of war. I could not see how war was ever to be reconciled with Christian belief, and I felt convinced pacifism was implicit in Christianity. And how, I asked myself, was the desperate plight of those around me to be improved by war, which was more likely to impoverish them further and even destroy them and their community? I was quite wrong. About a twelvemonth before war broke out I remember sitting by the fire in a large bus garage at the derelict top end of one of the valleys, chatting to a group of unemployed miners. They were cheerful. As we talked one of them got up, went to the work-bench under the window and returned with half a pint of engine oil which he poured on the fire. The flames went up bright and yellow, illuminating the gloomy barn-like garage with their brilliance. This was a celebration. The men, after years of unemployment, had been promised jobs within a matter of days. One, a miner who hadn't worked for fifteen years, was the next day to start in an arms factory.

Pacifism was no new creed to me, thought up during the thirties. As a schoolboy I knew that Merthyr conscientious objectors to the First World War, of whom there were several, were being ill-treated and imprisoned and were suffering social ostracism; but I never at home, although my own father was serving in France at the time, heard any word of disparagement or condemnation or contempt for the stand of these men; rather the reverse, admiration for their courage and tenacity in the face of so much mass scorn, derision and ill-treatment. Merthyr in fact had a strong pacifist tradition, a combination of the pacifism of Welsh nonconformity and of left-wing politics. Here the old ILP with its influential anti-war element had flourished. One of Merthyr's members of Parliament had been the near-pacifist Keir Hardie, and an earlier one was Henry Richard, the Apostle of Peace. Some of the nonconformist ministers of the town had preached pacifism from their pulpits with great courage even when the First World War was in progress. The Cardiff pacifists in the thirties, Quakers, Peace Pledge signatories, members of *Urdd y Deyrnas* and the Fellowship of

Reconciliation,[23] had a propaganda stall in the busy Cardiff market, and it was in attendance here during the thirties that I spent my agonized Saturday mornings.

In 1934, as I describe in a later chapter, I first met Dylan Thomas. In 1936 I received a letter addressed from Crouch End, London, and signed 'Keidrych Rhys'. That letter was the first of more than forty that were to arrive at our house from Keidrych in the next three years. Later in 1936 Keidrych, accompanied by a friend, himself turned up, tall, handsome, beautifully-dressed in country tweeds, as was his companion, and speaking disconcerting Welsh with the accent of the English public schools. This visit was the beginning of a friendship between us which lasted for many years. *Wales*,[24] the first literary magazine of any standing, and standards, for Welshmen writing in English, had not then appeared, and Keidrych, its founder and editor, was looking around for suitable contributors. He had heard of me, he told me, through Dylan, whom he had met in London, and what he had seen of my work made him think I might be the sort of poet he intended to publish in *Wales*. Other contributors to the first eleven numbers – *Wales* ceased publication in 1939 because war had broken out – were Dylan Thomas, Vernon Watkins, Idris Davies, Margiad Evans, Rhys Davies, Emyr Humphreys and Caradoc Evans, as well as the non-Welshmen James Hanley, Hugh MacDiarmid, George Barker, Julian Symons, Philip O'Connor and D. S. Savage. Keidrych published something of mine – story, poem or review – in most of the eleven issues, and he was also kind and encouraging about my work in his letters, which was a fine thing for one beginning to write. Also he got the late Margiad Evans to review my first book, *The Blue Bed*, in the second number of *Wales* in 1937, and that review, from a sensitive and generous poet, was one of the most perceptive and enthusiastic I received.

One of the rare intellectual and artistic meeting places in South Wales in the early thirties was the Three Valleys Festival of music, held in the valleys town of Mountain Ash. Late one night in 1935, when I was returning to Cardiff by train from this festival, I spoke for the first time to two other writers with whom I have been friendly ever since. The train, almost empty by then, drew up at Rhiwbina, the Cardiff suburb in which my wife and I, recently married, had taken a house. Three people got out into the pouring rain, myself and two other men who appeared to know each other. As we walked along the deserted platform we got into conversation. The shorter, more buoyant of the two friends I knew by sight as Jack Jones, ex-miner, ex-soldier, ex-parliamentary candidate, ex-cinema manager, author at that time of *Rhondda Roundabout* and *Black Parade*. The other was Gwyn Jones, who had already published his huge and exciting historical novel *Richard Savage* (1935). In 1939 Gwyn founded and edited *The Welsh Review*, another magazine which, like *Wales*, intended to publish the work of Welshmen writing in English. The first number appeared in February. In September of the same year the Second World War broke out, but before the magazine closed down in November (it was published again between 1944 and 1948), it had published work by Geraint Goodwin, Jack Jones, Alun Lewis, W. H. Davies, Huw Menai, Ernest Rhys, Wyn Griffith, Brenda Chamberlain and, in translation, Kate Roberts. Gwyn Jones asked me to contribute, which I was glad to do. I have tried to say earlier how much I am in his debt for encouragement and criticism over many years.

At this time, during the thirties, although I was publishing regularly in *Wales* and *The Welsh Review*, I was also sending my work to London, New York, Paris and Chicago. *Life and Letters To-day*, under the editorship of Robert Herring, published some of my stories, and *The Adelphi* some stories, poems and reviews. *Poetry Chicago* not only published my work but paid me what I thought was remarkably good money in return. I saw my fellow countryman Rhys Davies appearing in the Paris-based *This Quarter*, and this decided me to send some stories to Edward Titus, but the magazine, as so often happened, seemed suddenly to fold up. One other magazine that interested me I ought to mention. In 1934 H. E. Bates, with Arthur Calder-Marshall, Hamish Miles, Edward J. O'Brien, L. A. Pavey and Geoffrey West, founded *New Stories*, to provide a magazine for the work of short-story writers, and much to my satisfaction a couple of my early pieces appeared in it. I spent my school holidays at that time in London picking up obscure 'little magazines' that I could send my work to and meeting young writers with whom I would discuss books by writers of the type of Djuna Barnes, Flann O'Brien and Samuel Beckett. In 1936 the late Hamish Miles, having seen some of my short stories in the magazines mentioned above, wrote to me from Jonathan Cape's asking me if I had a sufficient number of stories available to make a volume. I had not, but I wrote some more and in 1937 *The Blue Bed* appeared. 1937 was, in fact, a very fruitful year in Anglo-Welsh writing, perhaps its most fruitful ever. It saw the publication, among other books, of the novels *A Bridge to Divide Them* by Goronwy Rees, *The Wooden Spoon* by Wyn Griffith, *A Time to Laugh* by Rhys Davies and *Cwmardy* by Lewis Jones; of Geraint

Goodwin's short stories *The White Farm*; of Jack Jones's autobiography *Unfinished Journey* and his play *Land of My Fathers*; of David Jones's *In Parenthesis*; of Rhys Davies's *My Wales* and of Ernest Rhys's poems *Song of the Sun*. In the same year the first anthology of Anglo-Welsh short stories appeared, *Welsh Short Stories* (Faber), and Keidrych Rhys founded *Wales*.

Until I was twenty-five I had taken no special interest in Wales or in Welsh. When the First World War broke out my father volunteered for the army – surely the most positive act of his life – and on his demobilization he moved to Cardiff where he had a clerk's job in the post office. When the war ended I was thirteen. A little short of twenty-one I started to work in Cardiff myself as a teacher and I became a member of the church to which my parents already belonged, a church in which every activity, on Sundays and on weekdays, was carried out strictly in the Welsh language.[25] A notice on the wall of the minister's room warned visiting preachers against using any language other than Welsh in the pulpit. But this intensely Welsh atmosphere, the intense Welshness of the members, failed to awaken any response in me at all. I lived in a sort of isolation, so obsessed with my own problems and with the modern English literature I was reading that I was quite indifferent to the atmosphere and activities of the Welsh community to which my parents belonged. The combination of ignorance and arrogance is a guarantee of insensitiveness, but in time I began to know some of the young Welshmen and Welshwomen who were members at the church of my parents, and their friends – students, for the most part, studying Welsh as part of their academic course – and their proud Welshness affected me profoundly. Some of them were political Nationalists, and all of them, by their conviction, their knowledge and understanding and their devotion to Wales, shamed me. I began in time to find it intolerable that I should be a Welshman, living in Wales, and yet ignorant of my Welsh heritage, the first in a seemingly endless family descent who was unable to speak the language of my ancestors, and so excluded from the Welsh community. English literature I knew I should always be interested in, but what did I feel about the literature of my own country? The answer was nothing, because I knew nothing about it. I began to read Welsh, commencing with our hymn book, which is immeasurably richer in poetry than any similar collection in England, since the hymn has been the chosen form, the lyric, of some of the greatest of Welsh poets.[26] In 1932 a series of Welsh paperbacks, entitled collectively *Y Ford Gron* (*The Round Table*) began to appear and I bought and read these volumes as they were published. These books were not, like the early Penguins, cheap editions of modern novels, but volumes of selections and anthologies, with introductions and notes, of older Welsh literature – in Welsh of course. One was a selection of poems by Dafydd ap Gwilym, another an anthology from the *cywydd-wyr*,[27] another some tales from the *Mabinogion*, another a marvellous collection of folk poetry. This series was a revelation to me, and I read some of the volumes in a sort of blaze of glory. Also not without a sense of resentment. Why had I never heard of the staggering beauty of this material before? All of what I read I did not completely understand, because after twenty years of indifference my Welsh was uncertain and limited; but I could take in enough to be swept off my feet by the unfamiliar music of the *cywyddau*, by the brilliance of their imagery and by their sharp response to the visual beauty of the world. I got out my grandfather's copy of *Yr Ysgol Farddol* and began learning the *cyng-aneddion* from it, and I employed two young Welsh scholars to read the *cywyddau* with me so that I could understand them better. As well as studying privately I joined a class run by one of my new friends, by then a teacher in Cardiff, to learn, or rather to relearn, to speak Welsh with greater ease; and later, classes in Welsh literature of various periods.[28] Everything Welsh became of enormous interest to me. The fact that my mother's father had attended the school of Iolo Morganwg's son was for the first time of special personal significance, and the picture of my father's father in the *Gallery of Welsh and Welsh-American Poets* was a matter of strange satisfaction, although I was well aware that most of the poets represented, my grandfather probably included, could not be regarded as writers of any great distinction. But I took pride in the fact that someone closely related to me was a master of the *cynganeddion* and was able to compose *cywyddau* and *englynion*, as well of course as verses in the free metres.

In addition to writing my early poems and stories at this time I began to attempt Welsh literary journalism. I was in Paris in 1937 and on my return I wrote an article for *Tir Newydd*[29] on Surrealism, the only Welsh article I ever saw on the subject. I gave a radio talk on G. M. Hopkins in a series designed by Aneirin Talfan Davies to bring the significance of English, American and continental writers to the notice of Welsh-language listeners. I reviewed Welsh books and, a little later than the period I am speaking of, I regularly translated English articles into Welsh for *Y Tyst* (*The Witness*), the weekly journal of the Welsh Independents. As a result of such writing and reviewing, I suppose, I was on two occasions invited to adjudicate Welsh prose at the National Eisteddfod. What I was quite incapable of doing was myself writing prose or poetry that seemed to me to be of any value or distinction at all in Welsh. I said earlier that the language of adolescence, not the mother tongue, appeared to me the one the artist will be likely to use for his creative purposes.[30] Twenty years of English were too much for me. The unconscious rules the poet and the language stewing in the juice of my unconscious, if that mysterious brew has a language at all, is English; every line of poetry that has arisen unsought and unexpectedly in my mind, the words of every image and description, almost every beautiful and striking individual word, have all been English. I, and those Anglo-Welsh writers brought up in circumstances similar to mine, certainly did not reject the Welsh language. On the contrary, the Welsh language rejected us. This is true even of those of us who are deeply conscious of and love our Welsh heritage. On the other hand, while using cheerfully enough the English language, I have never written in it a word about any country other than Wales, or any people other than Welsh people.

III

BACKGROUND

Wно are the Anglo-Welsh? I defined them first simply as Welshmen who write in English. Later I qualified this, and I ought to qualify the definition further by confining the term to those Welsh men and women who write in English about Wales. But how do poets, especially lyric poets, whose subject is so often themselves, fit into this definition? Surely consciousness of being Welsh ought to find a place somewhere in a complete definition. Also the term for my purpose in this book, as I have previously indicated, means only writers of the twentieth century, more particularly the post-Caradoc Evans writers of the first half of the century.

Whom does this leave? Or rather, whom does it bring in? In the first two Anglo-Welsh anthologies of poetry published since the end of the First World War, *Modern Welsh Poetry*, edited by Keidrych Rhys (Faber, 1944) and *Presenting Welsh Poetry*, edited by Gwyn Williams (Faber, 1959), there are, between them, thirty-eight individual poets. In the first four anthologies of short stories[1] there are thirty-seven individual writers. This gives a total of seventy-five; but some of the short-story writers, being also poets, appear in both types of anthology, so if we subtract these nine duplicated names we are still left with sixty-six names. Novelists who are not poets or short-story writers do not of course appear in any of the six anthologies – e.g. Jack Jones, Richard Llewellyn (*How Green Was My Valley,* 1939), Megan Glyn (*Hovering Chariot*, 1951) and Richard Vaughan (*Moulded in Earth*, 1951). And writers who have appeared since the publication of the anthologies,

novelists like Ron Berry, Raymond Williams, W. H. Boore and Menna
Gallie, and poets like Harri Webb, Leslie Norris, Meic Stephens, Robert
Morgan, John Stuart Williams, Sally Roberts and Bryn Griffiths ought
also to be added to the number. As should the dramatists Emlyn
Williams, Alun Owen, Alun Richards and Eynon Evans. My own list of
twentieth-century Anglo-Welsh writers, restricted to those who have
published at least one novel, or an individual volume of stories or
poems, or a play, still totals over fifty.[2] But about a few of these, for
various reasons, I must confess myself a little uneasy. Is Richard Hughes
really an Anglo-Welsh writer? A Welshman, certainly, and living most of
his life in Wales; but this fine novelist's best work, *High Wind in Jamaica*
and *In Hazard*, is not concerned with his native land at all. And what
about David Jones and Emlyn Williams and Goronwy Rees and Alun
Owen, writers who seem from some points of view very much Anglo-
Welsh, but whose work, like that of Richard Hughes, is not invariably
about Wales? I very much want, naturally, to include figures of such
attractive brilliance in my list, and I have in fact done so, while cheerfully
rejecting writers of remote Welsh ancestry like Wilfred Owen, Charles
Morgan, Anthony Powell, Wyndham Lewis and the Powys brothers. One
can in fact find comfort if not justification in the reflection that very
seldom can writers, painters and musicians be placed with complete
tidiness and satisfaction into arbitrary groups and categories. There must
always be a few elusive and individual figures who for various reasons
refuse to be penned in comfortably with any group, however much we
might want to do this to them. On the other hand, there is, I think, a
central core of writers whose names would appear in everybody's list of
Anglo-Welsh, whatever their definition of the term might be, e.g. the six
authors I have chosen to write about at greater length later.

Attempts have been made from time to time to see throughout
Anglo-Welsh writing the existence of definable common qualities, of
special and characteristic ways of regarding life, of a certain generic form
of expression, all of which collectively are thought to be *Welsh*, or at least
Celtic, and which give the group unity. I think all such attempts to
impose homogeneity on these writers on a basis of race or style or
identity of vision or philosophy are bound to fail. It is in fact easier, to
use a phrase of Peter Elfed Lewis, to impose a pattern on the work of
these writers than to find one that already exists, although it is true that
some important negative generalizations can be made. The members of
the group are diverse and individual, varying in their styles, in their
subject matter, in their conceptions of the purpose of literature, in their

attitude to Wales. Obvious differences are shown by the fact that some are novelists, some poets, some short-story writers, some dramatists. One group, represented by Caradoc Evans, writes about those parts of Wales which are Welsh in speech, so that we have to imagine their characters speaking in a language other than the one in which their conversation is written down; indeed, with the exception of his novel *This Way to Heaven* (1934), Caradoc writes almost as exclusively about Welsh Wales (in Wales and in London), as do Welsh-language short-story writers like Kate Roberts and D. J. Williams. Others among the Anglo-Welsh, like Jack Jones and Gwyn Thomas, set their novels in the industrial, largely English-speaking, valleys. Eiluned Lewis, Geraint Goodwin, H. L. V. Fletcher, Raymond Williams and Margiad Evans are writers of the English-Welsh border. Nigel Heseltine is one of the few Anglo-Welsh (Richard Hughes, E. Inglis-Jones, Hilda Vaughan and 'Twm Teg' (C. E. Vulliamy) are others) who write about the squirearchy and its anglicized apers. Richard Vaughan, Richard Llewellyn and Alexander Cordell are concerned not with a different geographical area or a different social class, but with a different historical period – an agricultural and industrial Wales that no longer exists. Dylan Thomas was, as he says, 'a word man'. Jack Jones does not know, or pretends not to know, what a thesaurus is. Emyr Humphreys and R. S. Thomas are political Nationalists. The comment of Gwyn Thomas on some publicized Nationalist campaign was, 'Owain Glyn Dŵr rides again'. It seems to me that difference and variety rather than any uniformity of vision or expression or ideas are the marks of the Anglo-Welsh, and that nothing very meaningful and illuminating, except perhaps negatively, can be said collectively of a group that contains Jack Jones and Vernon Watkins, Caradoc Evans and Emyr Humphreys, Gwyn Thomas and Dorothy Edwards.

We ought not to expect to find what gives the Anglo-Welsh such unity as they possess in their style, or in their use of language, or in their subject matter, or in their attitude to what they write about. What they have in common, apart always from the basic fact that they are Welsh men and women who write in English, is their background. Earlier I described the sort of home and society in which I was brought up. The parents of some of the other Anglo-Welsh were no doubt more politically-active than mine were, more devout, better off, more learned, more cultured, more Welsh. And many, no doubt, were in each case less so. But I think the home of my parents did share features common in varying degrees to a large number, perhaps indeed to a majority, of the Anglo-Welsh.

More Anglo-Welsh writers of the first half of the twentieth century come from a background of Welsh-speaking radical nonconformity than from any other. I suggested earlier that this part of Welsh society has produced most of the country's leaders in whatever field during the last hundred or so years; here in fact we have the 'genius belt', or at least the talent belt, of the nation, the section in Welsh society, the creative, enlightened, literature-producing class that is the nearest thing existing in Wales to the creative, enlightened, literature-producing middle class in England, although our Welsh version is of course so far less wealthy, less privileged, less powerful and less ascendant in a social sense. Almost all contemporary Welsh-language writers, whether poets, novelists, dramatists or critics, also have this back-ground. The two groups of Welsh writers, Welsh-language and Anglo-Welsh, share this common origin if they share at present regrettably little else. The Anglo-Welsh are the often unwitting, as the Welsh-language writers are the conscious, inheritors of a specific culture. What happened to split the writers of modern Wales into two groups? The answer is, the same forces as have split our whole culture, our whole nation into two, namely anglicization. In industrial South Wales, as a result of mixed marriages, and under the pressure of non-Welsh education, thousands of parents gave up the struggle to continue speaking Welsh and gradually fell in with the common language of the neighbourhood or the community, which was English. One sometimes sees an illustration of this in those families, like that of Gwyn Thomas, in which the older children speak Welsh and the younger ones English only. In this situation an Anglo-Welsh writer is likely to appear – namely when a radical, nonconformist, Welsh-speaking family begins to speak English. The English speaking may sometimes be done concurrently with Welsh speaking, or far more frequently in preference to it. A very large number indeed of Anglo-Welsh writers are the first generation of the family to speak English as their first language, or their only language. I can think of hardly any writers, not more than five or six, who have come from those areas in Wales, whether geographical or social, which have long been anglicized, South Pembrokeshire and Radnorshire in the first instance, and the property-owning class in the second. (Gerald Morgan, reviewing in the *Western Mail*, 16 September 1961, *Beirdd Penfro*, an anthology of Welsh-language poems of Pembrokeshire, pointed out that more good poetry had been written in fifty years in north Pembrokeshire, the Welsh-speaking part, than in eight hundred in south Pembrokeshire, the English-speaking 'Little England beyond

Wales'.) On the other hand, many of the Anglo-Welsh were born in the industrial south, where the process of turning to the use of English took place most rapidly. Dylan Thomas, Caradoc Evans, Huw Menai, Jack Jones, Vernon Watkins, Gwyn Thomas, Rhys Davies, George Ewart Evans, Richard Vaughan, Emyr Humphreys, Alun Lewis, Idris Davies, Menna Gallie and many more are the children of Welsh-speaking parents, and several of these writers are the first generation of their families to be unable to speak Welsh themselves. It will be seen that in the matter of background the modern Welsh-language writers and the Anglo-Welsh are much closer together than perhaps some members of both groups sometimes realize; that some of the Anglo-Welsh in fact are Anglo only by the skin of their teeth.

This division, even in some instances the hostility, between Welsh and Anglo-Welsh writers, has always been to me regrettable and distressing. Welsh-language poets, conscious of the unbroken continuity of their literary heritage from the sixth to the present century, are inclined to look with a certain amount of coldness upon a literature which, it appears to them, hardly existed before 1900. I tried to show earlier that Anglo-Welsh writing is in fact a good deal older than this. But it must be conceded, I think, that no modern Anglo-Welsh writer would claim that those writers of previous centuries in Raymond Garlick's list meant anything to him as influences. The tradition the modern Anglo-Welsh writer really belongs to is not that tenuous one stretching between Ieuan ap Hywel Swrdwal and Sir Lewis Morris of Penbryn, about which he or she usually knows little and cares nothing. Their influences are to be sought in the contemporary literature of England, plus the literatures perhaps of France, Germany, Ireland and America. That is one cause of the lack of cordiality between the Welsh and the Anglo-Welsh, the reluctance of the custodians of an ancient literary tradition to admit real merit in the work of a new group which seems, although perhaps talented, also brash, ignorant, alien and rootless.

Another accusation levelled against the Anglo-Welsh concerns chiefly the prose writers – the novelists and short-story writers. The Welsh accuse them of falsity, of giving a hopelessly distorted picture of Wales in their writings, of not portraying or interpreting Wales truly and adequately to the world. The true Wales, the Welsh-speaker says, is nothing like the Wales of Caradoc Evans and Rhys Davies. I have myself, as a young Anglo-Welsh writer, been subject to this sort of criticism, and the first time I encountered it I was bewildered by its complete irrelevance to anything I had thought or attempted. The idea of undertaking anything so portentous as an interpretation of Wales to the world had never entered my head.[3] All I wanted to do as a young writer was to express what had moved me to delight, or horror, or laughter, or pity; to make my own statement about the Wales I knew; to impose some sort of pattern, acceptable to myself at least, upon the shoals of impressions pouring in upon me. In short, I was a writer whose impulse was primarily lyrical. I doubt if many Anglo-Welsh writers have consciously set out to interpret Wales to the world or to herself. This is true, but I do think there is substance in the complaint of Welsh critics that the picture of Wales presented by some early Anglo-Welsh writers is an almost unrecognizable distortion. But by today, it seems to me, that that note of contempt and mockery, so common in the work of Caradoc Evans and those who immediately followed him, has largely subsided, and the attitude of many present-day Anglo-Welsh writers towards Wales and her problems is responsible and deeply sympathetic.

This question of the resemblance between a writer's work and the society he depicts interests me greatly. I remember seeing once on television a programme about the painter Josef Herman, who at one time lived in industrial South Wales and painted many Welsh scenes and people.[4] Herman's paintings are characterized by a low-toned, almost sombre, range of colours, and to his massive human figures he gives a monumental and dour solidity. Some of the portraits of Welsh miners, which he had painted during his stay in the Swansea valley, were shown on the television screen, and they portrayed a sable-visaged race of torpid troglodytes, lumpish and impassive. Following the paintings the men we may suppose to have acted as models for them appeared, the volatile, laughing, vivacious Cwm Tawe miners themselves, with their expressive faces and their irrepressible liveliness of gesture. The difference between the paintings and the human beings on which they were presumably based was so startling as to be funny. But was Herman to be regarded as a poor painter because his works bore so little resemblance to the figures which they were supposed to represent? The problem as far as literature is concerned is not quite as simple, I know, since words are in some way intimately connected with the human psyche, with ethics and convictions and attitudes in a way paint, which is without adjectives, is not; words involve us in judgment and often cannot remain morally neutral as paint is able to do. I shall have further, probably equally unhelpful, suggestions to make about this matter, when I come to deal with Caradoc Evans, a writer whose work has for many Welshmen brought up this problem very sharply.

What traffic there is between Welsh-language writers and critics on the one hand and the Anglo-Welsh on the other has been almost entirely one-way. Welsh critics appear to read the Anglo-Welsh, often, for the reasons I have given above, with impatience, even hostility, with the contempt of those who see Wales as tragedy for those who see her as farce; but the Anglo-Welsh, apart from a small number, do not read Welsh at all, for the sufficient reason that they are unable to. Confronted by a poem or a story in their native language they can only respond as to a page of Magyar or Baltoslav. So that when the Anglo-Welsh have refrained from returning the attacks made upon them by the Welsh, this must be ascribed not to any special state of grace but to the fact that they are not even conscious, many of them, that the attacks have been delivered. With disapproval on the one side and ignorance on the other, the amount of cross-fertilization between these two vigorous and prolific literatures, flourishing side by side in a quite small country, was for many years almost nil. Recently, it seems to me, the situation has begun slightly to alter and to improve. I described earlier how my increasing awareness of Wales and Welsh coincided with the writing of my first stories and poems. But for the generation to which I belonged, namely the contributors to the early numbers of *Wales*, this dual development was unusual. Only Keidrych Rhys, Wyn Griffith and myself, as far as I know, were at that time really interested in the nationalist aspirations of Wales and in Welsh literature, although Idris Davies in time did develop an interest. Writers who began to publish their serious work a little later, Emyr Humphreys and R. S. Thomas, had come under the influence of Saunders Lewis, one of the founders of the Welsh Nationalist Party, and they were far more conscious of their Welshness and of Welsh nation-hood than Dylan Thomas or Rhys Davies, or Vernon Watkins or Caradoc Evans had been. (Though the fact that these writers chose to appear in a magazine called *Wales* is surely an indication of some national conscious-ness on their part.) This consciousness developed further among the Anglo-Welsh poets, associated with the magazine *Poetry Wales*, writers like Harri Webb, Peter Gruffydd, Meic Stephens, Tom Earley, John Tripp and Herbert Williams, some bilingual and active members of Plaid Cymru. Also the Academi Gymreig, the Welsh Academy, an association of Welsh-language writers, has opened its doors to certain Anglo-Welsh writers who have made a contribution to Welsh life and literature.[5] The outstanding example is Emyr Humphreys, who as well as publishing novels in English has also written a Welsh novel and produced several plays for Welsh-language television. He is in fact regarded by some Welsh critics as the finest prose, as R. S. Thomas is the finest poetic, interpreter in English of the dilemmas and the stresses and the contradictions of modern Welsh society. The material of our nationhood is often distressingly fissile, but what I have mentioned above are signs, small ones, of greater co-operation and understanding between the two literary groups in our country. One day perhaps a great Welsh publishing house will be established in Cardiff which will issue the books of Welshmen of both sorts, whether writers in English or in Welsh.

Attempts have been made to draw parallels between the Anglo-Welsh and the Anglo-Irish, the movement which produced Yeats, Lady Gregory, Synge, George Moore, Edward Martyn, Sean O'Faolain, etc. To me there seem few resemblances. One can call Yeats or Joyce an Irish writer without ambiguity in a way one could not call Dylan Thomas a Welsh writer. Certainly Irish society was split before independence, and Welsh society is split now, but there would appear to be marked differences in the directions of the divisions. The 'two nations' of Wales are composed not so much of the ascendancy and the peasantry of an agricultural land, but of Welsh speakers on the one hand and non-Welsh speakers on the other. Anglo-Irish writers were never, either beknown to themselves or unbeknown, shut out from a large part of the life of their own nation in the way in which, for example, a non-Welsh-speaking Welsh person may feel shut out by a Welsh-language television programme, even a current affairs programme, for and about Welsh Wales. Yeats, although he knew no Gaelic, could feel himself to be in the middle of Irish affairs in a way no Anglo-Welsh writer ignorant of Welsh could possibly do. Again the Anglo-Welsh are largely the products of an industrial society, and those with politics have given their allegiance on the whole, until recently, more to socialism than to nationalism. I doubt if any Welsh writer anyway, Anglo or otherwise, would endorse the hierarchic nationalism of Yeats; the concept of the 'big house' and all that it implies, is certainly not one that has dominated the imagination of Welsh writers. Perhaps a parallel can be seen between Anglo-Welsh and Anglo-Irish in the way both movements appeared at a time of increasing national consciousness. I cannot really claim that the magazine *Wales*, say, was the complete and dynamic expression in English of a new Welsh awareness of national identity; the influences behind the writing of much of it were English and American rather than Welsh, as I have already suggested. But I think both the politics and the writing were different manifestations of the same national and artistic stirring which has taken place in Wales in this century. Not only does Wales now have Nationalist members of Parliament; she has produced during the last half century more actors, singers, musicians, artists and writers who are conscious of their Welshness than probably ever before.

IV

INTRODUCTION TO SHORT STORIES AND NOVELS

THE first anthology of Anglo-Welsh short stories was published by
Faber in 1937 and shared an identical title with the three that
followed, namely *Welsh Short Stories*[1] – a misnomer of course, as I tried to
show when writing earlier about Anglo-Welsh poetry. This 1937 volume
contained the work of twenty-six writers, with a strict ration of one story
apiece, and included the work of Rhys Davies, Caradoc Evans, Gwyn
Jones, Richard Hughes and Dylan Thomas. But not quite all the contributors come within my definition of Anglo-Welsh. The compilers – the
book was not the work of a single editor – appear to have made a gesture
of conciliation towards their Welsh-language contemporaries, because five
stories, the work of Kate Roberts, D. J. Williams, Tegla Davies, Richard
Hughes Williams and J. Ellis Williams, appear in translation from Welsh. Of
the remaining twenty-one, the Anglo-Welsh, not all, for various reasons,
developed as short-story writers. In fact no less than ten of the twenty-one
do not appear again in any of the subsequent collections.

The anthology which appeared in 1959, edited by George Ewart
Evans, is ostensibly a revised edition of the 1937 volume but is in fact
virtually a completely new collection. It contains twenty-five stories,
one fewer than previously, again by twenty-five writers, and again with
translations (three this time) from the Welsh. But very few Anglo-Welsh
stories included in the 1937 volume appear again here – only five out
of the twenty-five in fact – and the list of authors differs very considerably also. Thirteen of the twenty-one contributors to the original

volume have disappeared, and their places have been taken by fourteen newcomers, including a by now well-known trio who had produced little or nothing when the first anthology appeared in 1937, namely Gwyn Thomas, Emyr Humphreys and Alun Lewis.

In between these two Faber anthologies, Professor Gwyn Jones compiled in 1940 and 1956 two further selections, the first a Penguin and the second one of the World's Classics series. Both these contain, in addition to the Anglo-Welsh stories proper, a few translations from modern Welsh, and the World's Classics volume is a little different from the other three in not confining its contributors to a uniform one story each. Although the stories and the authors included in these four anthologies naturally vary from volume to volume, it is perhaps worth mentioning that seven writers appear in all four collections. They are Rhys Davies, Caradoc Evans, Geraint Goodwin, Richard Hughes, Glyn Jones, Gwyn Jones and Dylan Thomas. But this should not of course be thought to indicate that these seven are necessarily the best among the Anglo-Welsh short-story writers. It might only mean they were born earlier or lived longer. In 1937 Alun Lewis was only twenty-two and Gwyn Thomas, a slow starter, twenty-four; Dorothy Edwards was dead by the age of thirty-one.

The anthologies and their introductions tell us a good deal about the Anglo-Welsh short story. The total number of individual writers appearing in the four books, excluding the Welsh-language writers, is thirty-seven, which seems to me a high figure, and prompts the question, why? That is, why should there appear in Wales, in this century, so large a number of short-story writers using English as their language? One good answer is that there are now more writers in every country. But I feel this is incomplete as an explanation of the number I have given above. When I was considering the Anglo-Welsh poets, the pioneer work of Raymond Garlick enabled me to point to over seventy Welshmen who had written English poems since Tudor times. I doubt if even so inspired and industrious a researcher as Raymond Garlick could find an equal number of short-story writers of comparable standing during that period. The short story seems to be largely a modern interest, and the Anglo-Welsh short-story writers appear to be the first of their kind in Wales.

To return to the question, why? Part of the answer has already been given, I believe, since the short-story writers have appeared as the result of those social and historical forces which have produced Anglo-Welsh writers in general, whether short-story writers, dramatists, novelists or poets. A very large number of these thirty-seven men and women belong to Welsh-speaking families. Many were born in democratic and dissenting South Wales, where industrialism has hastened on the process of anglicization. What I have not mentioned, or not stressed, is the vital part popular education has played in the appearance of the Anglo-Welsh.

In 1889 the Welsh Intermediate Schools Act was passed, and this virtually brought state secondary education into being in Wales, since before that date in Glamorgan, for example, the most populous county, there were only four grammar schools in existence, those at Cowbridge, Pengam, Swansea and Llandaff. That number would of course be multiplied many times by now; even by 1902, when a similar system of secondary education was adopted in England, ninety-five 'intermediate' schools had already been established in Wales – which means that since the beginning of the twentieth century, as a result of the Act, a vast number of the children of the education-loving Welsh have become pupils in these schools, and have so been educated at least to an age at which literature, English literature of course, might have some meaning for them.[2] The education of the Welsh secondary schools – grammar, intermediate, county or secondary as they have been variously named – has often, especially in the industrial areas, been an anglicizing influence, much more likely, as I tried earlier to show, to turn out writers of English than of Welsh. Of the thirty-seven Anglo-Welsh writers I mentioned earlier as contributors to the four short-story anthologies, more than half, I am certain, were products of the Welsh grammar schools; the exact figure will probably be found to be nearer three-quarters. (Of the background of writers like Ifan Pughe, David Alexander, Richard Pryce and Henry Mansel, who appear in only one anthology, I know nothing.) Also, of the seven writers who are included in the four volumes, five are products of the Welsh grammar schools. Only one of the seven, Professor Gwyn Jones, attended the University of Wales.

I doubt if there is at the moment in Wales a single full-time professional Welsh-language literary man, someone who earns his living by writing books and articles, supplementing his income perhaps by editing, and by work for television and radio. The great renaissance of Welsh-language literature of this century has been the work of brilliant amateurs; the poets T. Gwynn Jones, W. J. Gruffydd and T. H. Parry-Williams were university professors, Williams Parry and Saunders Lewis university lecturers, T. Rowland Hughes a BBC producer, Caradog Prichard a journalist, Kate Roberts and D. J. Williams grammar school teachers. This modern renaissance has been much more remarkable for its poetry and short stories than for its novels – only Rowland Hughes of the above would one think of *first* as a novelist. Perhaps amateurism in literature succeeds better when shorter works are attempted, since, for a man or a woman who has another job, writing a novel requires commitment and steadiness of vision and a quite unusual degree of stamina over a long period. This may be one reason for the number of short-story writers among the Anglo-Welsh, since the majority of this group also are, or began as, amateurs, without of course private means or allowances. The real weakness of this theory is that about half the thirty-seven short-story writers have also published novels.

Why so many short-story writers and so few dramatists, say? A sounder reason for the choice of the short story as a means of expression might be that when several of the Anglo-Welsh were beginning to write, in the thirties, the short story was enjoying something of a vogue in England. Volumes of short stories by new and unknown writers were published in those days and it was between the wars that writers like H. E. Bates, Liam O'Flaherty, L. A. G. Strong, A. E. Coppard and Malachi Whitaker really made their names as writers of short stories. Edward J. O'Brien's *Best Short Stories* appeared annually, chosen from work already published in magazines, and a glance through the indexes of the O'Brien selections will show the large number of periodicals of some standing in those days prepared to publish short stories. In 1934 also H. E. Bates and a few of his friends established *New Stories*, to which I have already referred. The two Anglo-Welsh magazines, *Wales* and *The Welsh Review*, together with *Life and Letters To-day*, published stories by, among others, Dylan Thomas, Caradoc Evans, Nigel Heseltine, George Ewart Evans, Rhys Davies, Geraint Goodwin, Llewelyn Wyn Griffith, Gwyn Jones and Margiad Evans. It was in this climate of interest and encouragement that many of the early Anglo-Welsh of this century began their writing careers, and the conditions prevailing in the world of publishing and criticism might have had their influence in helping them to decide what literary form to adopt.

I have already claimed that it is almost impossible to make general-izations, except negative ones, about the work of the Anglo-Welsh as a body. These writers belong largely, by birth and up-bringing, as I have tried to show, to Welsh, rather than to long-anglicized, Wales; and their surnames indicate that they are not either, most of them, the descend-ants of those immigrant English, Scottish and Irish of whatever class who have settled in their thousands in Wales in the last centuries.[3] They are in fact the products of a highly democratic society, one in which everyone who speaks Welsh tends to regard everyone else who speaks Welsh as a natural equal. This has given them the negative common characteristic of not having the results of class discrimination and consciousness among the constituents of their emotional stock-in-trade. Of the ninety-three stories in the four anthologies I have been speaking about, not more than two or three are concerned with class. 'Class distinction is no doubt a very cruel and a very reprehensible thing, but it is an evil that is deep-rooted in human nature itself, and it will only be eradicated at the call of the last trump. No champion of democracy, no Jack Cade, no Danton, no Lenin will be able to slay that dragon of caste.' So reflects Delia in Herbert M. Vaughan's story 'An Idyll Without an End' in the 1937 volume. She is Miss Delia Ward, a middle-aged English gentlewoman, falling in love with Mr Clement Thomas, a middle-aged Welsh carpenter she has met while on a holiday in Wales. The words have no doubt some truth in them, but how strange they sound in that volume of hopeless farmer Davis, Shacki Thomas the unemployed collier, Dylan's David Two Times and Meg the resurrected Rhondda whore. No 'Daughters of the Vicar' here, or 'The Real Thing', no 'The Garden Party' even.[4] Sex there is in plenty in Rhys Davies, Dylan Thomas, Geraint Goodwin, Gwyn Jones, Caradoc Evans, seen often as something of a mystery, sometimes disruptive, sometimes funny, but on the whole with mature acceptance as a natural part of human existence. An obsession with sex is not, though, one of the characteristics of the Anglo-Welsh short story. Stories in which childhood plays a central part are perhaps even commoner than those which have sex as their subject; stories about children are to be found, for instance, in the work of Dylan Thomas, Rhys Davies, Gwyn Jones, Margiad Evans, Alun Lewis, William Glynne Jones and Aled Vaughan.[5]

Anglo-Welsh story writers have been on the whole more faithful to the traditional politics of their background than to its traditional faith. What many seem in fact to have rejected is not so much nonconformity as organized religion, and yet much of the work of the Anglo-Welsh is inevitably permeated with Christian feeling, with a sense of humanity, with sympathy for the young and the suffering and the cheaply-held. Caradoc Evans's picture of nonconformity is indeed almost universally hostile, and most of the Anglo-Welsh who have written on this subject at all have followed him. It would be difficult to find Anglo-Welsh stories in which formal religion, or those who practise it, whether ministers, deacons or church members, is treated with seriousness, respect and understanding. (A remarkable *novel* which does this is Emyr

Humphreys's *Outside the House of Baal*, 1965.) There are, I think, several reasons for the frequent derision and contempt: the influence of a powerful pioneer like Caradoc Evans; the vulnerability at all times of the 'unco guid'; the general decay of religion in our time; the inability of the anglicized Anglo-Welsh to realize the positive role the chapel has played in the social, cultural and religious life of Wales; the fear in the young of not being on the jeering side. Almost one is tempted to say that the frequency and the ferocity of an Anglo-Welsh writer's attacks on the chapel are an index to the extent of his anglicization and his acceptance of English values. Modern Welsh literature, which understands the contribution of nonconformity to Welsh society, is not notable for such attacks.[6] The case of Caradoc Evans is the main reason for the 'almost' above. But Caradoc's sense of outrage is evoked less by religion itself than by the staggering discrepancies he sees between the professions of religion and the conduct of those making these professions – by hypocrisy, in fact. For the sincere Christian, e.g. his neighbour, the Rev. Tom Beynon of New Cross, Cardiganshire, Caradoc felt, personally, admiration and warm affection.

Humour is one of the most notable and constant qualities of Anglo-Welsh stories from the beginning. Satire is common too, or at least fun-making, and so is a sense of poetry, or a sense of language. And all these are to be found in the work of the man who Professor Gwyn Jones has taught us to regard as the first of the modern Anglo-Welsh, *viz.* Caradoc Evans. For anyone to have spoken about the Anglo-Welsh short story before 1915, when *My People* appeared, would have been almost an impossibility. It is true that Allen Raine (*née* Anne Adaliza Evans), the author of the best-selling novel *A Welsh Singer* had written about Cardiganshire before 1915, but her stories are not large in number (her one collection of stories, *All in a Month*, was published posthumously in 1908) and, excellent though some of them are, they lack that myst-erious seminal quality, that sort of glamour and strangeness arising from style and an individual vision, which make other writers warm to them and recognize their own capabilities in that particular field. In other words, inspired or not, they are not inspiring. Or rather, what they inspire is perhaps the line of whimsy and unreality we see as elements in the novels of Edith Nepean, Michael Gareth Llewelyn and Alexander Cordell, and which has its apotheosis in that staggering and accom-plished piece of literary hokum *How Green Was My Valley*.[7]

It is tempting, on the evidence of the poems and the short stories, to suggest that the Anglo-Welsh gift in literature is essentially lyrical and that longer works exhaust too soon the singing impulse. Anyway Anglo-Welsh novels seem to have impressed the critics on the whole less than the volumes of short stories and the poems and, with the sole exception of the work of Emyr Humphreys, no Anglo-Welsh novelist's work has received the acclaim of Dylan Thomas's poetry or Caradoc Evans's stories. And yet one could easily draw up a long list of Anglo-Welsh novels of quite outstanding merit. Here are ten, by ten different authors. *Bidden to the Feast* (Jack Jones, 1938), *Jubilee Blues* (Rhys Davies, 1938), *Border Country* (Raymond Williams, 1960), *Country Dance* (Margiad Evans, 1932), *The Heyday in the Blood* (Geraint Goodwin, 1936), *Times Like These* (Gwyn Jones, 1936), *A Toy Epic* (Emyr Humphreys, 1958), *All Through the Night* (Richard Vaughan, 1957), *The Alone to the Alone* (Gwyn Thomas, 1947), *Hunters and Hunted* (Ron Berry, 1960).

What have these ten in common except accomplishment and the fact that they are all produced by Welsh writers about Wales? Several of the points I tried to make in speaking about Anglo-Welsh stories are equally valid in a consideration of the novel. The Anglo-Welsh novel is not the place to look for sensitive examinations of class relationships, or descriptions of awakening or anguish at the public schools, or the ecstasies and miseries of homosexual love, or of skulduggery in big business, or intrigue in the week-end house party. Perhaps Dorothy Edwards, author of *Rhapsody* (Wishart, 1927) and *Winter Sonata* (Wishart, 1928) comes nearest to those writers who deal with artistic people at their week-ends in the country. One of her critics, S. Beryl Jones points out that her characters, middle-class, anglicized (English?) sensitives and intellectuals, never seem to have jobs.[8] Usually in Anglo-Welsh writing the only people who do no work are the ones on the dole. The Depression has perhaps played a greater part in the novel than in the short story.[9] The Anglo-Welsh novel has arisen very largely in an industrial area which knew widespread, perhaps unparalleled, unemployment, and during a period of violent unrest and bitter suffering. This we see from the work of Jack Jones, Rhys Davies, Gwyn Jones, Gwyn Thomas, Richard Llewellyn, Ron Berry and Lewis Jones. But that is not the whole story. Some of the finest Anglo-Welsh novelists were born far from the industrial south, and seldom or never concern themselves with that area in their books: writers like Emyr Humphreys, Richard Hughes, Geraint Goodwin, Caradoc Evans, Richard Vaughan. Variety is again one of the marks of the Anglo-Welsh novel, not uniformity, variety of style, treatment, emphasis, scope; it has its neutrals and its passionate advocates, its fine writers and its realists, its experimenters and its followers of tradition.

The first modern Anglo-Welsh novelist noted by Professor Lucien Leclaire in his *General Analytical Bibliography of the Regional Novelists of the British Isles, 1800-1950* is Joseph Keating, born in Mountain Ash, Glamorgan, and the author of six books.[10] Professor Leclaire goes on to give the names of more than forty novelists who have written about Wales, but several of these, like some of Brynmor Jones's writers, are non-indigenous, e.g. A. J. Cronin (*The Citadel*, 1937) and R. D. Blackmore (*The Maid of Sker*, 1872). By choosing from that thirty-odd that are left Caradoc Evans, Gwyn Thomas and Jack Jones to write about in more detail now, I do not necessarily mean to suggest that for me these three are the best among the Anglo-Welsh prose writers. But I do think that they are on many counts representative of the whole group. The most famous perhaps of all Anglo-Welsh novelists I have omitted. Richard Llewellyn is a highly skilled, and I believe a sincere, writer. Those who can swallow Caradoc's distorted picture of Wales and yet claim him to be a good writer ought, if they consider Llewellyn a bad one, to explain why they think so without quoting the sentimental falsity of *his* picture. Why is distortion due to sentimentality less acceptable than distortion due to some other emotion, say scorn or hatred? Because, apart from on this score of patent untruthfulness, and the dragging in of every cliché from quartettes of harpists to women in tall hats, *How Green Was My Valley* is a novel hard to fault. It has interesting characters, a profusion of incident, charm, tenderness, humour, drama. And yet it is a book I find it impossible to take seriously, although much of it I read with absorption. Everyone pretends to find sentimentality nauseating. It is my experience that written by a master like Richard Llewellyn it can often be fascinating, and this powerful hold of the book's sentimentality plus its genuine good qualities are what have given it its hundreds of thousands, probably millions, of satisfied readers.

I find I can only write at any length and with understanding about the books of men with whom I have made personal contact, and for whom I feel, or have felt, friendship or at least sympathy. Something in an author's work makes me wish for acquaintance with the man, and when this has been established I feel the desire, not to put the urge as high as necessity, to explain, even if only to myself, how the man and his work have struck me. I chose Jack Jones from among those Anglo-Welsh novelists I have known and liked because, like Huw Menai in a later section, he represents the self-educated working-class writer of high talent, prolific, dedicated, rooted in the community that has produced him, a type of writer who could not be omitted from any account of

Anglo-Welsh writing. With his wide range of experience and his knowledge of men and events, Jack seems to me an obvious figure to represent the Anglo-Welsh novelists of the South Wales coalfield, where half the population of our country is gathered. Caradoc Evans writes about the agricultural west and its people, and in his work is to be found at its most powerful that much-copied humour and that scorn and mockery of the tribal gods, missing from Jack's novels, which is an element in the work of many writers in this group. Jack, a Celt who has welcomed rather than rebelled against the domination of fact, writes faithfully of a community of which he is content to remain a part, whose history he is dedicated to recording and with whose values he does not feel himself to be violently at odds. Caradoc, the tough pioneer, the great *leaver-out*, the publicity-conscious journalist, turned upon the society which had produced him and, although he was always held firmly to Wales as by an unseverable umbilical of love and hatred, he derided or scourged his country for what appeared to him to be her hypocrisy and cruelty and corruption. This too is a voice that must be heard in any consideration of Anglo-Welsh prose. Gwyn Thomas represents for me another constant and prominent element in much Anglo-Welsh writing. Like Richard Vaughan and Gwyn Jones, he possesses, although he is exclusively a prose writer, something of a bardic quality in his concern for language, and in his brilliant use of jesting metaphor he is undoubtedly the group's finest comic poet. He is also a partisan; he represents at its most clear, intense and insistent, that element of protest and rebelliousness against social injustice heard so often, either implicitly or explicitly, throughout much Anglo-Welsh writing.

Between them these three writers seem to me to embody a good many of the characteristics, good and bad, of Anglo-Welsh prose writing. Whether they are the three who do this most completely and effectively I do not know. They do not include a writer concerned with the North Wales scene, although Emyr Humphreys, a distinguished figure of most impressive equipment and accomplishment, deals often with that area in his novels, works of enormous range, richness, insight and complexity. It must be increasingly difficult now, I feel, for any novelist to write well about Wales if he doesn't know something of the history and the language of our country. Wales was plundered in the thirties of her picturesque features; there is no longer novelty or quaintness in portrayals of her superficial differences from England, and her grotesques, cranks, oddities and eccentrics have long been creamed off for the exuberant and colourful pages of Dylan Thomas, Rhys Davies, Gwyn Jones and Caradoc

Evans. A younger generation, to which Emyr Humphreys belongs, is forced to look deeper into Welsh society if it is dissatisfied with a mere repetition of established patterns. Emyr Humphreys understands this very well, and he draws strength like a true artist from the dilemma in which he finds himself. Of all Anglo-Welsh writers he has, it seems to me, the profoundest understanding of the Wales that worships and carries on its daily life in Welsh, and of that life itself he is the truest interpreter. Emyr Humphreys seems important also as a representative of the growing sympathy between Welsh-language and Anglo-Welsh writers, since his own work has been done in both languages. (His Welsh-language novel, *Y Tri Llais – The Three Voices* – he translated into English under the title of *A Toy Epic*, which won the Hawthornden prize in 1959.) Geraint Goodwin, a novelist of rural mid-Wales and the English border, wrote in *The Heyday in the Blood* (1936), a book full of tenderness, poignancy, high spirits and Hardy-like humour, and of vivid descriptions of country activities like poaching, fox-hunting and market-going. But there is one important feature of this very gifted writer's work which marks him off from the ordinary novelist of bucolic buffoonery, local colour and Cold Comfort Farmism. Goodwin was an artist very conscious of the fact that he was writing about a Welsh community living in Wales. He did not, any more than Emyr Humphreys does, regard our country as a rather quaint area of England where lots of eccentric characters live, and where many amusing things happen. He saw Wales as a country with a history and with institutions different from those of England, and these institutions he respected. He shows us a peasant culture in being. He tells us about the local eisteddfod at Tanygraig, in which both Llew Morgan and Evan the Mill, his rival male characters, win prizes. He introduces us to Ben the postman, whose professor brother 'is a great Celtic scholar'. We learn about Llew's father, one of the preacher-politicians of an earlier generation. We learn about the books the people read and the plays they perform. Geraint Goodwin's Wales is not a fantasy, but a recognizable land inhabited by credible people. His understanding, I feel, would have deepened and become enriched as the years went by, and it was a great loss when this highly talented writer died in 1941 at the age of thirty-eight. Gwyn Jones, editor, novelist, short-story writer, playwright, is also in many ways a representative figure. When I look back over the work of this prolific and to me most attractive writer, it strikes me that here Anglo-Welsh writing lost a superb historical novelist. After four outstanding novels, Gwyn turned to the short story and achieved in this field remarkable success and a considerable and well-deserved reputation. But at this distance of time I do not now feel sure that short-story writing was really his true *métier*, in spite of the high accomplishment of almost everything he produced in this genre. The sweep and vigour of early books, like his *Richard Savage* (1935) and *A Garland of Bays* (1938), suggest that large-scale historical novels, action-packed and crowded with colourful characters, are really what he does best, rather than work of smaller scale and more lyrical quality. Welsh history, medieval and modern, has plenty of turbulent figures and tumultuous episodes in abundance, which Gwyn, with his vigorous, sensitive style, his sympathy, his knowledge and his tremendous stamina, could have used in the way he used so successfully the careers and the times of the Englishmen Savage in the eighteenth century, and Greene in the sixteenth, as a basis for a series of Welsh historical novels, colourful and rumbustious, which would have been unsurpassed as pictures of the bygone Wales which has produced our present society. He might have pioneered what Anglo-Welsh writing sadly lacks – a school of historical novelists.[11] Rhys Davies is another very prolific and accomplished writer, with something like twenty novels about Wales to his credit as well as ten or eleven volumes of short stories. A London-based professional all his working life, he gives us a vivid and highly individual picture of his native country, both the valleys and the agricultural west, the present and the past. It has never seemed to me that this writer, whose books, both novels and short stories, are full of passages of the most marvellous colourful writing, has ever received his true meed of recognition. From his earliest Lawrentian stories to the more sombre novels of his maturity, he has brought to his work the scrupulousness and the dedication of the true artist.

The number of novels written by Welsh men and women since the Second World War is very large. Three writers seem to me outstanding among the many, namely Menna Gallie, Raymond Williams and Ron Berry. Menna Gallie knew the mining valleys, particularly the Welsh-speaking families in them – she was herself Welsh-speaking – but she also wrote with verve and deep understanding about the migrant Welsh, the Welsh of the great diaspora, the brilliant naïve boyos from the mining valleys who go to teach in the universities of strange and foreign England. Her characterization is clear-cut and her books have humour and an attractive warmth, although her style lacks the sharp individuality of that of Gwyn Thomas, say, or Caradoc Evans.

Border Country (1960), Raymond Williams's first novel (he had previously written *Culture and Society, Drama from Ibsen to Eliot,* etc.) seems to me a very distinguished book indeed. It reminds me a good deal of the early Lawrence in its sense of intimacy, in being so clearly an inside job. To judge by the number who succumb to it, the temptation must be very strong for novelists to exaggerate working-class squalor and raffishness, or working-class bitterness, or quaintness, or oddity. To portray the dignity and decency and wholesomeness of working-class life is an achievement, and it is what Raymond Williams brings off in *Border Country*. One feature in the novel that helps to give this particular quality is, I think, the fact that the author's people – railway workers, jobbing builders and the like – are not an urban proletariat completely severed from the soil. Rather like Lawrence's miners, who looked out into rural Nottinghamshire and Derbyshire, they live in a valley on the border of Wales and England, and are conscious of industrial South Wales just over the horizon. The chief character, Harry Price the signalman, although sometimes headstrong, insensitive and selfish, is also a man of stubborn integrity, self-reliant, assured, the embodiment of all that is best in working-class life. He is a devoted gardener, and some of the finest scenes in the book, like those describing the hiving of the bees and feeding the fowls, underline the connection with the soil, the knowledge of country life possessed by Raymond Williams's people. The book is a record and a study of life on the border, the border between England and Wales, between working class and middle class, between the instinctive life and the life of the intellect; but to state the theme of the book in these terms seems somehow to diminish it and to rob it of much of its warmth and richness and colour.

The third writer is Ron Berry, whose first novel appeared in 1960. What Auden calls the 'glove-shaped valleys' of South Wales have by now become a sort of literary Klondyke, with all the claims to the richer territories, as it were, rigidly staked out and exploited right up to the horizon. What does a newcomer like Ron Berry do in such a situation? In his first novel, *Hunters and Hunted*, he just barged in among the old-timers and literary sourdoughs and located his book in an ordinary Welsh mining valley, Blaenddu, the sort that, although no longer green itself, looks up at mountains intersected with sheep tracks and trout streams, still the home of shy life like foxes, hares and hill-farmers. On top of all this, his three principal characters are just young colliers. But here, I think, resemblance to what has already been accomplished by other writers about the valleys abruptly ceases. No young colliers like Miskin, Beynon and Williams, it seems to me, have ever appeared before in Anglo-Welsh fiction. They are the disquieting products of a post-war Wales from which the grinding economic pressures of *Black Parade*,

Times Like These and *The Alone to the Alone* have been removed. They are more sophisticated, better educated than the moleskin heroes of Jack Jones, or at least they know more, and they are more cynical and far less committed politically than the dark philosophers of Gwyn Thomas. And these three, Miskin, Beynon and Williams, are certainly not the boys to bother with the political weeklies, or support the WEA. They exist in a world of booze, fornication and week-ends on the mountains with the dogs. They constitute part of that vast unshapable spiritual morass beyond the railheads of political awareness and Welsh non-conformity. They've *heard* of chapel – just about; they know a few words of Welsh – mostly swear-words. Two of them are ordinary sensual young men with a smattering of culture and no more morals than ferrets. The third is a sort of nihilist, a sour 'angry' from the coal-face, a poet who rejects poetry, a great clown also, besotted with language, his normal conversation like the abrupt, allusive, high-powered jabbering of Joyce's medicals. There's no tiredness or elegant lassitude in Ron Berry's writing; it bubbles up as fresh, as buoyant and as clear as those rocky mountain torrents through which his three young men pursue their bouts of idiotic horseplay. He is the jesting chronicler, particularly in his third novel, *The Full-Time Amateur* (1966), of a Rhondda in which coal, politics, religion and singing have lost their primacy. His hero in that novel is a portent perhaps, the prototype of the valley's man of the future, of a degutted South Wales without coal and without pits, whose people never meet together for political action, or singing, or worship, who are songless apart from their pop records and solitary apart from their strip-tease clubs and their bingo halls. 'Ichabod' is scrawled across the face of Ron Berry's Wales.

If I use the Christian names of those writers I have chosen to speak about in more detail, this must not be taken as an indication of lack of respect or of over-familiarity. Christian names come easily to the Welsh since all our names, even our surnames, are really Christian names (what are Thomas, Llewellyn, Morgan, Griffith, and even Davies, Williams, Hughes and Jones, but obvious Christian names?), and our surnames, fastened insidiously upon us since Tudor times, are part, an often irritating part, of our anglicization. To call Jack Jones, for instance, 'Mr Jack Jones', or even 'Jack Jones', every time I have to refer to him is cumbersome and unnecessary; to call him 'Jones', as one would refer to 'Auden' or 'Lawrence', is patronizing, as though one were trying to put him into the obsequious class of Victorian domestics; to call him 'Jack' is to show him warm affection and respect. It is nice to see that where

Dylan Thomas is concerned the English and the Americans have followed this practice.

V

THREE PROSE WRITERS

CARADOC EVANS

1878–1945

I first met Caradoc Evans in the company of Dylan Thomas in 1934. It seems to me strange now that I should at that time have sought him out, because, at fifty-six, he had been, for many years, a hated and notorious figure in Wales, the author of such works of calculated provocation as *My People, Capel Sion, My Neighbours, Nothing to Pay, Wasps* and *Taffy*. (I wonder if Caradoc's early books would have aroused such fury and attracted so much publicity if they had been given titles less jeering and inflammatory, say *Tales of Bygone Wales*, or *Remembering Aberteifi*.) He was regarded in Wales as the enemy of everything people of my upbringing and generation had been taught to revere, a blasphemer and mocker, a derider of our religion, one who by the distortions of his paraphrasings and his wilful mistranslations had made our language and ourselves appear ridiculous and contemptible in the eyes of the world outside Wales. But he was also one of the very few Welshmen at that time who had made a name for himself by writing in English, and in spite of everything commonly urged against them I read his strange stories almost always with curiosity and respect, often with considerable admiration.

In reply to my letter asking for permission to visit him, I received from Caradoc a cordial invitation to tea, written in a minute and rather spiky script in the central two or three square inches of a large sheet of writing-paper which had a list of Caradoc's books printed down the side. He was living then in a pleasant house called Queen's Square House, near the centre of Aberystwyth, in Cardiganshire, with his second wife Oliver Sandys (Countess Barcynska) and her son Nicholas.

I do not know enough about the nobility of Poland to judge whether Mrs Evans's title was genuine, or *soi-disant* on the part of her first husband. Did the Poles have counts, and were some of them Jewish? Certainly Mrs Evans was a fine and generous Englishwoman whom I always liked and admired very much, warm-hearted, merciful, tireless in her concern for the young, for outcasts and misfits, and bountiful towards her friends and dependants. Also she was an industrious and highly successful writer, the author, one of her publishers claims, of more than seventy best-selling novels. Caradoc's nickname for her was 'the sentimentalist'.

On the day of our visit Dylan and I were shown into a spacious drawing-room furnished with splendid antiques of varying periods and styles, the sort of place that, although roomy, seems overcrowded with too many exotic ornaments and large vases of fancy grass, and Buddhas, and icons with scarlet lamps burning under them, and too many damask curtains. Caradoc was sitting in the middle of this profusion, in the process of being interviewed by a local newspaper man. Mrs Evans was also present, looking like an ex-actress, or what I thought an ex-actress would look like; that is, her face was very much made up, she wore unusual and highly-coloured clothing and a good deal of conspicuous jewellery, including shoulder-length ear droppers. Her welcome to us, two complete strangers, was extremely cordial. I thought by the loudness and brusqueness of Caradoc's Cardiganshire English, and the violent pipe-brandishing, that he was quarrelling with his interviewer. I feel sure now that the truculence and the wrangling and the pontificating upon the absurdities of our National Eisteddfod were no more than an act. He knew well from his own considerable experience of journalism that his outrageous remarks and behaviour were good copy and good publicity for himself. Soon after our arrival the reporter departed and Caradoc's manner changed immediately, and he turned upon us the full blaze of his blarneying charm. His courtesy, simplicity and gentle manners have been remarked upon by many who knew him. He was not by any means a good-looking man. He had a large, ill-shaped nose and a too-long upper lip, and his face was at once very bony and flabby, with thin hanging skin. His lower lip pouted, and the hood-like lids, which he often slid forward and held down over his eyes, were of reptilian thinness. Mrs Evans talks in one of her books about his 'shaggy goat's hair', and that is a perfect description of the coarse, wiry, dirty-grey covering rising thick and upright on top of his head. In conversation he was a great encourager, a concentrated and smiling listener, an enthusiastic nodder and agree-er. And of course to a young and inexperienced writer like myself – I cannot speak for Dylan – much of his fascination was his familiarity with the literary life of the capital (that is, for the Anglo-Welsh writer then, London), his references to people like Norman Douglas, Mary Webb and Arthur Machen, whom he had known in Fleet Street. I recall little of our conversation apart from the goodwill of it. A few months later, early in 1935, having seen a story of mine in print, he wrote to tell me how much he had enjoyed it. After that I was prepared to listen very sympathetically to whatever was said in defence or praise of Caradoc and his work.

Caradoc's life began in 1878 at Pantycroy, a farm in Carmarthenshire, but his boyhood was spent in Rhydlewis in the next county, on a small farm called Lanlas-uchaf, to which the family had moved. The people of Cardiganshire, the Cardis, have in Wales a name for thrift, even meanness and parsimony, similar to the reputation of the Scots in England, and many stories are told, often by Cardis themselves, about what Caradoc calls their 'close-handedness'. Several tales are based on the allegation that the London water supply – pioneered, incidentally, by a Welshman, Sir Hugh Myddelton – is often unlawfully diverted by some of the numerous Cardigan dairymen of the capital into the metropolitan milk; and it is alleged that the wreath which appears annually on the Myddelton statue has been subscribed for by these same grateful tradesmen. One story says that the charge against a passer of dud cheques in Carmarthenshire stated that he had obtained credit by false pretences; when he crossed the county boundary and faced a similar accusation in Cardiganshire, the charge had to be reduced to *attempting* to obtain credit by false pretences. Many of Caradoc's short stories concern a peasant greed for money and possessions, but humour of this sort enters hardly at all into his treatment of this obsessive theme.

Caradoc's memories of his schooldays, his friends tell us, were painful, and embittered for many years by a deep sense of failure. But towards the end of his life he could depict his time in Rhydlewis elementary school like this:

> One of my schoolins [schoolmasters] used to stand sadly in front of me, cut a bit of spanish [licorice], pop it into his mouth, scratch his back head,[1] and say: 'There will be whiskers on eggs before the twelve times in your head.' He was short and slim and had whiskers all over his face and in his nostrils and ears, and he produced a child a year without outside help.

Another was a whipper-snapper who claimed to be able to count with his eyes shut and sing louder than any other man in the district. He said if there was a twp [dullard, dunce] more twp than me he would rather be Son Prodigal.

Though I never brought home a certificate merit or moved higher than the second from the bottom of my class and the porridge in the bottomer's head was not done, I knew one thing: schoolins got their jobs because they were religious Independents and the Independents were stronger than the Methodists.[2]

In spite of the teachers' alleged low opinion of him, Caradoc was invited to remain at school when his leaving time arrived, as a 'monitor' or apprentice school-teacher. Instead, like many youths of his time and situation, he left home to serve in a shop, in his case the Market Hall in Carmarthen town, a drapery store belonging to an uncle. He was fourteen at the time. Later, doing the same sort of job, he moved to Cardiff, and then at twenty-two he left Wales for London.[3] The management of the Holborn drapers where, after a period in Kentish Town, he found work, handed him a four-page brochure of the house rules governing shop assistants in their employment who 'lived in'. Caradoc's comment on this production was that he found Moses's ten commandments hard enough to keep, and Wallis's two hundred had him 'whacked'. 'Whacked' meant eventually sacked. At the end of two years he got a more congenial job in the drapery department of Whiteley's, 'the universal provider', at thirty-five pounds a year all found, 'living in' with about five hundred other men in a sort of civilian barracks. By this time Caradoc was beginning to feel a desperate need for privacy to read and write. While at Whiteley's he read Jerome K. Jerome and such books as Forster's *Life of Dickens* and Besant's *All Sorts and Conditions of Men*, but a cubicle shared with two or three other shop assistants made serious study impossible, and he determined to find a room for himself and live out. He got a job in an Oxford Street store and rented a room in Marylebone, in a street in which Trollope had once lived. He saved up ten pounds, applied for a job on a periodical called *Chat*, at three guineas a week, and got it, solely, he thought himself, because he turned up in his shop assistant's frock coat and pin-striped trousers for the interview. Unfortunately *Chat*'s proprietor was an eccentric who used to burn the linoleum to keep the office warm, and before long his paper folded. But Caradoc was now a journalist; at twenty-six he had finished with his hated shop-keeping for good, and he became in turn a sub-editor on the *Daily Mirror*, an assistant to Sir John Hammerton in his work on the

Harmsworth Encyclopaedia, editorial assistant on *T.P.'s Weekly*, editor of *Ideas* and *The Sunday Companion*. Thomas Burke, who worked in Fleet Street at the same time as Caradoc, says that he was 'everywhere popular', and that he made a deep impression upon the place.[4] A sharp distinction seemed to have existed between Caradoc's attitude to his journalism and to the writing of his short stories, which went on concurrently. His preference in journalism was for what was popular, of the widest possible appeal; he laughed at the *Sunday Times* and thought the *News of the World* a splendid job. His taste was in fact unaccountable. Although we know he owned a copy of Johnson's Dictionary, and read Dickens, Chekhov, Tolstoy, Balzac and Renan, and greatly esteemed the fastidious Arthur Machen, he yet admired some lady novelists 'several degrees inferior to Marie Corelli'.[5] It has been suggested that the twelve-year-long shop-keeping period of Caradoc's life, with its poverty and its humiliations, and its agonizing consciousness of wasted powers, explains the savagery of his writing, the sombre skill with which he exposes the sham and corruption of the human heart, especially the Welsh human heart. I think it possible that these things did increase a bitterness and a sense of injustice already present, but it is perhaps worth remarking that the people he satirized most cruelly and most frequently were not the snubbing ribbon-and-button-buyers, and the vindictive shopwalkers of Cardiff and London, but the peasants of west Wales, at whose hands, as far as we know, he had suffered no injustice. Caradoc was a man who, as we have seen, had been a failure at school. And yet like many failures conscious of great powers within them, he probably knew that his teachers' estimate of him was mistaken and undeserved; that his defeat had occurred in the particular type of education he was unlucky enough to have to endure because it happened to be in vogue in a certain place at a certain time. The mechanical, uncreative, arid, mock-English education of Rhydlewis at the end of the nineteenth century was almost bound to send someone like Caradoc to the bottom of his class.

In her book *Unbroken Thread* Caradoc's widow hints at another cause of bitterness. His mother's brother, a country doctor, died leaving £60,000, an enormous sum at that time, but it would appear that he never did anything towards the education of his nephew. Mrs Evans quotes Caradoc as saying: 'My mother never asked him [for financial help]. She didn't realize the value of education. But when I became a young man I did – and it was from then the rankle festered and was never healed. It became a running sore like all the root causes of my angers'. This message was received by Mrs Evans from beyond the veil, after her husband's death. Whether it is satisfactory explanation of Caradoc's famous bitterness I do not know. It certainly suggests that the journey to the other side has a debilitating effect on a man's expression.

Professor George Green thinks that the appearance of several satirical books in the early years of this century, *The Unspeakable Scot*, *The Egregious Englishman*, and so on, might have helped to create an atmosphere in which Caradoc's stories could be appreciated. They might have suggested to him the possibility of satirizing the Welsh.[6] We know that early in his career he had written stories of a very different sort from those he is usually associated with. 'I wrote Cockney stories', he says, 'after the manner of Edwin Pugh and Arthur Morrison. I showed them to my friend and he said: "You don't know what you're writing about. Tell stories about people you know – the Welsh". I filled a penny exercise book, both sides, with a Welsh love-story. "This doesn't sound true," I said to myself. "Any Welsh preacher could have written it." I let the years go by'.[7] His first story to be published appeared in *Reynolds News*, which paid him fifteen shillings. In 1915 the *English Review* under Frank Harris gave him five guineas for a story, and the same year his first book, *My People*, was published. He was thirty-seven years of age at the time.

Caradoc, after his period of journalism, was certainly not unaware of the value to a writer of shock and publicity. But whatever lay behind his work – personal bitterness, a sense of grievance or injustice, an ambition to do something out of the ordinary, the journalist's knowledge that wickedness is more sensational than virtue, the desire to attract attention to his gifts by methods of shock and sensation – his stories certainly could not be ignored. Thomas Burke called him the English Gorki, Hugh Walpole the most striking thing in English letters, Stephen Graham the sans-culotte of English literature and Naomi Royde-Smith the most savage satirist since Swift. (In fact one personal characteristic that Caradoc shared with Swift was bodily fastidiousness. Micturators who omitted to pull the chain after them aroused his ire.) To many of his fellow countrymen, after the publication of *My People*, he became 'the best-hated man in Wales'.

He says this of his early life in London:

> Now I came across a young man preaching the Shop Assistants' Union at shop doors and street corners. He said a shop-assistant lives without honour and dies as unhonoured as an ass. He came from Lampeter and named Evan Sydney Duncan Davies; and he was a very

argumentative young man. But he could argue many subjects and was
never hackneyed. He took me to the Poets' Corner in Westminster
Abbey, the Cheshire Cheese, where I sat in Dr Johnson's chair, old
City churches, Dickens' landmarks, Carlyle's house in Chelsea, and the
houses where lived Irving and Ellen Terry and Mrs Patrick Campbell.
He showed me the London he loved and seemed to be part of; and
there was born in me a deep and abiding love of London. He
introduced me to Hardy's novels, Ragget's stout in a pub in Oxford
Street, cod cutlets in a restaurant off Ludgate Circus, Defoe's *Plague*,
The Pilgrim's Progress, and to Robert Blatchford's writings in the
Clarion. It was Blatchford's simple grandeur that led me to discover
the English Bible. So what schoolins failed to do this young shop-
assistant from Lampeter did: educate me.

I joined a grammar class at Toynbee Hall, but I gave it up for grammar is the study of a lifetime. Then I joined a composition class at the
Workingmen's College . . . Somehow I came to read Genesis again
and when I was about the middle of it 'Jiw-Jiw this is English writing'
I said to me. On a Saturday night I went to the Hammersmith Palace
and there I saw Marie Lloyd, and 'Jiw-Jiw,' I said to me, 'she tells a
story not by what she says but by what she does not'. I kept up
Genesis and Marie Lloyd.[8]

One of the features of Caradoc's work which seems to attract critical
attention and cause sharp controversy, is this famous literary style, whose
origins he has just indicated. I am prepared to believe on the evidence of
the stories themselves that in the above account he is giving – as he
might himself have translated *calon y gwir* – the heart of the truth. The
rhythms and the vocabulary of Genesis in the Authorized Version are
everywhere in his work: 'In the foolishness of her vanity she curled her
yellow hair like a Jezebel, and she fashioned the front of her hair into a
fringe which she wore over her forehead.' 'These things Martha did; and
Danyrefail prospered exceedingly: its possessions spread even to the
other side of Avon Bern.' 'The night of the Hiring Fair Evan drank in the
inn, and the ale made him drunk, and he cried a ribald song; the men
with whom he drank mocked him, and they carried him into the stable
and laid him in a manger, and covered him with hay; and in the stall they
put a horse, thinking the animal would eat Evan's hair and beard. But the
Big Man watched over Evan, and the horse did not eat his beard.' This is
Caradoc's normal narrative style, direct, strong, unencumbered, biblical.
Perhaps the only non-biblical words in these three quotations are 'its' and
'ribald'. But Caradoc's world is not the nomadic and pastoral one of the
book of Genesis, but a modern society, settled, agricultural, even in some

cases urban and industrial, and this means that his seventeenth-century masterpiece is an inadequate model, at least where vocabulary is concerned, for his purpose. Even in his earliest work he is forced to use words like 'materialism', 'surgery', 'fripperies', 'ogled', 'trickish', 'tall-hatted', 'credited', 'India-rubber', 'song-like', 'shuddered', 'middle-class', and 'sapidness', and phrases like 'spirit laden eloquence' and 'togged in black gowns'. When Caradoc is writing about rural Cardiganshire he is naturally under less pressure to employ a non-biblical vocabulary than when he is writing about the Cardis of London.

Another feature of Caradoc's narrative style which has its parallel, if not its origin, in the Bible is the infrequency of extended passages of description, whether of scenery, weather or of persons. He rejects the detailed set scene as Genesis does. He lived much of his life in his native Cardiganshire, a county of quite outstanding natural beauty, of clear seas, bays, cliffs, green hills, magnificent rivers, but very little of this appears in his work. 'The sense of the beautiful or the curious in Nature', he says, 'is slow to awake in the mind of the Welsh peasant'; and I sometimes wonder whether this might not have been true of Caradoc himself, who confesses in his journal that 'God never meant me to live in the country'. Or his exclusion of natural beauty from his stories may have been for a reason I shall touch on presently. If a person is to be described in his work at all, which is uncommon, a sentence or two has usually to do the job. '. . . as they stood up in their pew you saw that . . . Lisbeth's body was as a billhook.' '. . . this short man with a large head, broad shoulders, billowy belly, bandy legs, and a smile that nothing drove from his face.' 'His face, school-slate in shape, was grey and pale yellow like cornland after harvest, and it was flat other than that his nose was like a sickle stuck into the ground. In season his hat stood on a scarecrow.' Seldom indeed does consecutive description reach the dimensions of this last, or of the following: 'He wore whipcord leggings over his short legs, and a preacher's coat over his long trunk, a white and red patterned celluloid collar about his neck and a bowler hat on the back of his head; and his side-whiskers were trimmed in the shape of a spade.' Scene setting he avoids too, although with his compactness of style he can make this vivid and effective when he does undertake it:

> The transparent china lamp on the tinsel-draped mantelpiece lit up the group on the hearth: Bern-Davydd, a loosely woven rope of whitish hair like a coil of sheep's wool which has been caught in a barbed wire, and exposed many days to the weather, extended from ear to ear; Lamech, the ball of his small nose glittering against swarthy

skin and bushy black beard and moustache: Puah, her feet resting on
the fender, and the tuft of red hair on the right side of her mouth
shivering like boar's hairs between the fingers of an ancient cobbler as
she turned over the leaves of the book she was not reading.

The influence of the English Bible on Caradoc raises the question
why he, a Welsh-speaking Welshman, chose the English language to
write in at all in preference to his own. English was for him, at least at
the level of art, laborious; but was the fascination of what's difficult part
of its attraction for him? Or was his choice the result of a sort of pride,
or even arrogance, a desire to make a name for himself, to be somebody,
and respected, among the rich, powerful and really literary English,
rather than among the Welsh, a small, culturally negligible nation with,
so in his ignorance he thought, insufficiently exacting literary standards?
('Any Welsh preacher could have written it.') Or was it that his scorn
expressed in English sounded more devastating than when expressed in
Welsh? I cannot help feeling that part of the answer lies in Caradoc's
education, which, whether in elementary school in Cardiganshire, or in
adult class in London, was entirely in English. It seems unquestionable
that the language of his awakening, as we have seen, and of whatever
literature he was acquainted with – the Bible, Hardy's novels, Defoe's
Plague, the *Pilgrim's Progress*, Dickens, etc. – was English.

Although Caradoc's descriptive passages have a biblical infrequency
and almost always a biblical brevity, he is a copious employer of
dialogue, and an element of this part of his practice has given very great
offence to many of his countrymen. Anyone ignorant of Welsh, the
argument goes, would assume that the conversations of Caradoc's
monoglot Welsh characters are, as rendered by him, direct translations
of their words into English. Certainly he has the problem, unknown to
those Anglo-Welsh authors like Jack Jones and Gwyn Thomas who
write about the anglicized industrial valleys of Wales, of rendering the
Welsh speech of his farm labourers and shopkeepers as effective English
dialogue. But it would be a mistake to assume, as is commonly done,
that what Caradoc did was to translate Welsh speech into English. He
does indeed sometimes translate – and even unintentionally mistranslate
– some Welsh idioms into English. When he writes phrases like 'head-
stiff', 'large money', 'red penny', 'kill your hay', 'rob me pure', 'forehead
of a house' and 'one hundred and a half', we can assume he had in
mind the Welsh phrases of which these are literal translations – *penstiff*,
arian mawr, ceiniog goch, lladd eich gwair, fy nhwyllo'n lan, talcen tŷ and *cant*

a hanner. But for the large majority of those notorious and outrageous sayings which he puts, in story after story, into the mouths of his characters, there are no parallels, not even remote ones, in Welsh. Nothing in Welsh, I would say, corresponds to *Big Man's Palace*, meaning, presumably, heaven; to *Dear Little Big Man*, meaning God; to *Little Holy Respected*, or to such monstrous locutions as 'Sober serious, mouth not that you . . .', or 'Glad day to you, Evan the son of Hannah', or 'old boy ugly', 'you wicked spider', 'Hold thy chin, little Dinah', 'What iobish do you spout?', 'the Great Male', 'Shut your chins, you dirty cows', 'move your tongue about Sara . . .' and so on. Why then did Caradoc use them, knowing them, as we may be sure he did, to be false? I think he saw in the necessity to translate his characters' Welsh speech into English a splendid artistic opportunity. What he did was to invent a whole language for them, and he invented it with one purpose, which was to create in his stories a certain atmosphere, an atmosphere of hypocrisy, stupidity, cunning and sham religion. This grotesque speech plays a large part in bringing about that powerful impression of universal falsity and uncouthness, which is the one he almost always wishes for, and for that purpose it is admirably chosen.

The second, and more serious, of the counts against Caradoc concerns the *matter* of his stories rather than the manner. The picture of our country he confronts his readers with, particularly in his early books, gave great offence in Wales and was of course indignantly repudiated. His play *Taffy* (1923) almost wrecked a London theatre. There was talk in Wales of publicly burning his books, and threats of physical attacks upon him were made from time to time. Is Caradoc's vision of Wales a true one? Only a non-Welsh writer, I feel sure, would regard this question as irrelevant.

An artist like Caradoc Evans does not concern himself with large and impersonal entities like nations. He deals only with a relatively small area of Wales during a short period and with only a handful of characters drawn from one social section of that area. He makes no Balzacian claims that these characters are chosen with deliberation as being the most significant and representative in the society depicted by him. On the other hand, when people laughed to scorn the more repulsive and squalid events of his stories as crude and malicious inventions, and declared they could not have happened in enlightened, nonconformist Cardiganshire, Caradoc replied that almost every incident narrated in his work was something he had seen, and known, in his own life in the county. They are, he maintains, authentic, and chapter and verse could be given for almost every one. But this, to me, does not in any way prove that he is therefore giving an accurate picture of the life and the community of this part of west Wales. For one thing, at this point, the second of the two influences which he claims formed his style must be taken into account. The first was his reading of Genesis, the other was Marie Lloyd: '"Jiw-Jiw," I said to me, "she tells a story not by what she says but by what she does not".'

What exactly did Caradoc mean by this? The statement is open to more than one interpretation, and I think Caradoc may have begun by having one meaning in mind, and that then he went on to another. I never heard Marie Lloyd, but Rob Wilton the comedian, it seems to me, was a master in his act of probably a similar sort of 'leaving out', the sort that in the first sentence of a story tells us that Charlie Evans has been having an argument and presently reveals that Rob is visiting Charlie in hospital. Caradoc may have employed a leap something like this at times, but his technique of omission goes much deeper. It is in fact the basis of his method. All authors inevitably 'leave out'; even the famous 'all-including chronicle' is necessarily highly selective. What Caradoc did was deliberately to suppress, beginning with the really marvellous beauty of Cardigan's natural scenery, everything he knew to be admirable in the life and circumstances of the people he was writing about, their hospitality and sense of community, their self-sacrifice, their devotion to their religion, their reckless and stubborn courage. Caradoc was brought up near one of the centres of Rebecca, and as a boy might easily have spoken to men who had taken part in those courageous, imaginative and effective disturbances; only nine years before he was born the radical nonconformist farmers of his county were being evicted from their farms for having the guts to vote – there was no secret ballot – openly against their own Tory landowners, although they knew the consequences would inevitably be eviction. Obviously the man who showed his courage and defiance in this way would find no place in a Caradoc story, not before *Pilgrims in a Foreign Land* (1942) at least. The point need not be laboured historically, but may be effectively illustrated from Mrs Evans's record of three small events which took place during her life in Cardiganshire during the last war:

> Big Head [chapel deacon, presumably] Cabbages tows his vegetable produce to town with an ancient car to the peril of every other vehicle and every pedestrian. Cabbages he sells at a price a cabbage should be ashamed to fetch even in war-time, and for onions no bigger than tennis balls he used to get fourpence each before they

were controlled. He is childless and has taken into his house an evacuee little girl whom he clothes and educates and hopes to make a teacher and to whom he has willed his house and his land. Will not God take this into account?

There is Big Head Whimey Moustache. He has a pretty tenor voice and when he sings he blows his moustache about as if they were fine strands of silk. He sold an old emaciated cow at an enormous price to a young Englishman who took up farming to dodge the Army. The day he did that he was marrying his servant girl who was going to have a baby by a sweetheart who never came back from Dunkirk. He made her respectable and the child of the man who died for his country has his name. He was turned sixty on the day of his wedding, and since the infant has come the clock of ages has taken him back twenty years.

There is Holyman Shon who used to sell − and would now if he could − dairy-cake with as much baked clay in it as cake. He gives his ration of butter to a soldier's wife. Two sons he lost in the Great War and if you ask him where his third and last son is he will tell you, 'I sent him after Hitler and told him not to come back till he has found him'.[9]

Here, in these three accounts by Mrs Evans, we have, obviously, Caradoc material, mixed up with matter which he would almost certainly reject. For most of his writing life he would have used approximately only the first half of these stories in every case, the unscrupulous money-grubber, the swindler who cheats the poltroon, the fraudulent Holy Joe. He would have regarded the elements of generosity in these anecdotes, the kindliness, the joy, the tenderness, *as what was to be left out* − the little evacuee transformed into a humble heiress, the unmarried mother married and her child given a name, the soldier's wife with her rations gratuitously doubled. This, it seems to me, is the way in which Caradoc employed the 'leaving out' technique whose beginnings he heard hinted at in the act of Marie Lloyd. A remarkable aspect of his achievement was that he managed to convince so many, by his art, that his small piece of the picture was really the whole.[10]

It was both a strength and a limitation of Caradoc's art that his deliberate narrowness of vision enabled him to deal thus with only a very small sector of the life about him. His peasants he represents as being largely without politics, which in the area he writes about they certainly were not, and without culture, which they might have been, although I doubt it. (I do not wish to be more dogmatic because I know that there are pockets in Wales, in spite of what I have said about a widespread culture, which are intellectually and culturally arid. I remember staying as a boy on the farm of relatives in Carmarthenshire. There, although my uncle was a dead shot and kept a hunter in the stable, the only books I ever saw were the Bible and the ready reckoner, and the second of these was in use much oftener than the first. And the farms around that I visited seemed to be at the same cultural level.)[11] Religion Caradoc grants his people, but far from being life-giving it is stunting and hypocritical. 'The Capels', he says in his self-portrait, 'keep the people down and chase the living God away'.[12] Surely the things that were keeping the people of rural Wales down were, as they thought themselves, not the capels, but the lack of education, and the oppressive and brutal landlordism and its resultant poverty, which drove thousands into the squireless but amply-chapelled industrial valleys, and to the United States, and into the Welsh 'colony' in the Argentine. Caradoc's complete ignorance of history, or his disregard of it, intensifies his vision, but it also helps to restrict it and to make its expression monotonous and predictable.

Every artist's understanding is partial, but Caradoc's is surely much more intentionally circumscribed than is usual. Hypocrisy, lust, double dealing, he sees with great clarity, but to tenderness, nobility, idealism, joy, he is as a writer, as we have seen, indifferent; not entirely so, because by the time he has reached *Pilgrims in a Foreign Land*, published in 1942, he has mellowed somewhat; he has become freer and more fanciful and he writes in this volume stories which have elements of grotesque or amusing fairy tales. But the characters he shows us in, say, *My People* are, it seems to me, too grim even for his own artistic purpose. Because often in Caradoc's stories, when one is likely to experience stirrings of compassion for some brow-beaten, wronged or cheated creature, Caradoc will underline the corruption of this victim also, or show us his physical repulsiveness, swindled and outraged though he may be. Variety, contrast or counterpoint there must be in any work of art, but Caradoc does not achieve this by presenting us with themes of moral tension, or contrasts of beauty and ugliness, or even variations of social or intellectual background. His world is almost universally joyless, a vision of physical and moral squalor, and the only variety in it arises from two things: first, the biblical dignity of the narrative passages in contrast with the idiotic and ludicrous buffoonery of the dialogue; second, urbane language of dead-pan solemnity used to describe situations of complete absurdity or farce like the drunken man in the manger whose hair might have been eaten by a horse, in the passage I have already quoted. But these devices have never been for me sufficient to dispel tedium from an extended reading of his stories, especially when the strain upon him of maintaining the rather artificial idiom becomes apparent in the writing.

Caradoc, so often in anger and journalism called a 'realist', does not seem to me to have created a realistic world at all. If we go to a *petit maître* like him for a 'true picture of Wales', whatever that might mean, we won't find one. He shows us not Wales but Welshmen; not even Welshmen, but a few peasants only in a restricted area. T. S. Eliot has a phrase somewhere: 'the desert of the exact likeness to the reality which is perceived by the most commonplace mind'. Caradoc's vision, which sees certain sins of flesh and spirit with blinding clarity, is too narrow, too partial, to present us with a lifelike and realistic picture of Wales. The world he shows us is not lifelike, but it is very much alive, and quite homogeneous; and this organic vitality of a work of art itself is surely what we should judge the work by, and not its resemblance to what we conceive to be the 'exact likeness to the reality'. Of course unless fantasy is intended common sense tells us that there should be some correspondence between the description and the thing described. (Even Upward and Isherwood, the authors of *Mortmere* in the 1930s, felt there should be some connection between life and their description of it.) But Caradoc's work is not documentary. In the world of statistics and sociology his stories are valueless. Not in the world of the imagination and knowledge of the depravity of the human heart. Do we read *Anna Karenina* for a true picture of Tsarist Russia, or *Scarlet and Black* for a true picture of 1830 France, or *Bleak House* for a true picture of Victorian England? Do not these great works engage and enliven and fill out and occupy our imaginations, and deeply satisfy our inner life, our feelings, what is still left to us of our childhood, rather than give us information about foreign countries? Isn't this the reason for their greatness? Much of the adverse criticism of Caradoc has come about because Wales is a small nation fighting desperately for her life, and Caradoc, because of his scurrilous portrait of her, and his guiding principle of never writing anything that could be construed as praise, was seen as a traitor, joining in the attack upon what was held dear, and was being desperately defended. This is understandable, at least to Welsh people. It is all very well for still great, assured and confident England to laugh at those plays and books by Englishmen that deride her, to join in the self-mockery and to make pets of her satirists. Wales, her language, her national identity threatened with extinction, feels herself unable to afford such tolerance. Art may be the lie which reveals to us the truth, but when the 'lie' is uttered by a Welshman about his own country, it is the lie itself for many which will have overwhelming power and not the truth which it is intended to demonstrate.

But all this obviously does not mean that in a few stories like 'Be This her Memorial', and 'The Way of the Earth', Caradoc is not a master of this form. Here is part of the first of these stories which tells of Nanni, a desperately poor and very old woman, crooked, wrinkled, toothless, who lives alone in a mud-walled hovel. The minister of her chapel, Josiah Bryn-Bevan, is soon to leave for a bigger church, and Nanni decides to present him with a large and ornate Bible. To pay for this she, a pauper, starves herself of normal food. Such is her devotion to him that instead of giving her customary help at hay harvest, she hammers hob-nails into her boots and tramps the countryside to wherever he is preaching. This angers the farmers who want her cheap labour:

> One night Sadrach Danyrefail called at her cottage to commandeer her services for the next day. His crop had been on the ground for a fortnight, and now that there was a prospect of fair weather he was anxious to gather it in. Sadrach was going to say hard things to Nanni, but the appearance of the gleaming-eyed creature that drew back the bolts of the door frightened him and tied his tongue. He was glad that the old woman did not invite him inside, for from within there issued an abominable smell such as might have come from the boiler of the witch who one time lived on the moor . . .

> Two Sabbaths before the farewell sermon was to be preached, Nanni came to Capel Sion with an ugly sore at the side of her mouth; repulsive matter oozed slowly from it, forming into a head, and then coursing thickly down her chin on to the shoulder of her black cape, where it glistened among the beads. On occasions her lips tightened, and she swished a hand angrily across her face.

> 'Old Nann', folk remarked while discussing her over their dinner-tables, 'is getting as dirty as an old sow.'

> During the week two more sores appeared; the next Sabbath Nanni had a strip of calico drawn over her face . . .

> At the end of his farewell sermon the Respected Josiah Bryn-Bevan made reference to the giver of the Bible, and grieved that she was not in the Capel. He dwelt on her sacrifice. Here was a Book to be treasured, and he could think of no one who would treasure it better than Sadrach Danyrefail, to whom he would hand it in recognition of his work in the School of the Sabbath.

> In the morning the Respected Josiah Bryn-Bevan, making a tour of his congregation, bethought himself of Nanni. The thought came to him on leaving Danyrefail, the distance betwixt which and Nanni's cottage is two fields. He opened the door and called out:

'Nanni.'

None answered.

He entered the room. Nanni was on the floor.

'Nanni, Nanni!' he said. 'Why for you do not reply to me? Am I not your shepherd?'

There was no movement from Nanni. Mishtir Bryn-Bevan went on his knees and peered at her. Her hands were clasped tightly together, as though guarding some great treasure. The minister raised himself and prised them apart with the ferrule of his walking-stick. A roasted rat revealed itself. Mishtir Bryn-Bevan stood for several moments spellbound and silent; and in the stillness the rats crept boldly out of their hiding places and resumed their attack on Nanni's face. The minister, startled and horrified, fled from the house of sacrifice.[13]

The last time I saw Caradoc was in the summer of 1944, a few months before he died. Professor Gwyn Jones, with whom my wife and I were staying in Aberystwyth, invited him and Mrs Evans to tea from their home at New Cross, a hamlet outside the town, where they had been living since 1940. How Caradoc, in the ten intervening years since my first sight of him, had changed! His clothes were as outlandish and colourful as ever; he was wearing black corduroy jacket and trousers, a magenta shirt, a cable-stitch cricket sweater and a brimless straw hat shaped like a smallish beehive. But his body at sixty-seven was old, and his face, with the droop-lidded eyes and the blunt, bulby, long-nostrilled nose, seemed gnarled and scooped out, the cheekbones in particular standing forth with prominence under the thin skin. But the day of this last meeting he set himself out to win us, he used all the Welsh charm and blarney he was master of, he listened with a concentrated pleasure that suggested he wanted to do nothing else, he acted, he told us scandalous tales about the literary eminent and, mixing in the most comical way the accents of Aberteifi and London clubland, described encounters with Frank Harris, W. H. Davies, Sean O'Casey and others. When we left Gwyn Jones's house for a stroll I had the chance to tell Caradoc I thought his character sketches of Mary Webb and W. H. Davies, then appearing in The Welsh Review, among the most interesting things he had written. He grinned through his pipe-smoke, rugged and momentarily bright-eyed; he seemed glad I had said that. Five months later I felt glad myself I had said it, because going to my job by train one cold winter's morning in 1945 I read in the newspaper that he was dead.

JACK JONES

1884–1970

RHIWBINA – it rhymes with Heine – is a pleasant, bushy suburb to the north of Cardiff. Its nucleus is a delightful garden village of white houses and green spaces, and in so far as Cardiff had a literary quarter, from the 1930s to the post-war period, Rhiwbina would appear to have been it. Here have lived, among others, Dr Kate Roberts, Welsh short-story writer and novelist; Professor W. J. Gruffydd, Welsh poet, essayist, scholar and editor of the Welsh literary magazine *Y Llenor* (*The Littérateur*); Professor Gwyn Jones, novelist, short-story writer, Icelandic scholar, editor of *The Welsh Review*; Dr Iorwerth Peate, poet; Dorothy Edwards, Anglo-Welsh short-story writer and novelist. Another who lived there was Jack Jones, one of the most famous, popular and successful of the Anglo-Welsh and, in his last years, the doyen, as he liked to say, of this group of writers. (Adding, perhaps, 'What's doyen?')[1]

Although I knew Jack for thirty years, we did not become close friends until he was gone seventy and I was gone fifty. By this time, a remarried widower, a respected inhabitant of suburbia, the great days of his life were over. His remaining three children – two of his sons were dead – were grown up, and grandchildren, even great-grandchildren, were beginning to appear. He no longer took any active part in politics and only one book, the novel *Come Night, End Day* (1956), appeared during the time I am referring to. I can claim to have known Jack Jones well only in the serenity of his old age, during what was probably the most tranquil and uneventful decade of a crowded life. Because no other Anglo-Welsh writer's experience came near to Jack's in variety, pace and richness. He was, in the words of his one-time boss, Lloyd George, miner, forester, navvy, soldier, communist agitator, trade union official, political propagandist, book salesman, cinema manager, lecturer, free-lance journalist, playwright and author. (Lloyd George left out a few like film actor, lamp salesman, script writer, broadcaster and television personality.) We think of Jack as a writer, but we must remember that he was in his fiftieth year before his first book was published, and if, remaining in politics, he had never written a word, he would still be an eminent figure among us in Wales – a life peer at the very least, probably Lord Jones, and not the first to bear that unlikely title.

Jack was born in what he himself described as a 'bug-ridden hovel' in a dreadful row of double-decker cottages called Tai Harry Blawd in Merthyr Tydfil in 1884, the eldest to survive of the fifteen children ('nine were reared') of a coal-miner and his wife, Welsh-speaking David and Saran Jones. Jack's father, the 'Glyn' of *Black Parade* (1935), was hard-working, highly skilled at his job, near-illiterate, rough, puritanical and very fond of his beer. His life was brutalized by its narrowness, by gross over-work, by the poverty and degradation of his home conditions and the surrounding squalor. He had begun his working life underground at eight years of age, and his ten hours a day in the pit, six days a week, meant that during the winter months he, and thousands of children like him, never saw daylight at all except on Sundays. Jack's mother, about whose life, when he was gone eighty, he wrote a further 120,000 words, was always for him both the tender, devoted, inspiring mother of his childhood, and the great all-mother, Saran, Elizabeth Tewdwr, Aunt Emily, Megan Davies, the beautiful, fecund, mythic figure of his novels, the imaginatively inexhaustible. She too was illiterate and had worked before her marriage in the local brickyard, but, unlike her husband, she found solace and refreshment in visits, when she could raise the necessary threepence, to the town's wooden-walled and canvas-roofed theatre, and occasionally to one of the local chapels. Her life was one of endless and laborious toil, of child-bearing and bringing up a large family in appalling conditions of poverty, and in a degradation for which she was in no way responsible. But she remained always loving, although masterful, towards her family, gallant, life-giving, undefeated. The more we read of this handsome and bountiful woman the more must our admiration for her energy, love and courage be.

One of the most moving and revealing incidents in Jack's childhood is related by him in the first of his autobiographical volumes, *Unfinished Journey*, to me the best book he ever wrote and the most quotable of his autobiographies. As a little boy of six or seven he was knocked down by a coal cart, which ran over his leg and broke it:

> Before dad came home from the pit my leg was well and truly set [in plaster of Paris] . . . As soon as [he] got home and heard about it from our mam, he came upstairs in his pit-clothes to see me. Not right up, but high enough up the stairway to bring his face level with mine. He smiled a tired smile, his teeth showing white in his grey-black face. 'Never mind,' he said. His face was also streaked where rivulets of perspiration had during the day been running down . . . This I could see because his face was close to mine . . .

With my leg in plaster of Paris I lay on my back watching the bugs walking upside-down across the ceiling. The days were long, and the nights were longer. My leg was itching worse than ever. People brought me things . . . Fruit, and illustrated papers. The light was bad, the one window being so small. Our mam sat with me for as long as she could . . .

Whilst I was lying in plaster of Paris another new baby came. Came quietly to mother in the room the other side of the partition, the room in which mother said she was going to lie down for a bit. The old midwife passed my bed in and out, going in to our mam and coming out, and it was she told me I had another brother. I had heard him crying . . .

Our mam, looking lovelier than ever, got up on the Sunday afternoon. She stood, smiling, and holding up the new baby, against the footrail of the bed I shared with [my brothers] Billa and Frank at night.

'Do you like him, Johnny?' she said. 'His name is David – after your father. Lovely, isn't he?'

'Yes, he's grand,' I said indifferently. My leg was itching. 'My leg's itching awful,' I said.

'They do say it's getting better when it itches.'

'Do they?' I said . . . 'I'm glad you're better again, mam. I wish I was better too, then I could go to the theatre with you.'

After she had gone down I concentrated on the pictures in an effort to forget the itching, but it was no use. The days were bad enough, but the nights, with Billa and Frank one each side of me, were worse. Now I suppose we'll have Blodwen at the foot of the bed . . . The itching. If only I could get at it to scratch it. After I had cried through one night our mam sent down to ask the doctor to call in when he was passing.

When he came our mam said: 'He's been nearly off his head, doctor. Crying an' screaming. You said it was time the leg wanted, so I didn't like to bother you.'

'That's all right, Mrs Jones. To tell you the truth, I'd forgotten all about him. Now, Johnny, let's see what we can do for you. Oh, heavens,' he cried as he started stripping my leg of the hardened casing of plaster of Paris. 'It's alive. Itching? It's a wonder he hasn't been eaten alive. If I had my way I'd blow up this lousy, bug-infested – Let me get my coat off – Don't put it down there. Take it out to the trap to my man.' Our mam did, and the doctor went on stripping my leg. What a relief. 'Yes,' the doctor said when our mam came back upstairs, 'we're getting on with it . . . Could you get me a bucket or something to put this stuff in?' Our mam fetched him the ash-bucket . . .

'Oh, look at them,' said the doctor shudderingly as he dropped pieces of plaster of Paris into the big bucket.

'Yes, I know, doctor,' our mam said, 'but indeed I can't help it. I've tried everything – '

'No doubt you have. Now we can see the leg.' He ran an experienced hand over it. 'Johnny, we've made a good job of it . . . Get rid of that stuff in the bucket. Will it burn, I wonder – My coat – oh, yes, out in the trap . . . Bring him down the surgery next week . . . Goodbye, Johnny . . . Oh, this stairway. Good day, Mrs Jones.'[2]

Jack attended the local church school, but at twelve years of age his formal education came to an end and he went to work underground with his father. This meant for him also, while still no more than a child, a ten-hour day in the pit, twelve hours if his father decided to work overtime for a bit of extra money. This is how Jack describes his father's working place on his first day underground:

I followed dad until we got to a hole in the side of the road, into which dad turned, and where he stopped and began to undress. 'This is my stall,' he said. 'Give me your spike.' I handed him my ringed spike, which he drove into a wooden post, and in which he placed my naked-light lamp to rest.

'Strip,' he said.

After having stripped ready for work and rolled my shirt-sleeves up I looked up at dad, who smiled down on me and said: 'Yes, you'll do.'

Then he spat the 'bacco out of his mouth, took some fresh out of his 'bacco box and put it into his mouth, and with his lamp in his hand went forward to where there was about two feet of coal sandwiched between two-feet layers of rock top and bottom.

'This is it,' he said, taking a mandril with which he crawled on his stomach towards the coal. He tapped the rock-roof with the mandril, listening carefully to the sound. Along the length of his working place – about twenty yards from end to end – he crawled tapping the rock roof before he lay resting on his elbows, smiling towards where I was waiting instructions. 'Yes, the top's all right. Get your lamp, son, then come on here for dad to show you the coal the British Navy likes best.'

This was a dad I had not known before, a jolly, protective and kindly dad. With my lamp in my hand I crawled forward under the rock-roof to where he lay on his side.

'There it is, Johnny. That's what we've got to get from where it grows into that empty tram. Three shillings a ton large coal, Johnny – we give the bosses the small-coal for nothing to help them to keep their families out of the work-house.' He laughed.

'The coal is not the same here, dad, as it is in the trucks in front of Tai Harry Blawd.'

He laughed. 'Not by a long shot. Here we've got to lie on our sides between the rock top an' bottom to beat it from there – ay, an' often to blow it from there with powder.'

'Is it all like this then?'

'No, no. In some places the coal is so thick they've got to get ladders an' on to staging to beat it . . . Here it's not two feet . . .'

(*Unfinished Journey* 71)

Soon after this, unable because of an accident in the shaft to leave the pit by means of the cage, the miners are told to find their own way to the surface as best they can. Jack and his father with Gyp, their Skye Terrier bitch, and a few other colliers try to make their exit through some old and long-abandoned underground passages:

Dad went confidently into the old workings, in which the almost rotten timber had grown whiskers of a sort of pit-moss . . . The upright timbers along the footway were covered with it, and it made them look like shrouded sentries on guard. There was running water under our feet which had been dyed red either by the ironstone or by some other dye in the rock of the roof. The background of continuous, but not loud, sound of the earth's unrest was punctuated by the snap of rotten timber, fall of stones, and droppings of water. There was also a faint whistling sound of straying air-currents, some of which were foul-smelling. In this decayed air the flames of our naked-light lamps weakened.

To scramble over falls of roof we had to fix our lamps in loops which most of us had sewn on the pokes of our caps. The lamp carried on our foreheads left us with both hands free to negotiate the difficult and dangerous passage over the many falls of roof, some of which were mountainous, and left only room for one to crawl over at a time. One false move would most likely start the roof above and bring another fall down to bury the crawler and those nearest him.

'Careful, son,' said dad, as he waited for me to come through the hole he had first crawled through. One fall of roof after another safely negotiated. Then we arrived at a [long] expanse of water . . . The lamps we carried could not show us the far end of the water which looked menacing to me. 'The swamp the old men used to talk about,' dad . . . murmured. 'It's not too deep on the right-hand side.' He fixed his lamp with which he had been viewing the water in the loop of his cap again. Then he tutted down. 'Get on my back, son, and hold tight. Don't be frightened, and whatever you do – even if I stumble – don't put out your hand to touch the side-timbers. Hold fast round my neck.'

I did, and dad waded into the water with me on his back, and our Skye Terrier bitch swimming in front. When the water was up above dad's middle I did get a bit frightened and my naked-light lamp fell into the water. 'My lamp.' 'Never mind the lamp now, son, you hold fast round dad's neck,' dad said in a way as calmed me.

Slowly he won his way through the expanse of ancient water, which at its deepest point, on the high right side along which our dad and the other men with boys on their backs travelled, was up to about our dad's chest. After they were all across safely, dad started up a steep incline. 'Shan't be long now,' he said. After we had climbed for some time he stopped, knelt and pointed. 'Look, son.' There was what seemed to me to be a bright disc, about the size of a florin, on what appeared to be a distant mountain. 'That's what we've been looking for, son, the light of the world, the world where your mam is. Come on.' The disc of light grew in size as we climbed our way to the world's surface.

(*Unfinished Journey* 79–80)

Jack stuck it underground for five years, and then, lying about his age, quit and enlisted in Cardiff in the Dragoon Guards. At least he meant to join the Dragoon Guards, but he found himself instead, to his disgust, in the militia battalion of the Welch Regiment. He protested. 'Shut up,' the corporal said to him, 'you shrimp.'

The Boer War had just ended and Jack, tattooed, and broke after a few sessions at the Crown and Anchor, was shipped off with his regiment to South Africa for mopping-up operations. There, finding the stupidities of military discipline intolerable, he deserted and flogged his uniform to the Kaffirs. Back with the regiment, court-martialled and imprisoned as a result, he was posted to India, to the North-West Frontier, where his bosom pal, Edmund Buck, was killed on sentry-go by the wild tribesmen. At twenty-two he is out of the army and back in Merthyr again, and once more down the pit. As a young collier on his summer holidays in Builth Wells, a small mid-Wales spa, he meets Laura, who was to be his wife, comforter, adviser, inspiration and deflator for the next thirty-nine years. But although Jack's devotion to Laura was total, relations between them at first were not always tranquil, because early in his marriage Jack was seized by a terrible mania for gambling and he began playing faro in a Merthyr gambling club instead of going to work:

Next day I lost what I had won, and a few pounds of my own money, or rather Laura's and her sister's money. For she had her own

home, and there was a couple of hundred pounds got for the Builth
Wells house and shop, half of which Laura got, and all of which I
gambled away before starting to pawn all that was pawnable of her
home. I made [my brother] Dave my unwilling accomplice in the
robbing of her home. Pawned all her wedding-presents, even the
sewing machine. All in less than two months, two months during
which I hardly ever ate food more than once a day. I pawned my own
clothes and hers. Told her lie upon lie, for she was easy to deceive,
being from the country. I borrowed all I could, told our mam a lie
about Laura wanting five pounds, to send to Builth Wells to [her sister]
Lizzie . . . Got the five pounds – lost it. Same trick on my brothers Billa
and Frank; tricked my aunt Marged out of a few pounds. The last thing
to go was Laura's wedding ring. Having pawned that and lost the
money I hung about the club – club, be damned! – till midnight, until
I was thrown out. Dave, my shadow, my dupe, my tool, followed me
home – home? – from the place of the damned.

Our mam was there with Laura, who had cried herself ugly. A sight
she looked, with her swollen, tear-soddened face and her bulging
body. I stood in the doorway, Dave behind me in the passage. I was
afraid to go nearer, for there was that in our mam's face . . .

'Well, John?' she said. 'Are you satisfied?'

I didn't speak – Couldn't.

'You're a dirty s——, that's what you are, John,' she said; and I knew
that when that word left her mouth that I was nothing more in her
eyes. 'I could forgive you if it was to me you had done what you have;
but it's to this gel, with her baby coming and a dying sister on her
hands that you've done it. You've done for yourself, John . . . Don't
cry, my lovely gel. I'll see you through your time, then you shall take
all he's left you to take back to Builth with you. You can make him pay
towards you and your baby . . . Don't cry, lovely gel. He's my son,
worse luck, but he's not worth a tear from you . . .'

(Unfinished Journey 131–2)

Jack's mother, always stiffening Laura against him, gets hold of the
pawn tickets to redeem the wedding ring, and sees Laura and her baby
off to Builth. 'As for you two', she says to Dave and Jack. 'It won't pay
you to come near my house, for I'd brain the pair of you . . .'

Jack, unable to endure his rejection and remorse, and the anguish of
his separation from Laura and his child, walks all the way from Merthyr
to Builth, singing hymns in the towns he was passing through to get a
few pence for food. Wonderful, gentle, forgiving Laura takes him back.
The gambling fever is over, never to return. Jack gets a job as a bark-
stripper, later as a haulier and a navvy, in Builth Wells, where three of

his five children are born. And then in 1914 the First World War breaks out and Jack, as a reservist, is immediately re-called to the colours, and is caught up in the appalling retreat from Mons:

> About three days and nights we were holding that trench before we were relieved. What a time we had. Just as we were getting out of the blasted trench, looking forward to the first drink of tea for eighty hours, young Evans copped out. He screamed as the bullet tore its way through his belly. Captain Berkeley said: 'Get him back if you can, Jones.' I managed to detain three other chaps who were getting off the mark. With them I dragged young Evans behind the shelled farm-house, where one of the doors was hanging. Having plugged young Evans' wound with our field-dressings, we laid him on the door and hoisted him up on our shoulders. Crying like a kid he was.
>
> Bullets were whistling, and it is doubtful if ever we would reach the hard road. But we did. Young Evans crying . . . for his mother. 'Mam,' he cried again and again – and the shoulder I was carrying with was aching like hell. Couldn't change over, for if once we lowered him down from our shoulders it was doubtful if we would be strong enough to put him up there again. Stick it, Joney, I kept on saying to myself. I had young Evans' rifle as well as my own. His pack was serving him as pillow . . .
>
> 'Shoni, Shoni hoy,' was what he was crying now. 'Shoni,' that was my name in the South Welsh tongue. 'Shoni hoy,' and as he moaned it above my head [his] life's blood dripped down off the door on to the base of my neck . . .
>
> 'Stop squirming up there, for Christ's sake,' one of the two chaps carrying in front shouted. "You're throwing all the bloody weight on me. Lie still, mun.'
>
> Presently he did lie still. When we lowered him down off our shoulders in front of a roadside dressing station he was dead. I took his identity disc. When we found the regiment a couple of hours later I reported to Captain Berkeley, who said: 'Well, you did what you could – and it was a damned fine performance to bring him back dead through that. I shan't forget to mention . . . '
>
> It was a drink of tea I wanted more than the mention in dispatches I got for that performance so I hurried off . . .
>
> (*Unfinished Journey* 149–50)

Presently, outside Ypres, Jack is wounded, a blighty in the head and hand. Back home, war-weariness has not yet set in and Merthyr gives him a hero's welcome; and at a packed and tumultuous recruiting meeting in the drill hall he makes from the platform what was probably his first public speech. He managed to stay on in the town with the red, white and blue ribbons of a recruiting officer in his khaki cap, and in his heart the secret determination to delay his return to France for as long as possible. Up to the middle of 1916, he tells us, with a candour which is one of the most endearing qualities of his autobiographies, 'I dodged the column . . . I played for safety for all I was worth'. As a result of addressing almost nightly recruiting meetings, sometimes sharing a platform with celebrities like Mrs Pankhurst and Mrs Flora Drummond, he became a fluent and effective public speaker, an accomplishment to be of decisive importance in his later life. Before the war catches up with him again it is 1918 and the Armistice is signed. Jack is thirty-four, minus a finger and plus a Mons Star. He returns to the mines.

But the 'Land fit for Heroes' hasn't materialized by a long chalk in the South Wales valleys. Before long there is much short working and unemployment. Times are so bad in the early twenties that one day Jack, weeping (by now he is the father of four children), tries to touch a conchy ILP-er for a bob.[3] This chap invites him to hear Noah Ablett, the syndicalist miners' leader, speaking on 'Who are the coal-owners?' Jack accepts. At that meeting he sees the light. For the next twelve years he is a dedicated party politician, although his dedication seems to have been to politics rather than to party. But let us not be too self-righteous about Jack's political changes. He has always had the faculty, commendable in a novelist, damaging to a politician, of understanding and sympathizing with a wide variety of points of view, even with his opponents'. Could the young soldier, who in South Africa in 1902 felt shame and deep compassion at the plight of the Boer prisoners-of-war, ever turn out to be a really successful party leader? Or the recruiting sergeant of 1917, who had admired and respected the conchies he was escorting from Merthyr to Wormwood Scrubs, ever develop into a blind or unscrupulous partisan? Jack was a man for whom the sorrows of this world are far more real than the political tinkering we sometimes employ to set them right.

The measure of the change in Jack's thinking and allegiance by 1921 is well illustrated by his reaction to an invitation to rejoin the colours for the duration of the miners' strike of that year, following the government's decontrolling of the mines. 'Like hell I will', he shouts, and rips up his papers. Instead he goes off to attend a political conference at Manchester. His presence there makes him a foundation member of the Communist Party of Great Britain. Regardless of the fact that the conference has officially liquidated God, Jack spends part of his train journey back home to Wales in silent prayer.

Nevertheless as the missionary comrades, the big names among the post-war Reds, Walton Newbold, Tommy Jackson, Harry Pollitt, Tom Mann, Palme Dutt, Saklatvala, begin to arrive in South Wales, Jack arranges meetings for them. A Welsh newspaper advertises for a secretary-representative, a miners' agent in fact, in the Garw, a deadend coal-mining valley in Glamorgan, and Jack, although a known Communist, gets the job out of a hundred and sixty candidates. His wages shoot up from thirty bob to three pounds ten a week. Immediately he takes over his job, instructions for the comrade secretary begin to arrive from Moscow in the little office under the stage of the Workmen's Hall, and these in time Jack learns to treat like the offer of sergeant's rank and all allowances a few months before. As a boy Jack had shared his mother's love of the stage, and he had in fact been a regular theatre-goer while still on the breast; later he had appeared in Merthyr both before the stage, selling pop and oranges, and on it, playing such parts as one of the trolls in *Rip Van Winkle*. Now he begins to use his Blaengarw Workmen's Hall as a theatre, bringing Shakespeare and Shaw to the valley – *Julius Caesar, Man and Superman, Mrs Warren's Profession*. And here in Blaengarw, while still a miners' leader, Jack began, in a tentative way, to be a writer. He entered a one-act play competition in Manchester and won a three-guinea prize.

But the year, 1926, was not one propitious for the beginning of the literary career of a miners' agent. The bitter and ruinous miners' strike, following the collapse of the General Strike, was on, and Jack was not only giving leadership and encouragement to his own miners, but was also stumping the country, the Forest of Dean, Notts, Derby, Staffs, Warwick, wherever there were coal pits, stiffening the morale of the strikers: 'Not a penny off the pay, not a minute on the day'. After seven months the miners, those who were able to get work at all, returned to the pits defeated, disillusioned and embittered.

And early the next year Jack performs one of those acts of outstanding courage, or cynical betrayal – according to whether he was joining you or abandoning you – which marked his career as a politician. At a Labour meeting in Swansea he declared that both the General Strike, and its continuation in the miners' strike, were a tragic mistake. 'Renegade' and 'bourgeois hack', scream the Communists, and their journal *The Worker* demands his removal from his job as miners' leader. Jack counters by putting on his third Shakespearean Festival at the Blaengarw Workmen's Hall.

Rejected now by the Communists, he becomes one of the panel of
Labour speakers, which includes J. H. Thomas, Jimmy Maxton, the
Mosleys and Oliver Baldwin. Soon, at the Market Harborough by-
election, speaking on behalf of the Labour candidate, he takes time off to
listen to his fellow countryman, Lloyd George, delivering on the Liberals'
behalf a more than usually spellbinding oration. The experience is too
much for Jack. He is converted to Liberalism. Back home in Blaengarw
they want him to explain a newspaper article he has written advocating a
Lib-Lab front. With his usual guts he attends a packed and hostile
meeting in an attempt to justify himself and to convince his hearers. He is
requested to give an undertaking not to write again for the boss press. He
refuses and is fired from his job as miners' agent. He is on the dole.

The Liberals use him as one of their staff speakers and he stumps the
reddest areas of red South Wales. 'Judas', yell the Communists when he
appears on the platform, and drown his voice with the strains of the
'Red Flag'. Snapped with Lloyd George entering a Cardiff hall to make
a speech, his photograph appears in the *Tatler*. A little later, speaking in
Tylorstown in the red Rhondda, a Communist in the audience holds
up the magazine and shouts: 'Here he is, comrades, here the traitor is.
On the front page of the bloody *Tatler*, the boss-class picture-paper.
Easy to see where he's going, comrades'.

Not only does Jack speak for other Liberal candidates; he becomes
one himself, and in 1929 fights the Neath division in South Wales.
Defeated by Labour by 12,000 votes, he is again unemployed and, to
the jeers of the Communists, signing the dole.

Cardiff seemed a better proposition for an unemployed man of drive,
courage and ability than a derelict mining valley like the Garw, so in
1930 he moves with his family to Rhiwbina, and finds a place to live in
on top of and behind a boot-repairer's shop and workrooms. He is forty-
six, and because of his unemployment he has time on his hands. The
Depression for most of us in South Wales, although a good time to write
of, was a bad time to write in; but Jack decides to have a go again at
getting something down, something 'substantial', not the piffling little
newspaper articles on politics and drama he has been doing occasionally
up till then. With characteristic gusto he produces in a year, to the heavy
pounding of the boot-repairer's machinery the other side of the wall, a
quarter of a million words, a novel about the lives of his parents in
Merthyr from the eighteen-eighties to the nineteen-thirties. This saga of
'the illiterate, the unsung, unknown woman of the coalfield', which he
called *Saran*, was rejected by three publishers and then, reluctantly, for

the time, laid aside. Jack continues every morning to search for work in a Cardiff where there are twenty thousand unemployed. He signs on regularly at the Labour Exchange, and the family endures the periodic snoops of the means-test man. Many people in Cardiff ironically believe Jack to be well off, a sharer of the Liberal millions said to have been amassed by Lloyd George through the sale of honours.

In 1931 Sir Oswald Mosley starts his New Party. Jack is still on the dole, no one wants his novel, his typewriter is sold, his wife and three of his children are still dependent upon him, and the rent is in arrears. He offers the New Party his services as a speaker and is accepted at a fiver a week. He goes round with Professor Joad, Peter Howard, John Strachey, etc. At Ashton-under-Lyne only a strong police guard prevents the lynching of the whole platform, including Jack and Mosley. On a matter of expensive principle a now uneasy Jack, seeing the direction towards Fascism the party seemed to be taking, quits and takes a job selling the *Encyclopaedia Britannica*. This is no good – even navvying's better, which he does for three or four months on the new building site behind the boot-repairer's in Rhiwbina. For eight articles under the title 'The Autobiography of an Agitator', Sir Ernest Benn's *Independent* gives him twenty pounds and, his appetite whetted by hard cash and success, he starts another novel, although his first is still unpublished. With money, borrowed chiefly from his son, he has it typed and the second publisher he submits it to accepts it and advances him twenty-five pounds. When *Rhondda Roundabout* is published in 1934 Jack is nearly fifty, and the only author on the books of the means-test man in Cardiff.

As a result of publication he is invited by Lady Rhondda to a literary luncheon at the Gargoyle Club in London, where he meets among others Sean O'Casey, Winifred Holtby and Mrs Bernard Shaw. But this is no more than a pleasant and slightly unreal interlude. In the eyes of the local public assistance committee he is still officially destitute, and when a Liberal friend actually *offers* him a job, an astonishing, almost unimaginable, piece of good fortune in the South Wales of the thirties, as an assistant cinema manager in Swansea, at four pounds a week, he accepts. But the eternal dinner-jacket and black bow-tie, the non-stop smiling and the urgencies of the job's trivialities, plus, no doubt, dreams of further literary success, put an end to this in a matter of months. With time again on his hands he attacks his thrice-rejected, quarter-of-a-million-word novel about the Merthyr of his parents, and reduces it to about eighty thousand words. It is accepted first go and published in

1935 under the title, not of *Saran*, but of *Black Parade*. The novel had an enthusiastic press and H. G. Wells, who called it 'a great book', wrote to Jack about it twice. Only the *Merthyr Express* dissented, protesting that Jack's picture of Merthyr, drunken, brutal and filthy, was likely to 'injure the town's fair name'.

One might reasonably suppose that Jack's circumstances would now improve. Through his speaking and writing he is one of the best-known figures in Wales, and with two highly successful novels to his credit his name is becoming familiar in English literary circles. But the year is 1935, and before long Jack is peddling electric lamp bulbs on commission. Also his next book *Behold They Live*, a sort of Welsh journey, is rejected as being too gloomy by London publishers, expecting no doubt, even in the thirties, another *Wild Wales*. Unbeaten, he tries a third novel, *Shadow-Show*, about his experiences in the cinema, and this too is rejected – a bitter blow to a man in Jack's desperate situation. In his box of unfinished manuscripts he finds a piece of autobiography written seven years before. This he rewrites and extends and in 1937 the first of his autobiographies, *Unfinished Journey*, is published, a Book Society recommendation and the choice of the Readers Union for its twenty thousand members.

It was a little before this time that I first got to know Jack and some of his family, his wife Laura, his daughter and her husband and his youngest son, David. I had seen Jack on his daily walks in Rhiwbina long before and had been impressed by his appearance. He was perhaps a little below medium height, but so compactly built, so slim and erect and well proportioned that I have always been a little uncertain on this point. He walked in those days habitually with a springy, buoyant step, jaunty and rapid. Good looks are frequent in his family, and Jack had his share of them. He had the sort of head that seems attractive to artists, and I know of at least four who have found this so. His dark hair beginning, in the late nineteen thirties, to turn grey, was dense and wavy, and his long, well-boned face, lean and mobile, had a finely shaped hooked nose rising out of it. During his last years he fulfilled an old ambition and grew a rather curly beard which, with his thick grey hair, gave his whole head an appearance of distinction and impressive benignity. He was the sort of figure at which, in our walks through Merthyr and suburban Cardiff, people took a second look, even when he no longer wore his famous broad-brimmed American hat.

Unfinished Journey was published in the same year, 1937, as my own first book, and the fact that Jack was an author was reason enough for me to find him interesting. We met occasionally between that date and the outbreak of the Second World War, usually in the presence of Gwyn Jones, who had published his first novel, *Richard Savage*, in 1935, and his novel about the Depression in South Wales, *Times Like These*, in 1936. Gwyn, to whom Jack dedicated *Some Trust in Chariots*, was in fact much more intimate with him in those days, and for many years to come, than I was; with his customary generosity to other writers Gwyn was friend, proof-reader, advisor, critic and general encourager. (Not prodder; Jack was always a shamingly conscientious worker at his writing; no doubt he found authorship relatively undemanding after his 'treblers' in the pit, when he would dig coal for thirty-two hours nonstop without coming to the surface.) We sometimes, the three of us together, went for rambles in the lovely hills behind Rhiwbina, allowing Jack, the most articulate and uninhibited of the three then, I felt, to entertain us with his splendid mimicry, and his descriptions, clear-eyed and often jeering, of his encounters with the eminent. One such concerned T. S. Eliot, at that time Jack's much-admired publisher, and was a marvel of character-drawing in miniature; Eliot, reserved, courteous, shrinking, offering a placatory and rather fishlike hand to the strange phenomenon confronting him out of Wales, brash, buoyant, irrepressible. Gerald Gould called Jack a 'born writer'. He was certainly a born actor, a much more flamboyant and authoritative one than the two appearances he later made in films would suggest. 'What's "additional dialogue", Jack?' I would ask. 'You know, you see it in the credits before the films – "Dialogue by So-and-so. Additional dialogue by So-and-so".' Jack would explain, and supply a couple of pages of impromptu additional dialogue so funny that Gwyn and I were soon speechless. And he would go on to describe to us the lunacies of the world in which, by 1939, he was earning his living, the fantasy world of motion pictures, to me incredibly prodigal, cruel and lawless.

It is not generally known that Jack was an accomplished linguist, a fluent speaker of most European languages. I mention this in the context of his acting ability because I don't think he had a grammatically accurate knowledge of any language, not even the English he uses with such force and feeling. Most Sunday mornings during the last decade of his life he visited my house, and what my wife and I and any friends who happened to be staying with us always specially delighted in, were Jack's accounts of some play or film he had seen during the previous week. At such times his fluency in foreign languages was fully revealed. Because Jack was capable not only, like most of us, of outlining the plot of a film; he could also take all the parts. French waiter, German officer, English gentleman, Jack played them all with complete conviction, in their own tongues, on the hearthrug of our dining-room. It's true that a hypercritical and carping listener might suspect, no doubt correctly, that the only German word Jack had really mastered from end to end was *schwein*; but what of it? Those autocratic sentences barked out with their bunches of *au*'s and *ein*'s and, of course, *schweins*, were utterly convincing and comprehensible to all but some narrow-minded pedant or umlaut-grinding grammarian.

The extent of Jack's reading in his chosen fields was really staggering and should never be underestimated – English and American novels and plays, and European literature in translation, as well as biography and history. Not only did Jack act for us the films or plays that he had seen. He would give impromptu dramatizations of scenes from books he was currently enjoying. One of these was the Versailles memoirs of the Duc de Saint Simon, and to see Jack presenting the scene where one of the royal dukes, while using his commode, grants audience to the papal ambassador, I think it is, was to sense in ten minutes all the splendour, absurdity, arrogance and squalor of that place and period. Jack was superb as *grand seigneur, méchant homme*, and as suppliant emissary, and in his excitement his remarkable facility with foreign languages was sometimes inclined to desert him, and the ducal author might be anything from Duke Simon to the Duck dee Sang Simong. But of the skill, verve and complete identification with character there could never be the slightest doubt.

To return to our pre-war encounters. Sometimes we met with our wives at Gwyn Jones's house in Rhiwbina, and in company, in the presence of Laura, one saw Jack at his tenderest and best. Laura had by that time become very hard of hearing, but Jack saw to it that she was not in any way left out of the pleasures of conversation. After every remark or anecdote, Jack would turn patiently to her and say, while she watched his face with intense interest, 'Gwyn was saying, love, that when he was . . .' And so on. Another house at which we used to meet was that of T. Rowland Hughes, the Welsh-language poet and novelist, already in the grip of the paralysis which was to kill him within a few years.

But although the fact that Jack was a writer made him a person of interest, he was not the sort of writer who, when I was a young man, had much glamour for me, as Dylan Thomas, say, had. To begin with, Jack was essentially a prose writer, a novelist, and I found in poets and short-story writers at that time much more fascination and appeal. Further, even as a prose writer he appeared pedestrian and unexciting, his concern for language and style obviously nil. His prose seemed to me almost indistinguishable, apart of course from the matter of it, from the unawakened writing in the essays my reluctant and insensitive adolescents submitted to me for marking week by week in school. It was bare, factual, unadorned, with few of those marvellous life-giving graces, quirks, fancies, perceptions, images, embellishments and distortions of language we depressingly lump together under the term of 'figures of speech'. A phrase like 'down the arches of the years' in *Black Parade*, or even 'sweated like a bread tin' in *Me and Mine* (1946), stands out by reason of its complete unexpectedness, even inappropriateness, in so plain a style. Jack saw language – granting that he saw language at all – solely as a vehicle, not as something rich and beautiful in itself which had passed through the hands of thousands of artists. The vitality, the pace, the bounce, the colour of his books, were all to be in the material itself, the turbulent stories of the lives of his South Wales miners and their families and communities, not in the author's vision and treatment. In addition to the lack of concern for language, there appeared to be little evidence of reflection, or standpoint, or sensitivity, and the speed with which he wrote seemed to rule out polishing and rewriting. It seemed to me that he was content to put his stories down on paper without subjecting them to processing in a passage through his own personal filter. How could this be art, I asked, when no artist appeared to be operating between the fact and the written page? My worst fears were confirmed when he asked me one day what a thesaurus was for. (He pretended he couldn't pronounce the word first go.) When I explained to him (fool that I was) he said he couldn't see much use in a book like that, because as far as he could make out one word was as good as any other if it meant the same. I have already quoted from the first of Jack's three autobiographies, and the passages I think reveal how foolishly prejudiced and narrow my early judgment of his work was. He is a novelist of the type, if not of the order, of John Bunyan; not of course a conscious stylist like Carlyle or Meredith, but a writer who achieves style by not caring about it and by aiming, like the fast clippers, at some other excellence. His estimate of my work was more generous than was my – unuttered – judgment of his at the time, and in the Welsh-language little magazine *Tir Newydd*, in 1937, he wrote an encouraging piece about the only book I had then published.[4] Jack's article for this quarterly was written in English and translated for him. He would never claim that his Welsh, although no doubt more extensive than his actor's

German, was anything more than so-so. 'Jack can speak Welsh', Laura once said to his mother. 'Yes', the old lady, bilingual herself, replied, 'and so can some of the Italian ice-cream men about here'. It is only fair to say, however, that Jack in his last years spoke with remarkable confidence and fluency on several Welsh-language television programmes.

Jack's story after the age of fifty-three was one of widening experience and growing fame as a writer. When he was in Merthyr visiting his parents to show them some cuttings about his recently-published *Unfinished Journey*, some remarks of his father concerning the eighteen sixties became the seed of his next book, *Bidden to the Feast*. This novel, one of his best, written and typed in a year, and again well-received, was published in 1938, a successful but very demanding year for Jack. Right at the end of it he cracks under the strain. The family have moved into a new bungalow in Rhiwbina, called 'Sarandai', a combination of the names by which his father and mother were commonly known, Saran (Sarah Ann) and Dai; the climax of the year's stresses comes in the noisy and incessant lav. in the middle of the bungalow, used on Christmas Day by the fourteen people present for meals. The unending sound of it sends Jack fleeing into the hills. Jack was essentially a family man, and many of his novels are family sagas. But the presence of his loved ones in large numbers in his house when he wanted to get on with his work could drive him to uncontrollable outbursts of irritability and bickering which he bitterly regretted afterwards.

The mention of the new bungalow is an indication that, financially, things were not so bad as they had been for the family. Three novels, all of which had attracted a good deal of attention, have been published, in addition to a best-selling volume of autobiography. Jack had also won a play-writing competition with *Land of my Fathers*, which was put on at the Fortune Theatre in London (1937). Later the same year it is translated into Welsh and performed to a packed and enthusiastic audience at the Prince of Wales Theatre, as part of the National Eisteddfod of Wales, held that year at Cardiff. So many amateur companies perform the play, and so much money rolls in from the fees and royalties of his other work, that before the end of the year Jack has to endure another new experience, unexpected and unpleasant. He receives a demand for income tax for the first time in his life. This was the less agreeable part of being successful, a celebrity, a bungalow owner, a receiver of as many as twelve letters in one day.

But Jack was never the man to forget his origins, or to be complacent in the presence of the appalling poverty, deprivation and unemployment that surrounded his small enclave of success and prosperity in the South Wales of 1938. Invited to speak at the *Sunday Times* National Book Fair at Earl's Court, he mesmerizes his comfortable, book-loving London audience with talk, not about literature but about his father spending fifty-five years of his life underground from the age of eight, and the two thousand children in the Merthyr borough *at that moment* without boots or shoes. At a Foyle's Literary Luncheon to launch a book by another South Wales author, E. Picton-Turberville, entitled, of all things in 1939, *Life is Good*, Jack boils over talking about the distressed valleys and, as he says, scalds his audience.

He dramatizes both *Bidden to the Feast* and *Rhondda Roundabout*, the first to be done on radio and the second for performance at the Globe in London, produced by Glen Byam Shaw. This period, partly because the Depression had focused attention on South Wales, was one in which works about Wales were sympathetically received by the critics. Emlyn Williams's play *The Corn is Green* and Richard Llewellyn's novel *How Green was my Valley* both appeared and were enthusiastically welcomed at this time. But in spite of this, and of good acting, much goodwill and many good notices, Jack's play folded after sixty-three performances. But before this disappointment it had been seen by Pen Tennyson, who approached Jack with an offer to work at Ealing film studios, writing dialogue for *Proud Valley*, a film about South Wales, starring Paul Robeson. Jack accepts, but after two unsuccessful attempts at the job he begins to feel frustrated, and out of his element up there in London, lonely, and a long way from Laura. For probably the only time in a life which has shown consistent and outstanding physical and moral courage, he quits and runs home. He is coaxed back, and the film, with Jack acting in it in a supporting role, is completed, and has considerable success in this country, and some in the USA, as well as being granted general release throughout the USSR during the war.

When war comes, Jack's four sons and his only son-in-law are in it. Lawrence, the third son, a brilliant historian who had been at Balliol on a scholarship, in 1942 wins the MC and dies of wounds in North Africa, a bitter blow to Jack. David, the youngest, is discharged from the army with tuberculosis and dies, incurable, some time later. Jack himself becomes deeply involved in what was called 'the war effort', speaking in support of War Weapons Weeks, Wings Weeks and Battleship Weeks, and so on, normally six times a day, sometimes more; and this, with his own broadcasting and writing – he has begun a book on his former leader, Lloyd George – works him to a standstill. Before an expectant audience of Monmouthshire Rotarians he breaks down and weeps. But Jack is nothing if not resilient, and soon after, in 1941, he accepts an invitation to undertake a three-month tour in America, not at that time in the war. He is to put the British point of view to American audiences, and works under the direction of Harley Granville Barker, head of the Speakers' Section of the British Information Service in New York. He does two such tours in fact, the second one, of five months' duration, after Pearl Harbour. He speaks at Washington, Atlantic City, Cleveland, Chicago, Toronto, Detroit, Baltimore, Boston, etc. etc. etc., addressing garment workers, teamsters, carpenters, Baptists, students, Rotarians, theatre-club members, in churches, halls, colleges, trade union headquarters and theatres. Once he addressed from the ring a crowd who had come to see professional wrestling. He met Lord and Lady Halifax, Isaiah Berlin, Alfred Noyes, Elsa Maxwell, Malcolm MacDonald and Reinhold Niebuhr, and narrowly missed (avoided?) meeting Auden. He bursts into the presence of the unwilling and over-whelming John L. Lewis, whose Welsh mam was still alive, and secures a cordial interview with that formidable old volcano. In Newark, New Jersey, at a vast rally complete with loudspeakers, trousered usherettes and a twenty-piece orchestra, Jack followed Governor Edison, Burgess Meredith, Tamara and Maggie Bondfield on the platform. What the audience really wanted by the time Jack rose – it was 10 p.m. – were the between-speeches singers with their numbers from *Rio Rita* and *The Desert Song*. This is how Jack handled them:

> The singer was going to oblige with an encore, after all, and the audience simmered down to enjoy it. Then, after that and the applause I was called upon to speak, and there was a dribble of applause as I stood up. I held up my hand and shouted, 'Silence! I'm going to speak of the dead, the glorious dead,' I told them, 'and I won't have you insulting with cheap applause the memory of those who have died for us and for freedom. Their blood has enriched the waters of Russian rivers and the sands of deserts and the good earth of China. Those I take pleasure in reminding you of died without applause, in places out of the limelight. Do you know how many British merchant seamen have given their lives in the battle of the Atlantic so that others may live? Did I say they were dead? No, they are not dead. It is we, the living, so-called, who are dead . . .'
>
> I may have spoken for twenty minutes before I said that a few moments' silence in remembrance of our earthly saviours would be more to our credit than cheap applause. 'I've nothing further to say.

Please sit still and keep your noisy hands quiet.' I walked backwards to my seat and they all sat still and no one present made noises with his hands. 'God bless you, Jack,' said Margaret Bondfield. 'May God bless us all,' I said . . .[5]

On the whole Jack's two tours are a great success, in spite of the harrying tactics of a fiercely anti-British section of the American press. In fact Jack began to feel at one time that his journalist interviewers, so hostile and perverse were their questions, had been personally coached by William Randolph Hearst.

On his return from America Jack goes overseas to address British troops, first in Belgium and Holland and then in Italy. All this talking and travelling have meant that he hasn't done much fresh writing for a very long time. In fact in 1944 he could look back on five years in which he had not published a single book. But before the end of the war in 1945 he had buckled down again and written *Our American Cousin* (a play) and the enormous *Me and Mine* (the second section of his autobiography). He had also completed *The Man David*, his biography of Lloyd George (1944), and begun his third Merthyr novel *Off to Philadelphia in the Morning*. Also by then, both his parents and one son were dead and another son was dying, Laura was unwell and he himself had suffered several illnesses from overwork, including shingles and a sort of stroke.

By this time, it seems to me, Jack's best work had been done, namely the three working-class novels *Rhondda Roundabout*, *Black Parade* and *Bidden to the Feast* and the autobiography *Unfinished Journey*. Much more was yet to happen to him both as a man and as a writer. He was to complete his boxing of the political compass by speaking on behalf of a Cardiff Tory candidate; he was to receive the CBE; to survive three heart attacks; to endure the agony of his son David's long dying, to lose Laura and to marry as his second wife his charming and gifted librarian; to undertake another American tour, this time on behalf of Moral Rearmament. In addition he was to write his three enormous family-town novels, *Off to Philadelphia in the Morning* (1947), *Some Trust in Chariots* (1948) and *River out of Eden* (1951) as well as *Lily of the Valley* (1952), *Lucky Lear* (1952), *Time and the Business* (1953), *Choral Symphony* (1955) and *Come Night, End Day* (1956). During his writing career of less than thirty years he wrote eleven published novels, three volumes of autobiography, three plays and a biography, in addition to innumerable radio scripts, speeches, newspaper articles and masses of unpublished material. Jack's work accounts for 167 items in a schedule at the National Library of Wales, Aberystwyth.

I find it easiest to think of Jack's novels when they are divided into three sections. In the first, both by reason of chronology and merit, I put *Rhondda Roundabout, Black Parade* and *Bidden to the Feast*. These three novels have a freshness, a gusto, a spontaneity which Jack never fully recaptured in his later work, the verve, and innocence and brilliance of week-end paintings of high talent. The understanding of and sympathy with Welsh working-class life in them is complete. The dialogue, apart from, occasionally, a kind of trade-union-official pomposity and a rather strange literariness, is authentic. (I doubt if any of Jack's people would really have used 'summoned' rather than the almost universal 'summonsed'. And stilted locutions like 'that which you've got', and 'townships in which there's', seem unlikely ones for South Walians. A few habitual phrases in Jack's narrative passages sound rather inappropriately dainty for him also, e.g. 'one and all', 'each and every one', 'ever so tall', 'ever so plentiful', etc.) The characterization, if not profound, is crisp, convincing and memorable; Jack's instinctive creatures of passion and impulse live to the full in action, even violence. They are without self-analysis, without reflection. How remarkable and unexpected is that contemplative moment of Saran in *Black Parade*, when, holding the coal bucket in her hand on Armistice night, she gazes for a moment in wonder up at the pearly sky. There is humanity in these books, pathos, fun; the vision is clear and uncomplicated by theory or hypothesis. Several Anglo-Welsh writers, it seems to me (Caradoc Evans, Dylan Thomas, Gwyn Thomas, Vernon Watkins), did some of their best work at the beginning of their careers, and Jack is among them.

Some, almost certainly Jack himself, would make out a case for the inclusion of the three 'family-town' novels in this category. 'Huge, sprawling things without very much depth to them. Mixtures of laughter and tears, rather coarse mixtures but with backgrounds no social historian could find fault with.' That is Jack's description of his own novels, and it is, alas, only too accurate where the 'family-town' books are concerned. What Jack has done in these with more or less consistency is to parallel the history of a family with that of the growing South Wales town in which the people he has created live; the Parry family and Merthyr, at the head of the Taff Valley, in *Off to Philadelphia in the Morning*; the Tewdwrs and Pontypridd (which he calls Pontyglo), half way down the valley, in *Some Trust in Chariots*; and the Regans and Cardiff, at the mouth of the Taff, in *River out of Eden*. But I have never been convinced that this particular formula of Jack's for novel-writing is a good one. For one thing, to undertake the history of a large family, with all its ramifications by the third generations spreading into the middle class, plus the social, industrial and economic history of the rapidly growing and changing South Wales town in which these people live, is bound to result in an enormous book. Especially, as Jack himself confesses, 'Brevity has never been my strongest point'. *Black Parade*, as we have seen, was at first 250,000 words long. Jack reduced it for publication to about 80,000 and, judging by its appearance now, I would guess that what he cut out were the parts about the history and rapid development of the township of Merthyr, paragraphs, perhaps chapters, on coal-mining, iron- and steel-making, on trade unionism, local politics, religious controversy and so on and so on. This left the condensed, exciting novel of rich human interest which we have now. When *Some Trust in Chariots* was finished Jack's splendid publisher found that also much too long, and asked for a cut of about 50,000 to 60,000 words. But by now, in 1947–8, Jack was, I believe, writing self-consciously to his plan, and what he cut out this time, one would guess, were some of his characters and the incidents in which they were involved, rather than information about the novel's historical background, the industrial and social development of Pontypridd which, as he says, 'no social historian could find fault with'. Jack has generous praise for the helpfulness of the Cardiff Central Library towards him and his researches, but I am not sure that his visits to that admirable institution, where he amassed Zola-like mountains of fact about the coalfield, were altogether beneficial to his writing. The necessity for drastic shortening of his novels after they were completed, in a sense an acknowledgment of the failure of his plan for writing them, is bound to result in a certain perfunctoriness in his dealings with some of the swarms of characters he has inevitably to introduce, the almost unheralded marrying off of some, as in, say, *Some Trust in Chariots* and *River out of Eden,* and the pushing of others with very little ceremony into their graves.[6] Also Jack is essentially a novelist of the working class, and narratives whose scope lands him outside this *milieu* are inclined to be, as he says himself, without much depth. It is an indication of his skill as a novelist that in spite of what seems to me the disastrous plan to which these three impressive novels have been written, their humanity yet holds the interest and they have been highly popular and successful; for instance, *River out of Eden* sold 10,000 copies and a second edition of *Off to Philadelphia in the Morning* was printed almost immediately after publication; and this book, like *Bidden to the Feast*, was later reissued as a paperback. But then *Off to Philadelphia* has as one of its themes the Dickensian situation of a devoted slum child caring for her blind, drunken and disfigured genius of a ballad-singing father. And of course it also has the marvellous and unforgettable story of Harry Half-a-man.

The novels after *River out of Eden*, namely *Lily of the Valley*, *Lucky Lear*, *Time and the Business*, *Choral Symphony* and *Come Night, End Day*, although full of admirable scenes and situations and characters, and of vivid pages of writing (especially in *Choral Symphony*), do not for me approach the six earlier novels in interest and conviction.

I heard Jack speak in public several times, but never at the exalted level of his famous oration at the Cardiff Cory Hall in 1928, the occasion when he shared with Lloyd George not only a *Tatler* photograph and a platform, but the response, enthusiasm and esteem of the audience. At times, he told me, when facing a sympathetic meeting, he forgot his surroundings and spoke out of a sort of trance. This, I believe, happened to him sometimes as a writer also. Jack's narrative style is in a way part of the heritage of his life as a miners' agent; it was formed, like the long speeches in Shaw's plays, on the political platform or soapbox, and is haunted by the sound of the human voice, the orator's or the actor's. He described himself as a mile-a-minute talker and he is that sort of writer too. But when the trance overtakes him his prose falls into new rhythms. The sufferings of this world, not only the many sorrows of his own life, lay heavily on Jack's heart, and I remember his saying to me once, after telling me that one of his young neighbours was dying of a brain tumour: 'In the midst of tragedy we write comedy'. But not always. Here is Jack, in the middle of the record of the domestic details of *Me and Mine*, suddenly moved, writing in compassion and sorrow of another's grief, after he has himself received news of his own son's death at El Alamein:

> Last night, when I went to the Butcher's Arms for a pint of half and half there were three men in the bar with me who had lost the one and only son. There was another who had lost a son quite recently and he showed the lad's photograph to some of us. He did not say anything, nor could he hear our sympathetic murmurs, for he was a deaf-and-dumb cobbler, and the boy who had died fighting in Normandy had for years been his father's voice and ears. The deaf-and-dumb cobbler nodded as he read the sympathy in our eyes and he put the photograph back in his inside-pocket. He picked up his pint and drank a little of the beer and as he put his pint back down on the

table he sighed, closed his mouth tight and shook his head and felt
desperately for a cigarette. Someone snapped a lighter aflame and held
it to the cigarette the deaf-and-dumb cobbler had placed between his
lips. He nodded his thanks and took a long and steady and steadying
pull at the cigarette. He has had or will in due course have a letter
from the King, but who will speak for him and hear for him the way
his boy used to? . . . It's no fun being a cobbler at the best of times but
to be one alone and deaf and dumb into the bargain in wartime is a
job and a half . . . Then what about our friend the deaf-and-dumb
cobbler, whose son and one-time helper and spokesman now lies as
deaf and dumb as his poor father somewhere in Normandy? . . . Oh,
forget thou not the deaf-and-dumb cobbler, ye people of high
degree.[7]

I have written more in these notes about Jack the man than about
Jack the writer, and this in his case is an easy trap to fall into because he
spoke about himself on a hundred platforms and wrote well over a
quarter of a million words about himself, about his irascibility, his
goatishness, his dedication to his job of writing, his unshakable belief in
an afterlife, his own estimation of his standing as a writer, his great love
of the cinema. It is unlikely that a future researcher will discover any
aspect of Jack's life or character that Jack himself has not already revealed
somewhere or other, because he was never, as he says, a shy man. And yet
one mystery remains. The great marvel about him for me is not that he
has written so well but that he has written at all, he, the son of unlettered
parents, himself with hardly any schooling, in a life of worry, conflict,
hardship and frequent poverty, real poverty, not the sort that follows an
overspent allowance. But his work does not invite criticism tempered
with this knowledge. His novels have the variety, the restlessness, the
vitality of the valleys they are concerned with; they swarm with incident
and with unforgettable characters – Bandy Bowen, Llew Rhondda,
Evans the draper, Uncle Shoni Lloyd, Dai Hippo, Big Mog, Saran,
Steppwr, Harry, Shon Howell, Megan and Moriah, Myfanwy and Blind
Dick, Will Full-Moon, Harry Tewdwr, Lucy Escott, Lena Jenkins. They
have the poignancy of the pastoral visits paid by faithful old Harry
Morgan, the converted mountain-fighter, to the workhouse imbeciles;
the terror of Rhys Davies's vigil, greeting his errant daughters with the
buckle-end of his strap; the comedy of the Cork Club's outing, and of
Harry Tewdwr's two complaisant mistresses tossing to decide who is to
enjoy his favours for the night. They have mountain fighting, massed
bare-fisted battles, rough-house punch-ups, underground accidents,

domestic upheavals, booze-ups, strikes, they have sexual love, maternal love, ambition, trickery, unfaithfulness, devotion, anger, magnanimity. The element I myself chiefly miss in these teeming works I can perhaps describe as poetry, the visionary element, the sense of poetic tension one experiences from time to time in works as diverse as *Almayer's Folly*, *Great Expectations*, *Scarlet and Black*, *Titus Groan*, *Sportsman's Sketches*, *Moby Dick* and so on; the footprint-covering episode in the first of these, the childhood encounters of Pip and Estella, Julien's determination to hold Madame de Renal's hand by ten o'clock, the fight of Flay and Swelter, the unearthly tavern singing of the drunken peasant, the nailing of the golden coin to the Pequod's mast or the first appearance of Ahab. Jack's novels are enacted in the light of common day, clear, wholesome and disenchanting. He is well aware of course that this visionary element exists in literature, but only once or twice, it seems to me, has he brought it off himself. When Amy Meredith high on the hill on her black horse in *Some Trust in Chariots* follows with her eyes Rhys Tewdwr whom she has just seduced, Jack comes near to it, and when the two old men at the end of the same novel watch the young couple making love in the field while the sun sets behind them. In *Unfinished Journey* he achieves it. The little collier boy in the gloom of the old pit workings with his father, looking up the dark tunnel at the disc of daylight at the far end, the light of the world where the life-giving mother is, has always seemed to me one of the most moving passages in the whole of Anglo-Welsh literature.

GWYN THOMAS

1913–1981

SOME critics and reviewers have tended to see in retrospect Anglo-Welsh writing as one of the less predictable results of the Great Depression of the nineteen twenties and thirties. This is an understandable, although wrong, conclusion, arrived at probably for the reason that many Anglo-Welsh writers first appeared in the very much depressed South Wales of the thirties, and frequently wrote about unemployed workers and their families. But what the Depression really did was not to create the Anglo-Welsh, but rather to provide some of them with a theme, or even a passion. Gwyn Jones, Jack Jones, Lewis Jones and Rhys

Davies have all made it the subject of novels; Idris Davies devoted two of his volumes of poetry exclusively to it; George Ewart Evans, William Glynne-Jones and Alun Lewis, among many others, wrote short stories or poems about it. It plays a large part inevitably in the admirable autobiography of B. L. Coombes, and in that of Jack Jones, who has also used it as the basis of a play.[1]

The amount of Anglo-Welsh writing about the Depression is understandingly considerable, and much of it, the work of men who experienced it at first hand, is of great immediacy and power. Not for the Anglo-Welsh that unreal, patronizing attitude to what was at the time a fashionable subject which Dylan Thomas satirized in 'How to become a poet',[2] but rather a sense of involvement and agonizing concern.

The writer most profoundly affected by the Depression, on the evidence of his books, is Gwyn Thomas. When short working and unemployment first began to be felt in the valleys in 1923, he was ten years of age; when prosperity was restored with the outbreak of the Second World War, he was twenty-six; so that part of his childhood and the whole of his youth and young manhood were lived in a period of crippling poverty, emigration and unprecedented unemployment, and the widespread frustration, bitterness, suffering and despair that inevitably followed. The fact that during part of this time Gwyn was away from the Rhondda at Oxford and Madrid universities did not lessen the impact of the disaster upon him. Indeed his absence might even have increased his awareness, since it gave him both an external viewpoint and a standard of comparison. He wrote some eleven novels, five volumes of short stories and essays and several full-length plays, besides innumerable radio scripts, articles and television programmes, and a considerable part of this great mass of material was concerned with one quite small area in Wales and with one relatively short period in that area, in fact with the time, and often the condition, of unemployment in the Rhondda of the nineteen thirties.[3]

Gwyn Thomas was born in the Rhondda in 1913, which made him a year older than Dylan Thomas. But Gwyn, although an outstandingly brilliant and precocious student at his grammar school, and ultimately a very prolific writer, was as a novelist rather a slow maturer. Dylan's first book appeared when he was twenty, Gwyn's not until 1946, when he was thirty-three.

Dylan's father was a school-teacher, Gwyn's a collier, but the differences between the two Thomas homes, the one in suburban Swansea and the other in the coal-mining Rhondda, need not necessarily on that account have been culturally very great. Dylan's home had the advantage of a salary which, although not large, was constant and assured, uninterrupted by strikes, lock-outs and bouts of unemployment. In the matters of language and religion, the Swansea home was divided between English and Welsh, agnosticism and nonconformity. Politically, peopl᷈ with a background similar to that of Dylan's parents were traditionally Liberal. The pervading culture was literary, English and suburban, superimposed upon a pattern involving the Welsh-speaking radical dissent of the parents' rural ancestors. In Gwyn's home in the Rhondda the parents and the older children – Gwyn was the youngest of twelve – were Welsh-speaking, and as a child he himself attended a Welsh Sunday school and chapel belonging to the Independent denomination, whose theology, he said, 'had a kind of bland and easy-going tolerance which would have won a nod of approval from Montaigne'. Music, which Gwyn loved deeply, appears to have been the art best appreciated by him in his attendance at the chapel and most popular with his family. Endless debate, much of it political, went on inside and outside the Rhondda home; the group of three or four young men in discussion in the local Italian café, or on somebody's back wall, is a recurrent feature of Gwyn's stories. In the course of a half-hour radio interview with me in 1950, Gwyn made the following remarks about himself and his background. I quote them here because they seem to me not only important in what they say, but because they illustrate also Gwyn's amazing gifts as a spontaneous speaker. (The interview was scripted, based on discussion.) His writing has always seemed to me only a slightly more condensed version of his brilliant conversation. I remember his describing a mild-mannered Conservative solicitor in Cardiff to me once as being 'to the right of the Pharaohs'! I cannot remember whether St Paul became 'that steady foe of the gonad' in a novel or in conversation, or in which I learnt about the unemployed tenant threatened with eviction who had 'thought more about rent than anybody since Ricardo':

> The people among whom I grew up spoke with a boisterous artistry. On certain levels of deprivation, life and speech cease to be cautious and hedged-in; humour then can express itself without inhibitions. Life in the valleys when I was a boy was a precarious and disquieting thing which encouraged an amazing vitality on people's tongues. We talked endlessly. That was one way of keeping up our spirits in a universe that did not seem very encouraging. A cracked world and a love of the poets gave us all the spiritual incentive and mechanical facility we needed. If we lacked sixpence for the pictures

we could always float on a sea of metaphor in a session of high Socratic debate under a lamp-post in Porth Square or outside the Tonypandy Empire. Our imaginations had a ferocious quality. They roamed through our cosmos like hungry wolves, free to feed on whatever they fancied, finding nothing to make them fall back into a reverent hush. There's another thing. People tell me there are comic undertones in even my most sombre imagery. I can easily believe it. Humour is a sense of the incongruous or absurd, an aggravated sense of the contrast between man's divine promise and his shambling, shabby reality. There was enough incongruity between the way my people lived in the Rhondda of my early manhood, and the way in which they would have wanted to live, to have nourished at least ten thousand humorists of the first rank. But of course about the humour produced from such a situation there will be hints of the most extreme savagery; and the artist into whose spirit it may have entered too deeply will find his main task to be the rendering of his anger bearable to himself and acceptable to others.

Each of the mining valleys of South Wales has its own special characteristics. Gwyn Thomas's valley, the Rhondda, is really two valleys, Rhondda Fawr and Rhondda Fach, Great and Small Rhonddas, which meet at Cymmer (the confluence of two rivers of the same name), Porth (a doorway, an entrance). Up to the outbreak of the Second World War it was upon coal that the Rhondda depended almost exclusively for its prosperity, such as it was, because there was almost no other industry or manufacture carried on there, not even iron- and steel-making as in the Merthyr and Ebbw valleys, or tinplate as in the Swansea area. The Rhondda's output was coal, house coal and some of the finest steam coal in the world, but after the First World War the overseas markets for it had very seriously dwindled. The United States had captured the Canadian and the Central and South American trade. France and Italy, to which Wales used to sell much of her output, were now receiving vast supplies from defeated Germany by way of reparations. In 1921 the British Government decontrolled the mines and this was immediately followed by a miners' strike lasting three months. In 1926 the miners were out for a further seven months following the nine-day General Strike. The British Navy, once a great and steady consumer of steam coal, switched to oil, and so did most of the other navies of the world, and in time the merchant fleets began to follow suit. All these factors helped to reduce the demand for Welsh steam coal, and to hit very hard the economy of those areas which depended entirely upon it for their prosperity. In the Rhondda, at the height of the Depression of the thirties, it is estimated that 42 per cent of the insurable male population was unemployed.[4] This was the by now almost incredible extent of the Depression in the South Wales of the inter-war years.

The Rhondda population is a very mixed one. The descendants of immigrants from rural north and west Wales have intermarried, as in Merthyr and elsewhere, with the descendants of the few original inhabitants of the valley, the aboriginal Welsh who lived there before coal became big business. Other immigrants came from England, from the Forest of Dean, Hereford and Shropshire, and from the other side of the Bristol Channel, viz. Somerset, Devon and Cornwall. The Scots, Irish, Jews and Italians came too. An indication in Gwyn Thomas's books of this mixture of origins is the large number of characters in them with non-Welsh surnames, especially with English surnames preceded by Welsh Christian names, which would probably indicate a Welsh mother and an English father – Caradoc Dando, Bodvan Hemlock, Teilo Beveridge. This type of name, like the large number of biblical names (Omri, Matthew, Salathiel, Naboth, Uriah), Gwyn almost always uses for comic effect, as he does the incongruity of dignified or aristocratic Christian names once common in the valleys, names like Denzil, Ewart and Picton, bestowed upon the shabbiest victims of unemployment and recession.

Gwyn attended the local elementary school and the Rhondda Intermediate School in Porth on which he perhaps based in part his sixth novel, *A Frost on My Frolic* (1953). From there he proceeded on scholarship to St Edmund Hall, Oxford, where he studied modern languages, principally Spanish, because the alternative subject in the grammar school had been 'physics, at the time a dismal and under-publicised field of knowledge. I had also heard that Buenos Aires was a place where sun and sin were high in the charts'.

He passed through Oxford, he says, 'with the arrogant loneliness of Isaiah, but without the dogma', harassed by his two chronic disabilities, namely 'social bewilderment and nicotine poisoning'. Gwyn's humour does not conceal the fact that from first to last Oxford was for him 'a kind of muffled nightmare'. Everything would seem to have been against him; he was lonely, ill, homesick and short of money. His Spanish tutor later became the Poet Laureate of the Fascist Spanish Phalanx of Franco's Spain, and with him Gwyn existed predictably, 'on terms of classic antipathy':

I was one of the people in the thirties who managed to rise – if that is the word – from the lower reaches to Oxford . . . I was to be a bridge, the sort of swaying, straw bridge you see scaring the wits out of the natives in documentaries about Peru. My mind still tinkles with icy little bits of terror. I was one that the Establishment never really assimilated from a genuine lack of desire to do so. A less likely recruit could not have been found. My father was ostensibly a collier but he made the most staccato contribution to mining in the history of the pit . . . He was one of the most mature of our unemployables . . . I was so short of money [in Oxford] that the ghosts of mediaeval students called on me . . . I was the first tenant in 400 years with whom they felt genuinely at home. I kept away from the college dining hall and subsisted on meat pies which obliged me, years later, to buy my own magnesia mine . . .[5]

This reaction to Oxford seems highly unusual and individual, and refreshing after the almost routine expressions of bland satisfaction and fulsome gratitude which so often follow attendance at the university. But in Gwyn's case at least it is surely one with which we can sympathize profoundly. One feature that has often astonished me in reading reminiscences of life at Oxford, and Cambridge too, is the assurance, the maturity, the worldly wisdom of the students. The undergraduates seem to talk with the aplomb of cabinet ministers, and in place of the diffidence and uncertainty we usually associate with youth, they have the arrogance, the hauteur and the snobbery of *seigneurs*. Are, or were, the young men actually like this? Perhaps some of Gwyn Thomas's generation really were, and perhaps many more were able to impose this image of themselves upon those around them. Gwyn, sensitive, desperately poor, socially inexperienced, immature compared with many of the rich and privileged and well-connected young men around him, but conscious undoubtedly, even then, of considerable and unrealized gifts and powers, was bound to feel an outsider in such an atmosphere, to experience affinity only, as he says, with 'the statue of Shelley, who was thrown out of the place'. Gwyn was relieved to leave Oxford, and to get back to the Rhondda Valley where the people, instead of being large and confident as Martians, were 'short, musical, irreverent and flat broke, with not a thing on this earth to be haughty about' (*A Hatful of Humours* 70).

Gwyn spent six months in Madrid after leaving Oxford. Back in Britain he did various lecturing jobs, including a period with the Workers' Educational Association, and finally, in 1940, he joined the staff of Cardigan Grammar School as a teacher of Spanish and French. Two years later he moved to Barry, near Cardiff, in Glamorgan, again to teach in the local grammar school, and in 1962 he finally abandoned teaching to live by his writing and his work for radio and television.

I first encountered Gwyn's work in 1946 when I read his second book, *Where Did I Put My Pity?* This seemed to me unquestionably one of the best collections of Anglo-Welsh short stories ever to have appeared. Three things immediately attracted me to them. First, the extraordinary vigour of the style, the brilliance, the gusto, the torrential language, the inexhaustible imagery; second, the humour, both of situation and of language, strange, fresh, fantastic, contemporary; and third, the compassion, the profound humanity, out of which, later, were to be written *All Things Betray Thee*, and stories of terrible poignancy like 'The Teacher'. Another impressive feature of this book was its complete newness of style and attitude. The material of these stories, i.e. the condition of industrial South Wales during the Depression, was, as I have indicated earlier, shared by Gwyn with a very large number of other Anglo-Welsh poets, novelists and short story writers; but no one treated this material with the brilliant combination I describe, the amalgamation of gusto, compassion, humour and poetry that Gwyn brought to his writing. I have seen over many years, both as ordinary reader and as adjudicator and selector, hundreds of Anglo-Welsh short stories, large numbers of them in manuscript, and the majority of those that showed any promise at all appeared usually to be written by disciples either of Caradoc Evans or of Dylan Thomas. Gwyn Thomas did not so much avoid the pervading influence of these two spell-binding predecessors as write, even in his earliest books, as though he had never read a line of either of them.

The identification of his outlook throughout his work with that of the workers, in his case the miners, is complete, and he has a more profound understanding of Marxism and left-wing politics than most of those other Anglo-Welsh writers whose emotional involvement in the disasters of the coalfield is every bit as passionate as his. This gives his writing an intellectual dimension which is lacking in the work of, say, Idris Davies, and one feels, reading him, one is in contact with a mind much more adult, masculine and robust than that frequently revealed by Dylan, for instance, in his fiction. One of Gwyn's reviewers describes him as the 'greatest proletariat novelist since Lawrence'. I believe Gwyn to be a proletarian novelist of outstanding gifts, but the mention of Lawrence puzzles me. I find it difficult to think of Lawrence, the author of *The*

Plumed Serpent, as a proletarian writer at all. No one in this century has written with greater warmth and understanding about working-class people than Lawrence, in *Sons and Lovers* and in early stories like 'Odour of Chrysanthemums' and 'The Sick Collier'. But the class-consciousness of the English society in which he lived, and his position in it, turned Lawrence, it seems to me, into a sort of *sufi* at whose feet the restless rich and well-connected, disenchanted with orthodox religion and accepted values, found it soothing or stimulating to sit. The reformer is in Gwyn Thomas, too, but he has nothing fanciful or mystical to advocate like salvation through sex and dark-godism. His standpoint is firmly and consistently socialist and working-class, untouched by bourgeois or petit-bourgeois ideals and aspirations. By 'bourgeois' I don't intend a pejorative term for what some Bohemians and 'artists', themselves in some cases rentiers, find distasteful in conventional society. I mean it to convey an acceptance of a static, pyramidic conception of society, and of ruling-class values, such values as are expressed or perpetuated by manifestations as diverse as children's classics like *Tom Brown's Schooldays* and *Children of the New Forest*, hunting, the prep. and public schools and the older universities, the concept of the *gentleman*, grouse-shooting, the hierarchy of the Church, clubland, Debrett, *Country Life*, Ascot, the College of Heralds – a list so preposterous that its recital, I feel sure, would bring about in Gwyn Thomas long before its ending one of those bouts of uncontrollable laughter that what seem to him the basic absurdities of bourgeois society always engender in him. Upper-class values, by whomever held, were to him irresistibly comic; his comedic sense was a disinfectant element in him that leaves his work free of any impression of envy or frustrated ambition. He did not share either those nationalist aspirations which many admirable Welshmen today cherish, perhaps because he saw in nationalism a threat to the international unity and strength of the working class. His attitude seems to give point to the generalization that in South Wales the Lefter a man is the less Welsh he is likely to be. (The Welsh are radical and rebellious, not revolutionary.) Anyhow, I am sure Gwyn was a better Welshman than many of his more austere and dedicated compatriots gave him credit for being. He never attempted to groom himself into a middle-class English intellectual, as many gifted Welshmen before him have so successfully done, and neither did he become a London comic turn, or a 'wild pet', in Eliot's words about Blake, 'for the super cultivated'. Anyone who knew Gwyn Thomas for any length of time must have sensed in him a deep love of the country in which he was born and in which he chose to spend his life.

Paradoxically two of Gwyn's best novels are not about the Depression in the Rhondda of the thirties at all. One of them, *The Love Man* (1958), is set in the Spain of Don Juan, and is really a sort of 'sport' in his work since its chief characters are ruling-class Spaniards, a bishop, the governor of a province, a wealthy merchant and his daughter and the Don himself. No proletarian buffoonery here, no class struggle, no Birchtown, Mynydd Coch or Meadow Prospect, no Edwin Pugh the Pang, or Silcox the Psyche, or Leyshon the Law, or that 'lover of the head-voice', Matthew Sewell the Sotto. *The Love Man*, although in the characteristic Gwyn Thomas idiom, is a strange book for him to have written. This does not prevent me from thinking it one of the best. The other novel not about the thirties, *All Things Betray Thee* (1949), concerns events in what could be the Merthyr of the last century. The book has for me every good thing of which Gwyn Thomas is capable, and marks the peak of his achievement in the field of the novel, as distinct from the play or the short story. It is less shapely perhaps than *The Alone to the Alone* (1947), or than *The Love Man* for that matter, but it is given a sort of organic unity by being written around an obsessive contemporary theme, namely the class struggle and the place of the artist in it. The story concerns Chartist-like disturbances (post-Rebecca anyway) in and around Moonlea, a town in the iron-smelting area of south-east Wales; one of the characters says of it:

> For as far back as we can remember the big farmers and the landlords have been putting their own special brand of boot into the small field-folk, making them flow like rivers from the West lands into valley towns like Moonlea. Towns like this one here have grown up all in a space of about ten or fifteen years. Streets, churches, chapels, courts, taverns, all around and serving the foundries. At first it was fine. It stayed fine for as long as Penbury and his friends were riding their particular tide and the world kept calling out for iron and more iron . . . Then some time back its gullet seemed to be choked with [iron] and hundreds of furnaces went cold . . . Penbury has tightened his grip and wages have shrunk . . . There's hunger in Moonlea and not only here . . .[6]

Into the seething, often violent situation in the town, into the squalor, the exploitation, the savage repression, comes Alan Hugh Leigh, the wandering harpist, in search of his friend, John Simon Adams, whom he has not seen for two years. Alan wants only to practise his art and to get John Simon away from the dangerous valley with its informers, narks and paid bullies, its hatred and violence and unremitting tensions, to the 'lush nook' in North Wales which he has inherited, the 'painless paradise where the sun and the stream sing to each other all the day'.

Entering the valley in his search, Alan sees beside a stream in a dingle that has still managed to stay green a girl of striking beauty, not, oddly enough for an Anglo-Welsh novel, bathing in the nude, but elegantly-clothed and engaged in painting the scene around her. She turns out to be Helen Penbury, the daughter of the Moonlea iron king. The encounter between harpist and heiress is purely dialectical, because Alan, although attracted by the girl's beauty and intelligence, is repelled also by the arrogance and insensitivity her immense family wealth and her reactionary upbringing have given her. Like all Gwyn Thomas's characters, regardless of station or period, this carefully-nurtured young woman speaks in the special and universal Thomas idiom. When the harpist tells her that any man who accepts a master's hand or a rented hovel is fit for the boneyard, she replies: 'You're a savage or a radical. You ought to say those things to my father. He'd have you sitting over a furnace learning elementary logic in less than a minute'. John Simon Adams, now an agitator and a greatly-loved leader of the oppressed iron-workers, she describes in the same interview as 'Moonlea's leading thorn'.

The harpist is at first, because of his art, welcomed into the Penbury home, a fine, huge mansion above the town, to play to the sick and neurotic iron-master, Richard Penbury, the girl's father. Penbury represents the rising industrial class, newly-rich, ruthless, grasping. Another ruling-class figure powerful in the valley is Lord Plimmon, the local squire, also rich, but by inheritance, handsome, assured, masterful. He has, like others of his class, 'made a name for himself with a few radical speeches in the Parliament about the crime of working kids to death in mines'. But where his own interests are concerned he is as grasping, brutal and ruthless as the new capitalist class whose increasing wealth and power he envies and denounces. Gwyn, although showing the conflicts between these two men and the classes and interests they represent, does not play up the virtues of the squire in an attempt to gain our sympathy for him at the expense of the industrialist. Plimmon is in fact a far less sympathetic character than the sensitive and bewildered Penbury. Dashing, clever, aristocratic, Lord Plimmon is still seen steadily as a reactionary ruling-class figure, an oppressor and equally a vulgar grabber on the make. He aims, one of the men he has dispossessed of his farm declares, 'to become one of the greatest landowners since Darius the bloody Persian'. Before the end of the book he has married Helen Penbury, a union not without elements of misalliance for the bridegroom, who was at one time rumoured to be the betrothed of a royal princess; Helen is very rich, very beautiful, very accomplished and very strong-minded, but she is also the grand-daughter of a farmer and belongs to a family still engaged in trade.

Penbury and Plimmon are surrounded by informers like the 'cheese-dweller' Lemuel Stevens, by bullies like the gigantic and mutilated Bledgeley, whose 'brow did not even make a struggle to appear', and by more respectable lieutenants in the persons of Radcliffe the works manager, Jarvis the lawyer, Bowen the preacher and Wilson the captain of the local yeomanry. Against these are ranged the badly-housed, half-starved, overworked or unemployed ironworkers and the leader of their resistance to their masters, John Simon Adams, together with his friends in the valley and beyond.

The artist finds himself unwillingly in the arena. Alan the harpist feels powerfully the pull of an ideal artistic world, symbolized by his 'glen in the north', but his love for the completely dedicated John Simon, his compassion for his suffering fellows, his sense of outrage at the cruelty and the savage exploitation he sees around him, stir his conscience and give him a growing desire for involvement so that finally he abandons his neutrality and throws in his lot with the iron-workers. A great torchlight procession over the mountains is organized to link up the workers of twenty towns in the valleys around, a gesture of protest which John Simon, one of the leaders, insists must be peaceful and non-violent. Before the iron-workers can reach their objective, Penbury's mansion above Moonlea, they are met by Plimmon, Radcliffe and Captain Wilson, all mounted and armed, and backed by a strong troop of yeomanry drawn up across the road to prevent the workers' passage to Penbury's house. The street there is narrow, and as more and more demonstrators pour into it, it becomes a closely-packed mass of bodies filling the highway. A scuffle breaks out between those at the head of the procession and Plimmon and Radcliffe, and foot soldiers, concealed in the upper rooms of the houses along the route, begin pouring musket fire from the windows into the dense and helpless crowd of workers below. John Simon and the harpist escape, but are eventually caught and lodged in the castle jail of the border town of Tudbury. The harpist, after trial and sentence to hanging, is pardoned and released. Once outside and back in Moonlea, he organizes a raid on the castle to rescue his friend. The raid itself is successful, but when he and his comrades enter John Simon's cell they find they are too late – their leader has already been hanged that morning.

In addition to being a remarkable novel, *All Things Betray Thee* is a moving affirmation of allegiance. Much of it deals with bitterness, betrayal, frustration and defeat; compared with a great guffaw in the face of human absurdity and pretentiousness like *The World Cannot Hear You* (1951), it is a sad book. But it is not a book without hope. There is plenty of comedy in it, of character, speech and situation. This is how we first see Floss Bennett the local whore, 'as steady an industry in Moonlea as iron, but she works at a slightly lower heat . . .' No sentimental harlot's heart of gold here; Floss Bennett is the corrupt and perjured creature of the bosses, 'one solid block of interlocking betrayals'. She enters the hill tavern, 'The Leaves After the Rain', frequented by John Simon Adams and his friends and kept by Abel Jefferies who is sympathetic towards them:

The door opened and a man wearing a rabbit-skin cap and a yellow 'kerchief around his neck came shooting in out of the twilight as if he had been kicked. After him came a woman who looked as if it was she who had done the kicking. She would have been about thirty five and wearing clothes that had seen their best when she was twenty five. Her face was the finest lump of tumbledown loveliness I had ever seen. She stood in the door with her arms on her hips and her head flung back, her nostrils dilated almost to breaking and breathing so loud I could hear all the tiny details of its passage even where I stood. Abel the landlord slipped from behind his counter and made for her.

'Outside, Floss Bennett. I've warned you about coming here before. Where you are, there trouble is, and if it's trouble I want, I'll make my own.'

'Put the bung in, Jefferies,' shouted Floss, and lowered her head, her dull eyes fixed on Abel as he advanced towards her. She looked for a moment as if she were going to charge him. Then she grunted feebly, turned on her heel and slammed the door behind her. Abel came back to join us. As he passed the little man with the rabbit-skin cap, who had taken his seat at a table and was mopping his face with his 'kerchief and taking sups at a friend's tankard, Abel said:

'And you, Oliver, for God's sake stop playing the goat. The next time you come in here bring only the draught. Leave that Floss behind. She's an outhouse of sin itself, that woman, and if you don't give up dickering with her you'll be landing up with the year's largest catch of French Evil and that 'kerchief will be the only thing holding you together. Why don't the pious join hands in a real snorting decree

about that woman and banish her to the very deep darkness under
one of the furnaces?'

(All Things Betray Thee 41–2)

The situation of John Simon and the harpist in Tudbury jail awaiting
execution is made a little less grim by the presence there of a richly
comic character, Bartholomew Clark, the caretaker of the castle, who
acts as their jailer; Alan says:

'Bartholomew was a notable man and he had leavened a large part
of my misery's lump since I had been brought into the gaol.' He was a
bulb-nosed, cheerful, waddling man, about fifty, wrapped in a huge,
sack-like coat which he never seemed to put off and fond of
drunkenness in any shape or form. Anything that would change the
key of consciousness suited his card. Ale, wine, gin poured into the jail
in a steady stream, and he made it plain to John Simon and myself that
as a liberal-minded turnkey he would always be willing to turn part of
these supplies over to us if we could arrange with him for payment
from somewhere outside. John Simon told him he was not interested
and was so intent on listening to the existing melodies in his mind
that Bartholomew looked upon him as an unpleasant freak. I was
more sociable.

(All Things Betray Thee 224)

Drinking together, the harpist and the jailer relate their life stories to
each other. Bartholomew has himself at one time been a radical, and he
still remembers a number of revolutionary hymns which, he says, 'he
had often sung in bitter burning protest beneath the walls of Tudbury
castle which he had always regarded as emblematic of oppression at its
most crass. But his strings had grown slack, tuneless and filthy'.
Nevertheless after a few drinks he would

peer outside the cell door to make sure that there were no spies in the
corridor; then he would bring his head close to mine and whisper
those antiquated songs of revolt that lay strewn along the gutter of his
fine, abandoned self, and after a night or two I got to know them as
well as he, and we made an impressive sight crooning this rhyming
litany of defiance and revenge against the walls in which I was
imprisoned, against the men who paid Bartholomew to keep guard
over us, while the tears ran fast down his face into his nearly black
cravat of greasy immemorial linen while I smiled up at the oblong of
sky I could see through the grating, pleased by the rich gravy of

absurdity this scene seemed to pour over the black dollop of what
appeared to be our forthcoming doom.

(*All Things Betray Thee* 225)

Bartholomew, of course, expresses himself with that rich fluency
common to all Gwyn Thomas characters, whether border jailers, Welsh
miners or Spanish aristocrats; he tells the harpist:

We soft ones who see life as a night to be got through in the cosiest
sort of fuddle, who drink the very slime our hearts are squeezed into,
we think we are bringing off a very smart deal to be as soft as butter
and beyond the reach of pain when kicked, quit of all the agony that
goes with decent hardness. But nothing's free, harpist. Somebody's
paying all the time. Even with a free bitch to bed on the straw in the
cellar of Slaney's gin shop down in Caroline Street and stupor at
twopence a time it's still too hellishly expensive. That's only the
down-payment, because for radiant boys like you who are setting your
faces towards the dawn and keeping fresh the parts of life that we
defile, breaking the silence in our acre of degradation, the paying's
never done.

(*All Things Betray Thee* 226–7)

One of the elements wanting in the characters in Gwyn Thomas's
books is social class-consciousness, or rather, perhaps, social deference.
The class struggle, in its industrial aspect, is ever-present in the minds of
his leading figures, but these men are unconscious of any human
differences between themselves and the leaders of those ranged against
them. No respect at all is due to their opponents because of their
wealth, or power, or superior social position, or exalted ancestry. Gwyn
Thomas grew up in a solidly democratic society where the idea of any
man 'knowing his place' was alien, and the people of his novels look
upon the rich and powerful and well-connected coolly and without
envy or deference, and they are totally unimpressed by wealth, position
and family. Penbury and Plimmon, for example, are seen with terrible
clarity as enemies, of course, but also in a sense as equals; in the way an
English general, I guess, might think of the German general opposing
him, as someone to be defeated, hated perhaps, perhaps feared because
of his superior striking power, certainly not to be mentally deferred to
or regarded as in any way intrinsically superior.

Part of this effect of equality is achieved by the language Gwyn puts into
the mouths of his characters in *All Things Betray Thee* and throughout

his work. Unlike Caradoc Evans, he uses virtually the same style and vocabulary for narrative and dialogue, and his most frequently used words, like clown, compassion, wanting (a noun), obscene, whittled, festooned, skulls, crass, tactic, perplexity, loon, squalid, layers, mania, antic, joy, witless, ecstasy, oaf, rapture, can be found in both. Clown and patrician use the same colourful, richly-metaphoric language, and this gives them a sort of equality, a common humanity based on identical speech. And this language, which makes the prose of many other comic writers by comparison seem pitiably threadbare, this vigorous, poetic, high-hearted, sardonic expression of his exploited and subjugated workers arouses our admiration for them, and protects them from our unwanted and sentimental pity. His miners and iron-workers, his unemployed, are never shown as people browbeaten into sullen silence, inarticulate through fear and deprivation, and without hope. Their marvellous inventiveness of language is an expression of their boundless will to resist, their unquenchable determination to assert in the face of the powerful and ruthless forces ranged against them, their human dignity and worth. This method has one disadvantage in that it can do nothing by idiosyncrasies of speech to distinguish one character from another. Unless Gwyn tells us, it is sometimes difficult to decide which of his people is speaking in any particular scene, and, under the gorgeous load of metaphor they carry, some of the characters in the later novels sink indistinguishable into the coruscating background.

Gwyn's identification with his own class has always seemed to me absolute. And yet I have spoken to people in South Wales who, on the evidence of his novels, have questioned the genuineness of his championship of the workers and the workless, and have seen in him rather a jeerer and a mocker than a passionate advocate. They point to such characters as Omri Hemlock in *The World Cannot Hear You*, and to that marvellous comic study of a man completely demoralized, degutted and reduced to near imbecility by the savage social and industrial climate in which he has to live – Morris in *The Alone to the Alone*. But to me it seems incredible that anyone could miss in Gwyn's work that great thundering note, that powerful underthrob of compassion that sounds throughout much of it. Surely Gwyn's humour at the expense of the poor and the underprivileged is uniformly genial and affectionate, never sardonic or wounding, never the sort to set a man apart from his community, to pillory him in his economic suffering, to deride him for his physical or social deficiencies. The term 'voters', a frequent synonym for 'workers' or 'unemployed' in his work, is sometimes quoted as an

example of Gwyn's underlying scorn or derision. The term as used by
him is sometimes seen as one of contempt. But Gwyn's employment of it
is surely ironic, not derisory. The people to whom he applies it certainly
have the vote, which suggests, according to most theories of government,
that they wield supreme political power; and yet these ostensible rulers,
Gwyn seems to be saying, these 'masters' in Disraeli's famous phrase, are
the poorest, the worst fed, the worst housed, the most vulnerable to
economic changes in the land. What I myself see in Gwyn Thomas,
underlying the rumbustious style and the poetry, and the knockabout
fun, is not scorn or derision but deep compassion. Once when I was
speaking about Gwyn in public, I quoted extensively as an illustration of
his brooding tenderness, from that deeply-moving short story, 'The
Teacher', which describes the visit of some grammar schoolboys to a
much-admired master of theirs, who lies mutilated and dying in hospital.
One of the more clear-sighted of my friends asked me after the talk was
over how much digging I had been forced to do to unearth such an
example of Gwyn's compassion. The point I had attempted to make was
that Gwyn is a poet, at once comic *and* compassionate, that poetry,
humour and compassion are everywhere in his best work, that they in
fact are the elements which make him the writer he is. 'The Teacher' was
quoted because it had in unusual and convenient concentration what is
in fact an important element of much of his writing.

Gwyn was in many ways an embodiment of the spirit of the valleys.
His attitude was comradely, egalitarian, socialist. Music and discussion,
the pubs, the workmen's institutes and the Italian cafés all play their part
in his novels, and that widely-used anodyne of unemployed South
Wales, the cinema. He was anti-imperialist and anti-war. Upper-class
characters when ineffectual, like the feudal Sylvester Strang in *The World
Cannot Hear You*, are shown without envy or deference as figures of fun.
Sex, not really important, is almost always comic, even absurd, although
love is treated seriously. Where he falls short of being a completely
representative figure, I think, is in his attitude to Wales and Welshness.
Wales has her own characteristic features and institutions, her language,
the Eisteddfod and the *eisteddfodau*, the chapels, the Welsh schools, the
Urdd, the Nationalist Party. Gwyn appears in his writing to have little
sympathy with the national aspirations and the indigenous culture of
our country. He sees the chapel, as one example, not as one of the
custodians of the language, or historically as the disseminator of culture
and education, of singing and music, of the poetry of its hymns, the
democratic training ground for oratory, for speaking and for organizing.

For him it is merely an object of derision, good for an easy laugh, and those who support it are represented, quite falsely in my experience, as little better than amiable imbeciles.[7] Many Welsh people find this insistence irritating, and resent a picture so patently, to them, the result of either ignorance or wilfulness. And yet to me Gwyn Thomas's values are very largely Christian; he has invariably the good word for human brotherhood, for love, for compassion, for simplicity as against cynicism, for tenderness as against cruelty, for warm-hearted reasonableness as against violence. And he has a mind to go along with this that uses metaphor as naturally, as abundantly and as persistently as do most of us the cliché, a mind that enlarges and enlivens and decorates, which shoots up all its material as it were into massive and spectacular fountains, and plays upon them always the dazzling illumination of his wit. To me, he is the supreme poet of the industrial valleys, the *cyfarwydd* (storyteller) of the working class, comic, compassionate, of inexhaustible invention, and of an utterance unequalled among the Anglo-Welsh for its richness, its consistency and its vigour.

VI

INTRODUCTION TO POETRY

A good case might be made out for the claim that the highest achievement of the Anglo-Welsh has been in the field of the short story. But no Anglo-Welsh writer's stories, not even Caradoc Evans's, have ever achieved anything like the fame of Dylan Thomas's poetry. And the names of Vernon Watkins, R. S. Thomas, Alun Lewis and David Jones might be quoted to support the contention that it is as poets rather than as prose writers that the Anglo-Welsh have really excelled.

If this is so, they and their Welsh-language fellow countrymen have in this a further point of resemblance, because the glory of Welsh-language literature is unquestionably its poetry. The representative Welsh literary figure would appear even today to be the poet, and not the novelist, the dramatist or the short-story writer. In the annual Welsh National Eisteddfod the poets are the important figures, and it is they who receive the greatest share of interest and acclaim and the largest measure of publicity from press and television. The really crowded days of the Eisteddfod week are still the Tuesdays and Thursdays, which traditionally are the days of the Crowning and Chairing ceremonies, when the winning poet is proclaimed with much pomp, colour and pageantry. The withholding by the adjudicators of the Crown or the Chair when none of the submitted poems has reached a sufficiently high standard, is always a disappointment, sometimes a bitter one, to the seven or eight thousand people who have packed the Eisteddfod pavilion to witness the ceremony, and to the thousands more crowding the field outside, listening to the proceedings on the loudspeakers, and to the perhaps hundreds of thousands who will read about the Eisteddfod in their newspapers, or watch its ceremonies on television. And although only a small minority of those present at the ceremonies will ever read the winning poem – *pryddest* or *awdl* – the crowd's sense of deprivation when no winner is announced is, I think, a measure of the pre-eminence poetry has established for itself in the Eisteddfod and of its popularity, or at least its acceptance, in the minds of the people of our country. It is true that now a gold medal is presented every year, on the Wednesday, for a winning prose work, but none of the glamour and the colourful circumstances attaches as yet to this ceremony.[1] It is certainly poetry which has counted in Wales, and for the reason that the highest achievements of Welsh literature have so far been in this medium.

Before I proceed any further in this section I feel I ought to explain in a little more detail the background of the two Welsh words *pryddest* and *awdl* which I used. The choice is open to a Welsh-language poet of writing his poems in one of two ways. First, he may employ blank verse, quatrains, couplets, sonnets, etc. etc., exactly as an English or American poet might do. These, and not 'free verse', are for him the 'free metres', although 'free verse' can be included too in this group. If a Welsh-language poet submits a 'free-metre' poem, called a *pryddest* (i.e. a poem in blank verse, or in a series of lyrics, or in free verse, etc.), to the National Eisteddfod and is adjudged first, he wins the Crown. But a Welsh-language poet may reject the 'free metres' and choose to write his poems in some of the twenty-four classical metres of Welsh prosody, the *cywydd* metre, the *englyn* and so on. The prosody here is based, not on foot stresses, on iambic and dactylic feet and the rest, but on a counting of syllables per line; and the choice of this type of verse, the 'strict' or 'unfree' metres, involves the poet in the use of *cynghanedd*, which is, briefly, an extremely rigid, line-by-line system of alliteration and internal rhyme, much more intricate and elaborate and dogmatic than anything in English, or, for that matter, in any other European language. For a successful poem, called an *awdl*, in this mode, the prize is the supreme literary award of the National Eisteddfod, the Chair.

Ieuan ap Hywel Swrdwal, that conjectural first in a long line of Anglo-Welsh poets, took one of the twenty-four Welsh metres, the *englyn*, and wrote his 'Hymn to the Virgin' in it, in English.[2] A poem in the English language, written not in any metre known to English prosody, but in one of the twenty-four strict metres of Welsh *cerdd dafod* or poetic art. But the work of this pioneer has almost never been used as a model by subsequent Anglo-Welsh poets. Dylan Thomas, Vernon

Watkins, Idris Davies, Roland Mathias and others use the ordinary forms of English verse, or their own personal variations of them. The most successful poet in the practice of introducing certain features of classical Welsh prosody into English verse was in fact not a Welshman at all; it was G. M. Hopkins, who during his stay in Wales learnt our language and the rules governing our 'strict' poetry and used them to give richness and music to his English verse, not in every line as a Welsh-language poet is obliged to do, but occasionally, when he felt that the need had arisen.[3] I suppose the modern Anglo-Welsh poet who has most frequently employed some of the ideas of *cerdd dafod* in his work is Anthony Conran.[4]

Two of the twenty-four metres still much used today are the *cywydd deuair hirion* and the *englyn unodl union*. This type of *englyn* consists of four lines, the first having ten syllables, the second six and the last two seven each. As far as *cynghanedd* is concerned the first of Ieuan's *englynion* can be analysed as follows:

> O meichti ladi owr leding – tw haf
> at hefn owr abeiding
> yntw ddy ffest efrlesting
> i set a braents ws tw bring.

In the first line *i* of *meichti* rhymes with the *i* of *ladi*, and the *l, d* of *ladi* alliterate with the *l, d* of *leding*. This is called *cynghanedd sain*. The *t, h* and *f* of *tw haf* then alliterate with the *t, h,* and *f* of *at hefn* in *cynghanedd groes*. When the accented penultimate syllable in a line rhymes with a previous syllable in the same line the *cynghanedd* is known as *cynghanedd lusg*, and this we have in line three. The last line has *cynghanedd groes* again, the consonants *s, t, br* in the first half of the line corresponding with the *s, t, br* of the second half. The rhyme-scheme is discernible if one remembers that an accented syllable can rhyme with an unaccented – *leding, abeiding, efrlesting, bring.*

THE GALE

> Searing the land with sorrow,
> With loud wail the gale doth go,
> Mad and loud o'er mead and lea
> I hear its wanton hurry.
> Whizzing around the houses
> And scourging the surging seas,
> I wonder if my windows

Can outlast its blast and blows.
Ha! how its currents carry
A loud song from the wild sea,
Now clouds of spindrift lifting
Forge aloft on fragile wing.
In fear of its wild fury
I view the surge of the sea.
With solemn mien the sailor
Dreads nearing the sheering shore;
Toiling at rope and tiller,
Setting and getting his gear,
Will he sink or lose anchor,
And shape for the horrid shore,
His deck all strewn with wreckage
And all around a dull rage?
Hear us now, thou fair Mary,
Whose Son calmed the raging sea,
Those who now range in danger
On the deep keep in thy care.

The above English poem, the work of Trefín, a former Arch-druid of Wales,[5] is another example of a poem in English written in obedience to the rules of Welsh classical or 'strict' prosody. The metre employed this time is the *cywydd deuair hirion* which has seven syllables in each line and an ultimate accented syllable rhyming with an unaccented. Each line has the obligatory *cynghanedd*. In the first *s* and *r* correspond to *s* and *r* in *cynghanedd draws*; in the second *wail* and *gale* rhyme and *gale* alliterates with *go* (*cynghanedd sain*); in the third the consonants *m*, *d*, *nd*, *l* correspond to *m*, *d*, *nd*, *l* in *cynghanedd draws*; and so on, line by line to the end.

Poetry was at one time in Wales the concern of a class, the *uchelwyr*, or land-owning class. These people, the princes of the Middle Ages and the later squires, were the supporters and patrons of poets, many of whom, like Dafydd ap Gwilym, Dafydd ab Edmwnd and Gruffudd Gryg, were members of that class themselves. As the *uchelwyr* over the centuries became more and more anglicized and remote, their fading concern for the poetry and the culture of their own country was, in some miraculous way, inherited, probably through the Eisteddfod, by the Welsh society at large that still continued to speak Welsh.[6] This society, the radical, nonconformist society to which I have several times referred, was on the whole not a wealthy one, and the culture diffused so widely in it was not associated with costly arts like drama, painting and architecture. Its productions were poetry, singing and oratory, chiefly preaching. Art in Wales, almost until this century, has been thought of in these terms. We still use the terms *cerdd dafod* (lit. 'tongue music') for poetry, and *cerdd dant* (lit. 'string music') for the art of music itself, and we have a great wealth of technical terms in prosody to distinguish the variations in the basic metres, etc. (*englyn penfyr, englyn milwr, englyn unodl union* and so on) and for the differences, often small, possible in the *cynganeddion*, as *cynghanedd groes gytbwys acennog, groes gytbwys ddiacen, groes anghytbwys ddisgynedig*. Our Welsh word for artist is, alas, *artist*.

The existence of the National Eisteddfod is in itself an indication of a widespread interest in culture in Wales. Every year about two hundred thousand people – which would, in proportion of population, represent the attendance of, at some time, about 2 million English people at a week-long cultural institution – attend the sessions of singing (choral, solo and group), reciting (individual and choral), dancing and instrumental music held during the seven days, and the concerts and drama performances in the evenings. The Crowning and Chairing ceremonies are, as I have indicated, still enormously popular and, although very little poetry is actually heard spoken on these occasions, their popularity indicates the respect and esteem in which poetry is held by the mass of the people. We are told that the literature of the twentieth century is increasingly a literature of revolt. It seems to me that the basic Welsh conception of the poet even today is not one of a man at bitter variance with the values and institutions of his country, or attacking the whole of Western civilization. Rather is it of a sort of craftsman, well integrated in the community of which he is a product, a conception which would appear to be an inheritance from the time when the poet was so much a part of Welsh society that he was actually a court official, with a 'chair' at his prince's council table. Protest certainly there is in modern Welsh-language poetry, but it is, or some of it is, in a sense conservative and nostalgic rather than revolutionary; protest against the disruption of a society and a traditional way of life seen by the poet as harmonious, cultured, egalitarian, religious, rural; not really perhaps a full-scale philosophic attack on Western industrial civilization, certainly not one delivered from a point, as some such attacks appear to be delivered, further out in the chaos and corruption than this civilization has itself yet reached. Here is what seems to me a typical example of this, a poem in free verse that I have translated into English from the Welsh of Gwenallt, a colourful modern Welsh-language poet,[7] a Chair-winner on more than one occasion in the National Eisteddfod:

RHYDCYMERAU

Saplings for timber for the third world war are planted
On the land of Esgeir-ceir and the fields of Tir-Bach
At Rhydcymerau.

I remember my grandmother at Esgeir-ceir
Sitting beside the fire fingering her apron;
The skin of her face as yellow and parched up
                              as a Peniarth manuscript,
And the Welsh on her aged lips the Welsh of Pantycelyn.
She was part of the Puritanism of the Wales of
                              the last century.
My grandfather, although I never saw him,
Was a 'character'; a lively, crotchety, bouncing little creature,
Fond of his pint;
A straggler from the eighteenth century.
They reared nine children,
Poets, deacons and Sunday school teachers,
Leaders all in their small community.

My uncle Dafydd farmed Tir Bach,
A country poet, a local versifier,
And his poem to the little cockerel was famous in the area;
              'The little cockerel scratching
              About the garden here and there.'
To him I went for my summer holidays,
To mind sheep and to compose lines of *cynghanedd*,
Englynion and eight line stanzas in the eight-seven metre.
He in turn brought up eight children,
The eldest son a Calvinistic Methodist minister,
Who also wrote poetry.
In our family we were a nest of poets.

But by today there is nothing but trees,
The arrogant roots battening upon the ancient soil;
Timber where there was community,
Plantations where there were farms,
The *argot* of the southern English where poetry was written and
                              theology debated,
The barking of foxes where was the cry of children and lambs.
And in the darkness in the centre of all
Is the den of the English Minotaur;
And on branches, as though upon crucifixes,

The skeletons of poets, deacons, ministers and Sunday school
                                                          teachers
Whitening in the sun,
Washed with the rain and dried up by the wind.

Pacifist, Christian, cultured, rural, menaced by war and English
barbarism, that is the poet's nostalgic and conservative vision of his
country. Among the contributors to the first numbers of the magazine
Wales the poet who most clearly in those early days shared this vision
was Emyr Humphreys, Welsh-speaking, pacifist, Christian and
Nationalist. The late Walter Dowding also wrote English poems in the
thirties on such topics as 'I'r hen iaith a'i chaneuon' and 'Wales – a
mourning'.[8] But the Anglo-Welsh poet who later most fully in his
poems expressed the attitude of 'Rhydcymerau' is surely R. S. Thomas.
(The work of Emyr Humphreys is by now almost entirely devoted to
prose.[9]) Among Anglo-Welsh poets a welcome move away from the
Symbolist aestheticism and political neutrality of their elders took place
in the 1960s, in the direction of the nationalism of their Welsh-writing
contemporaries.[10] This is perhaps the most striking difference between
the early Anglo-Welsh magazine *Wales* and a later one like *Poetry
Wales*.[11] The early contributors to the latter, poets like Harri Webb,
Peter Gruffydd, Alun Rees, Tom Earley, John Tripp, Herbert Williams
and its founder and first editor, Meic Stephens, all, explicitly or
implicitly, it seems to me, subscribed to the idea of Welsh nationhood,
or witnessed with sympathy or even anguish the crises of language and
identity with which Wales is confronted. These concerns are potent in
the creative part of their thinking, with the result that there appear to
be more poems about the condition of our country in the early
numbers of *Poetry Wales* than there were in the *Wales* of 1937 to 1939.

The widespread interest in, and knowledge of, poetry in Wales manifests itself in other ways than in attendance at the Eisteddfod. Some of
these ways are humble enough, although revealing. I remember the
Welsh-speaking friend of my parents who supplied us with house coal
in Cardiff. Below his name on his billheads, as a sort of motto, was the
line '*Dyma'r boi i dwymo'r byd*', which means, 'Here's the bloke to warm
the world'. But the point is that this line could, from a technical point of
view, appear in a classical *cywydd* or an *englyn*, since it has seven syllables
and contains *cynghanedd groes*, the consonants *d, m, r, b* in the first half of
the line being repeated in the same order in the second half. It was not
by accident of course that the poetic coalman had achieved this.

Recently I was speaking to a friend who has to do with organizing extramural classes of the University of Wales in Cardiganshire. He told me that in one Welsh-speaking class of about eighteen students, all of them were poets. Not very good poets, perhaps, but all were deeply interested and learned in the *cynganeddion*. They were farmers, farm labourers, garage hands, school-teachers and the like, and their concern with poetry would be no more remarkable in the community in which they lived than would standing for the council or being elected a deacon or church elder. On a summer holiday in Pembrokeshire I saw in the poetry column of the local newspaper a *cywydd* in English, similar in form to Trefin's 'The Gale', though on a different subject, written by a local resident. It also, like Trefin's, obeyed faithfully the intricate rules of classical Welsh prosody governing this type of poem. Although as poetry the achievement here, understandably, was no higher than in 'The Gale', the technical skill and knowledge involved were very considerable, and this verbal mastery was exercised by someone whose job was probably shop-keeping, farming or collecting insurance.

Although obviously to a modern Welsh poet the idea of the poet as seer or prophet is by no means unfamiliar, yet the conception of poetry as a craft plays a very large part. Whether he employs the 'strict metres' or not in his own work, he is almost certainly familiar with the rigidity and dogmatism of the classical prosody. The idea that Welsh poetry is a great undisciplined outpouring of emotion is completely mistaken.[12] It has nothing at all to do with 'Celtic Twilight'. It has been written variously for tough princes, for worldly and cultivated aristocrats, for an impoverished and struggling society, never for an aesthetic or literary class apart, rentiers and remote and cultured bohemians. This is the tradition in which the modern Welsh-language poet works. The connection of the Anglo-Welsh with this tradition is, as I have tried to show, social and historical rather than literary. For a literary tradition, being unfamiliar with their native language, the Anglo-Welsh poets tend to turn to England, to America and to Europe. Even those among the Anglo-Welsh who are familiar with the poetry of their own country have, until recently, tended to do this. Implicit in these notes is the wish that more of them would begin to look homeward.

The Anglo-Welsh have produced in this century, among a large number of other poets, Dylan Thomas, R. S. Thomas, Vernon Watkins, Alun Lewis, David Jones. The Welsh have produced during about the same period, again among others, Iorwerth Peate, Euros Bowen, Caradog Prichard, Waldo Williams, Alun Llywelyn-Williams and Bobi

Jones. I have already pointed out the striking fact that almost no sort of connection or interchange has ever taken place between these two groups, although they coexist in a quite small country, and I tried to indicate some of the reasons why this is so.[13] One of these contemporary literatures is addressed, perforce, to the Welsh-speaking community of Wales, because almost no one in the world outside that community is able to read it; the other seeks literary approval where it is published, namely in London and New York, in England and America, and only secondarily in Wales itself.

But to that minority of Anglo-Welsh poets to whom Welsh is not literally a closed book, e.g. R. S. Thomas, Idris Davies, Emyr Humphreys, Huw Menai, Ll. Wyn Griffith among the older generation, Meic Stephens, Harri Webb, Raymond Garlick, among those who came after – most of these, as far as I am able to discover, show in their English verse no traces, or rather very few traces, of having read Welsh poetry, although I know that all those named above have done so. It is obvious from the poetry of several of them that they are patriotic Welshmen, concerned with the condition and future of our country, angry at its ruthless spoliation and its neglect, and the menace to it of a modern industrial civilization which threatens to engulf and destroy its language and its culture. But the influences upon their work I would judge to be largely modern English, American and continental poetry rather than the traditional or contemporary poetry of their own country, Wales.[14]

How might the influence of Welsh literature be revealed in English writing? In more ways than one, I think. Possibly in reproducing in English verse some of the effects of the Welsh classical prosody I tried to describe above. But I think Hopkins's method of doing this, rather than Ieuan ap Hywel Swrdwal's, is the correct one. Attempts like 'The Gale' always seem to be failures as poetry. (I do not think Trefín imagined that his *cywydd* was poetry.) He would have to be a very great poet indeed technically who could write a good English poem about a gale in a poem composed of uniformly relatively short lines of seven syllables. Then the *englyn,* capable in Welsh of a great variety of effects, used for jewel-like imagism, for the expression of love, *hiraeth*, faith, or for epigrammatic utterance of unsurpassed point and conciseness, seems to be most successful in English when used like a limerick for comic effect. It would be difficult to imagine a series of *englynion* in English achieving the grandeur and poignancy of Williams Parry's 'Hedd Wyn' sequence. But the funny *englyn* does sometimes come off in some curious way. Here is one by Twm Tawe on the electric razor:

What a miracle, tomorrow – farewell blade,
Farewell bloody furrow;
My whiskers (à la Moscow)
By machine I mean to mow.

Strange that this crazy metre could also produce the stately movement of

Tyner yw'r lleuad heno – tros fawnog
Trawsfynydd yn dringo;
Tithau'n drist a than dy ro
Ger y ffos ddu'n gorffwyso.[15]

Poets in Welsh and in English have written about love, war, faith, death and loss and external nature, and so on, but there have been certain topics more common and certain traditions more frequently followed in Welsh-language poetry in the past than in English. At one time the *cywydd gofyn* (a *cywydd* of asking) was popular and the tradition still persists, although it has no parallel, as far as I know, in anything written in English. In such a poem the poet petitions his friend or his patron for a gift – a hound, a harp, a hawk, a sword, a horse, a jewel, a coverlet – or thanks him for one already received, and the poem is really a sort of ode in praise of a generous giver and a brilliant and detailed description of the gift. A modern Welsh poet like Waldo Williams would seem to be writing in this tradition when he composes a poem of thanks about the gift to him of a thumbstick.[16] Another frequent theme was that of the *llatai* or love messenger. In this type of poem the poet describes the beauty both of the girl he loves and of the messenger he sends to her with his declarations – the seagull, the swan, the salmon.[17] Had D. H. Lawrence and Ted Hughes, say, been Welsh-language poets they might have put words of eternal devotion into the mouths of their otters and turkeys, even their pikes and their goats.

An important theme of modern Welsh poetry, as I have already suggested, is the condition of Wales and her destiny in the modern world, which is seen by most Welsh-speaking Welshmen, whether Nationalists or not, as being bound up with the fate of the language. In a volume of poems by Waldo Williams, one of the finest of twentieth-century Welsh poets, there are three poems with the following titles – I translate: 'The Old Language' (i.e. Welsh), 'Wales in Unity' and 'Wales and her Language'.[18] Now no Anglo-Welsh poet of Dylan Thomas's generation, or an older one – Idris Davies, Vernon Watkins, Alun Lewis, Huw Menai, Roland Mathias, Brenda Chamberlain – would be likely to write poems on such themes, apart perhaps again from Emyr

Humphreys. We might of course expect them to be treated by R. S. Thomas, in some ways the most Welsh of the Anglo-Welsh. But he, although a year older than Dylan, really belongs to a more recent generation as a poet, since he did not publish his first book of poems until 1946, the year of Dylan's last volume to appear in Britain before *Collected Poems*. Again, I would emphasize that the tradition exists very powerfully in Wales that the poet is not a man apart, a freak, but rather an accepted part of the social fabric with an important function to perform. The type of writer who turns his back on society and abjures all responsibility towards it in a rootless Bohemianism is almost unknown in Wales. At the present time, when the Welsh language is relentlessly menaced, the idea of being involved in the nation's affairs, in her problems and her dilemmas, has fresh force for the Welsh-language writer. He sees himself as one of the guardians of an endangered heritage.[19] In fact it is this question, after language itself, which most sharply distinguishes the Welsh from the Anglo-Welsh, at least from the majority of the early Anglo-Welsh, this question of commitment, of where the writer feels his responsibility to lie.

In the mind of the Welsh-language writer, it seems to me, the relation between society and the literature written in it is always a matter of the deepest concern; and the preservation of the language, the future of Welsh nationhood, the continuance of a distinctive Welsh culture and way of life, even Welsh political autonomy, are all questions about which Welsh writers have to think. In England the situation is entirely different. Whatever fears and problems occupy the hearts and minds of English writers, they do not feel their language to be under relentless pressure from a powerful and attractive next-door neighbour, and they do not foresee and fear its extinction. Consequently such ideas as seem important to the Welsh-language poet are to the English or American of less concern. The average English writer, I would guess, would not feel his first responsibility to be to the English language as such, or to the community, or to his nation, or to a tradition. He would probably claim that his primary obligation was to *himself* as an artist, or to his art. Most Anglo-Welsh writers, at least most of the first generation, would agree with this. The Anglo-Welsh poets who came to the fore in the 1960s were much more conscious of their Welshness, as I have tried to point out, and have moved nearer in many of their attitudes to their Welsh-writing contemporaries; thus, Harri Webb writes in *Wales*: 'A Welshman writing in English only acquires significance when he is seen to be inextricably committed to and involved in the predicament of his country'.[20]

In 1917 the first modern Anglo-Welsh anthology of poetry was produced, *Welsh Poets* (published by Erskine Macdonald), under the editorship of A. G. Prys-Jones, containing work by such poets as W. H. Davies, Huw Menai and Ernest Rhys, as well as others much better known for their outstanding work in Welsh, like Silyn Roberts and T. Gwynn Jones, one of the very greatest of Welsh-language poets of any age. That A. G. Prys-Jones's anthology was not more interesting and lively was emphatically not the fault of the compiler. In 1917 the body of contemporary work to choose from, which is presupposed by an anthology, just did not exist. Keidrych Rhys's *Modern Welsh Poetry* appeared from Faber during the next war, in 1944, and in the intervening twenty-seven years a very considerable amount of verse in English by Welsh writers had appeared, both in individual volumes and in such periodicals as *Wales*, *The Welsh Review* and *Life and Letters To-day*. Keidrych was able to choose from the work of Dylan Thomas, R. S. Thomas, Alun Lewis, Emyr Humphreys, Vernon Watkins, David Jones and thirty others, without recourse to the inferior work in English of distinguished Welsh-language poets like those I have named above. Kenneth Rexroth, introducing his anthology of *New British Poets* (New Directions) to his American readers in 1949, says of the poetry in *Wales* that a 'heavy odor of the modernism of the Twenties still hangs over [it]'. The part about modernism is true (although I would see it as the modernism of the thirties rather than of the twenties) of the contents of the anthology *Modern Welsh Poetry* also. Keidrych's poets certainly knew what was going on in the poetical worlds both of London and New York. Some of them managed to combine their modernism with an awareness, at least, of their Welsh surroundings; Idris Davies, Walter Dowding, Wyn Griffith, Nigel Heseltine, David Jones, Alun Lewis, R. S. Thomas are all represented by poems about Welsh places or Welsh characters or Welsh affairs. Few of the poets again, only a tiny minority, showed that they knew anything about poetic developments of the Welsh-speaking past of our country or of the activities of the Welsh-speaking sectors of the population of their day, about Bangor or Aberystwyth or the literary tent of the National Eisteddfod. And yet this anthology could not have been produced by English poets. Conscious as it shows itself of English literature rather than of Welsh, it is yet in some, to me indefinable, way un-English. By now, of course, it is out-of-date. Some of those included in it like Rhys Davies, Goronwy Rees and Emyr Humphreys developed as prose writers rather than as poets; others failed to develop at all; Pennar Davies gave up English in favour of Welsh; Dylan Thomas and R. S. Thomas wrote some of their best poems after the collection was published; some of the contributors, admirable as poets, seem now to have connections with Wales of the most tenuous sort imaginable. But the volume is yet a repository of some very good poems indeed, including Idris Davies's 'O What Can You Give Me?', Alun Lewis's 'To Edward Thomas', Dylan Thomas's 'In Memory of Ann Jones', R. S. Thomas's 'A Peasant' and Vernon Watkins's 'The Collier' and 'Returning to Goleufryn'.

A further anthology of Anglo-Welsh poetry appeared in 1959, edited by Professor Gwyn Williams, and was entitled *Presenting Welsh Poetry* (Faber). Professor Williams's book attempted something quite different from that of Keidrych Rhys. About half the poems in *Presenting Welsh Poetry*, thirty-three in all, were translations into English of Welsh language poems, beginning with the sixth- or seventh-century work of Aneirin and Taliesin and extending right up to the work of contemporary poets like Euros Bowen (1904–88) and Alun Llywelyn-Williams (1913–88), the same span in fact as that in Dr Thomas Parry's *Oxford Book of Welsh Verse*, to which I referred in my opening chapter. The second half of Gwyn Williams's book consists of poems written by Welshmen, early and contemporary, in English, the Anglo-Welsh in fact. The first of these to be chosen by Professor Williams is not Ieuan ap Hywel Swrdwal, whom he discusses in his introduction, but no less a person than King Henry VIII. Others of the twenty-seven included are George Herbert, Henry Vaughan, George Meredith, Edward Thomas, W. H. Davies and Dylan Thomas. Although some of Professor Williams's candidates for Anglo-Welshness seem pretty questionable figures to me (if Meredith why not Donne and William Morris? But to be quite fair Henry VIII *did* have one Welsh great-grandfather), the basic idea of his book was sound and his introduction full of interest and good sense.[21]

I have chosen to write about Huw Menai, Idris Davies and Dylan Thomas at length because I knew and liked them and because they are dead, the second circumstance one which, however much a matter for private sorrow, has unquestionably a liberating effect on one's critical inhibitions. I do not of course by my choice wish to suggest that Huw and Idris are more important poets than David Jones, Vernon Watkins and R. S. Thomas, say, or than T. H. Jones, who died in 1965.[22] But it was with Huw, Idris and Dylan, for various reasons, some of them geographical, that I have been involved, a factor which has always been of importance to me. Alun Lewis, who also lived not far from Cardiff, to my great regret I never saw. Although I deeply admire his poetry for its truth and compassion and concern, I do not think he would have remained, or remained primarily, a poet. His most promising work it seems to me is to be found in his short stories, and no poem touches for me the marvellous accomplishment of 'Ward "O" 3 (b)' or 'The Orange Grove'.[23]

A poet who has never seemed to me to have had anything like his true measure of consideration is Roland Mathias, historian, critic and one-time editor of *The Anglo-Welsh Review*. Roland's poetry, full of striking lines and startling imagery, is strenuous, gnarled, thoughtful, highly individual and original. What has excluded it from a wider audience than it now enjoys, I think, may be its author's unremitting concern for truth, which seems to play its part in producing in some of his poems an impression of opacity or impenetrability. Although not a didactic poet, Roland gives the impression of a man who would reject out of hand anything which did not conform to or point up his profoundly experienced vision of reality. Life is an agonizingly serious matter, and so is poetry. So much honesty of thought and feeling packed into his poems give them, in spite of their marvellous diction and imagery, something of that rather compressed and baffling solidness one gets from time to time in Hopkins, although I am sure Roland owes nothing to the Hopkins technique. One would not wish Roland's poetry to be different. Its wholesome brilliance, its contempt for what comes easily, seem to me ineradicable elements in its make-up. I hesitate to use a shabby word like 'integrity' in speaking about work as genuine as Roland's, and yet it is the only one that really conveys the impression created by the poems in volumes such as *Break in Harvest* (1946) and *The Roses of Tretower* (1952).[24]

Many have written and will write about the poetry of Vernon Watkins, R. S. Thomas and David Jones, but I do not propose to say anything about their work here. Of the whole corpus of David Jones's work I cannot, in the present state of my knowledge of it, speak with any confidence, but he has returned to his roots, to the springs of Welsh poetry and legend and culture in a way and to an extent no other Anglo-Welsh poet has ever done. In the chapters that follow is the hope that something said in them will induce many other Anglo-Welsh writers of the younger generation to do the same.

VII

THREE POETS

HUW MENAI

1888–1961

WATCHING one day, not long before his death, the grave progress of Huw Menai across a Rhondda street, the tall gaunt figure, still erect at seventy-three, the pallid Eryri-rugged features, the imperious, long-legged 'Kaffir stride', I felt sharply the lack of some accompanying pageantry, of some poetic sodality or mysterious *urdd*, strangely and hieratically clad, to follow in attendance upon him. But his only follower, at a distance of three or four yards, and trotting to keep up with him, was an undersized Welsh novelist, described by Gwyn Thomas, who was watching the scene with me, as 'Huw's attendant gnome'. Huw Menai walked alone, as he had always done, remote in his own ideal world, a world of poignant natural beauty haunted for ever by suffering and death.

I had by that time got to know Huw quite well. I first heard his name when I was a poetry-mad schoolboy of fifteen in the Castle Grammar School, Merthyr Tydfil. The young French master, new to the job, quoted two lines of Huw's poetry during a lesson, in what connection I don't remember now, although the words impressed me so forcibly that after this one casual mention they have remained with me ever since. The lines were:

> Part-reading in the hard primeval sod
> The infinite biography of God.

These tremendous lines, with their startling rhyme and their cunning alliteration, had appeared, although I didn't know it at the time, in Huw's first book of poems, *Through the Upcast Shaft*, which had been published that year, 1920, by Hodder and Stoughton. In the following decade, as schoolboy, student and young teacher, I heard of Huw from time to time from people who knew him, and his fame and personality began to exercise over my boyish imagination a strange and powerful fascination; although I made no personal contact with him, I was acutely aware of his presence up there in the Rhondda Valley, not far from my new home in Cardiff, I saw notices of his lectures, I read his frequent poems and his letters in the newspapers and magazines. He was the first Anglo-Welsh writer of whom I became aware, as he was the first Anglo-Welsh writer of this century to make anything like a reputation for himself as a poet. His friend John Cowper Powys describes him, in his admirable preface to Huw Menai's *The Simple Vision* (1945), as 'the most striking looking individual I have ever had the privilege of beholding', and this remarkable physical distinction was no doubt what caused me to spot him, and to wonder about him, some time before I knew who he was. More than once on Thursday afternoons, when the excursion trains brought the shoppers swarming from the mining valleys into the centre of Cardiff, I noticed there a tall, spare, large-boned figure, well over six feet in height, walking bareheaded the busy streets of the city. It was the face that was unforgettable, gaunt, doomed, pallid, a countenance, Powys says, 'in which, as upon the face of some petrified Leviathan of Misery found in some antediluvian gulf, all the pain of all the tragedy of evolution has graven with its terrible rain . . . channels that no comfortable words from those who know not of what they speak can smooth away'. That was indeed Huw as he kinged it among the swarms of his dumpier fellow countrymen like a melancholy Benjamite; but I had no reason then to connect this remote and striking figure with the Huw Menai with whom for years I had felt so unaccountably involved, and whose fame and personality had so strangely captured and excited my youthful imagination.

And then one day in the studio of Alf Hall, a Cardiff painter, I saw on the easel an almost completed portrait, a painting of the tall figure whose brooding air of aloof distinction had so much impressed and intrigued me; there was the noble, long-lined face, the clustering grey curls, the pale blue shirt, the suit of snuff-coloured tweed, all set down with scrupulous faithfulness by this gifted but retiring artist. 'It's Huw Menai', he told me. 'You can come here some Thursday when he's sitting for me and meet him if you like'. But I put off an introduction then partly because, being young, I felt discouraged and overawed by the legend of Huw's eminence as a poet, and as time went on I began to lose interest, not in him, but in the type of poetry he was writing. Much of his second volume, *The Passing of Guto* (1929), although the book bore the imprint of the Hogarth Press and so, I argued, had presumably met with the approval of Virginia Woolf, I found old-fashioned, derivative and unexciting. It left me dissatisfied and, I am ashamed to say now, contemptuous; but about this time, 1929–31, I was discovering both the Welsh *cywyddwyr* and also the poetry of Lawrence, Hopkins and Roy Campbell, poets whose work, although so diverse, was much more appealing to someone of my age and temperament than the homespun broodings and sombre defeatism of Huw Menai.

I did not meet Huw until about 1946. An artist friend of mine, Elwyn Davies, was at that time engaged upon a series of caricatures of Welsh writers for Keidrych Rhys's magazine *Wales*, and I wrote to Huw on Elwyn's behalf to ask if we might visit him, and if he would consent to be sketched. Huw agreed, and I accompanied my friend up to Penygraig in the Rhondda Valley where Huw still lived, when the preliminary sketches were to be made. Huw, and indeed his entire family, received us, two strangers then, with the greatest cheerfulness and courtesy. Tea was brought into the front parlour for us by Huw's beautiful wife and two of his handsome daughters, and later, while Elwyn made what progress he could with his pencil, I listened fascinated to the guttural drone of Huw's unending monologue, a novel *lobscows* of reminiscence, some of it political, some bawdy, with poetical *obiter dicta* and lengthy quotations from standard works of philosophy, geology and religion, the whole delivered non-stop and dead-pan in that booming Caernarfonshire gargle which forty years of residence in the south had not diminished one sliver in thickness. Huw was indeed, in private conversation and in public speech, the great monologuist. Of his early poems he said that he wrote them because he had at the time no one to talk to, and the whole of his poetic output can be regarded as a kind of extended 'talking to himself' or self-communing. Listening to others, I believe, he soon found burdensome.

Then, and in subsequent conversations, I learnt a good deal about the life of this extraordinary figure, the man for whom John Cowper Powys's picturesque description was 'this *cawr* [giant] of the coalfield'.

Huw – his actual name was Huw Owen Williams – was born in Caernarfon town, on the Menai Straits, in 1888, the son of a ferociously independent mother and a gigantic poetry- and sermon-quoting collier of a father who earned his living not in his native North Wales but in the mines of the industrial south.

Twelve was the age considered suitable then for children of parents as poor as Huw's to start working, and at that age the poet's formal education ended. For the next few years he helped his wonderful mother with her fish baskets, delivered parcels for Suttons the carriers, bottled beer, stevedored in Caernarfon harbour and worked in a local printing office where he was taught, among other things, 'to "comp" a stickful of brevier without "pieing"', as he put it in his Introduction to *The Passing of Guto*. And in his spare time, then and always, he read with that inexhaustible and omnivorous gusto which seems to be one of the marks of those destined for literary eminence.

'Plato, Plotinus, Hegel, Kant and Hume. He'd read them all in his unlettered way', he writes of his own Guto, and the evidence of his conversation suggests that the lines may be autobiographical. The usual English classics, Scott, Dickens and so on, with *Literature and Dogma* and *The Age of Reason* were not neglected either. Both Huw's parents were practically monoglot Welsh, but what Huw found to read in his native language does not appear, and hardly any evidence exists in his poetry to show that he himself spoke Welsh fluently, read Welsh poetry and had some knowledge of the *cynganeddion*. Huw's intellectual life, like that of most Anglo-Welsh writers, was lived almost entirely in the English language.

A familiar figure, as I have indicated before, in Welsh-speaking Wales, where literary culture is often widespread, is the *bardd gwlad*, or *bardd cefn gwlad*, the country poet, the man usually of not very much *formal* education or schooling, a farmer, say, or a farmhand, self-educated, cultured, deeply versed in Welsh literature, rooted in and entirely accepted by the community about which, and for which, he writes; a man in no way cut off or regarded as exceptional, the opposite of the rootless Bohemian poet. Now it seems highly probable that Huw – sensitive, thoughtful, gifted – might, in spite of his predominantly English reading, have developed in time, had he remained in Welsh-speaking Caernarfonshire, into just such a typical *bardd gwlad*. Even in industrial Glamorgan he might still, when later he became a poet, have written in Welsh, since the language was widely used in the county in his youth. Indeed why Huw chose English as his medium of expression I do not fully understand. He and Caradoc Evans, both as young men fluent Welsh speakers and both of small formal education, are puzzles in this matter. Perhaps Huw's rejection of religion was an element in his choice, and also the practice in writing English prose which his political work had given him.

The reuniting of the family with the father in South Wales was decisive. Huw and his mother came to live in Merthyr Vale, a small mining town in one of the valleys of the vast Glamorgan coalfield. Whether, to the young Huw, the north, to quote Tennyson's couplet, had ever been 'dark and true and tender' is questionable. He certainly found the south very soon to be 'bright and fierce and fickle'; Huw was sixteen when he came south and he started work in the pits, but gave up after a few months and returned to Caernarfon. His permanent move to South Wales took place two years later.

The effect upon him, a young man of eighteen, of what he saw and experienced in South Wales must have been devastating. The mining valleys then – the year was 1906 – were characterized by such insecurity, intellectual ferment, religious emotionalism and industrial unrest as very soon banished from young Huw's head any thoughts of literature that might have lodged there. He had landed, he said, in a place of the 'isms' – Spiritualism, Secularism, Socialism. Poverty he had known only too well in North Wales, but not this widespread industrial squalor to be met with in the valleys, together with the ruthless exploitation, the strikes, the lock-outs, the victimization, the uncurbed economic banditry;[1] and it was the inhuman conditions in which he saw men, himself among them, living and toiling, that transformed the studious young North Walian into a bitter political agitator. Huw flung himself headlong into the tempestuous life of the valleys – into the political, not the literary, which would have been Welsh, life. He wasn't a poet yet. What he began to write now were not lyrics, but articles for the *Social Democrat* and the *Socialist Review*, then under the editorship of Ramsay Macdonald, and a weekly column for *Justice*, to which also contributed James Connolly, Karl Liebknecht and an inflammable young Italian school-teacher called Benito Mussolini. Huw, himself a miner, fiery and eloquent in two languages, a scourge of the boss class, was soon Organizing Secretary of the Welsh Division of the Social Democratic Federation (unpaid).[2]

After his daily stint in the pit, he spent his time attending meetings in the valley addressed by such demi-gods as Keir Hardie, Bernard Shaw and H. M. Hyndman, the old Etonian backer of *Justice*; or he was himself organizing and addressing street-corner meetings up and down the coalfield, and staging sham fights outside the pubs to attract the crowds for his speakers, and engaging in unpoetic attempts at countering what seemed to him the excessive zeal of the local constabulary on behalf of a manifestly tottering social order.

It was not to be expected that such unconcealed hostility, let alone open and organized defiance, should then go unpunished. Young Williams lost his job in the pit and, worse, became a marked man. But, jobless and victimized, existing on the charity of his parents, with calamity menacing him thus on all sides, he made the one final gesture of defiance and affirmation open to him. He got married.

The bookish and vaguely literary youth became, as we have seen, under the potent influence of those seething valleys, an agitator and a man of action. Dire economic necessity took the first step in turning him into a poet. The coal cut by each miner underground in those days was weighed twice on reaching the top of the pit, once by the weigher, who was an employee of the coal owners, and again by the check-weigher, a trade union nominee paid by the colliers themselves to ensure that they were not cheated by the stooges in the companies' weighing machines. It is often stated that Huw became a colliery check-weigher. The truth is, alas, that the word 'check' never appeared in the designation of his employment.[3] And it was his acceptance of this job, offered to him by D. A. Thomas – later Lord Rhondda, Welsh coal-owner, and Food Controller during the First World War – in that extreme situation of economic desperation which I have described, that appears to have put an end for good and all to Huw's life of active political agitation. When the 1914–18 war broke out Huw was twenty-six, and it was then, ten years after his first visit to the valleys, that he began to write poetry.

His first lyrics appeared in local newspapers and magazines, the *Merthyr Express*, the *Western Mail* and the *Welsh Outlook*, and in 1920, the year in which I heard Huw's lines quoted by my French master, his first volume appeared, *Through the Upcast Shaft*. The genuine merit of much of the writing in this book plus, no doubt, the intriguing novelty at that time of its authorship – 'a young Welsh miner', the preface says, 'of Welsh peasant parentage . . . who had worked in the coal-mines since he was sixteen' – plus a boost from the Prime Minister, Huw's fellow Caernarfon-ite, Lloyd George, ultimately sent the volume into three editions. The name 'Huw Menai' became known to the London literary world and to the poetry-reading public in general in England and Wales.

But considerable literary success and critical acclaim made very little difference to the economic circumstances and the way of life of the poet and his family. He continued to live and work – when he could get work – in the valleys. In fact for three years before the appearance of his second book of poems, published in 1929, he was unemployed.

The Passing of Guto, issued by the Hogarth Press, brought him into contact with Lady Gerald Wellesley and Virginia Woolf and other literary figures connected with that famous press, but a certain aloofness on the poet's part, a proud suspicion, I sensed, of even a suggestion of patronage, prevented any flowering of intimacy in that quarter. Huw was about as likely material for a pet as a starving timber wolf. He had not only the bearing but the pride and touchiness of a hidalgo. In 1933 came *Back in the Return* and in 1945 his last book *The Simple Vision*, which fifteen years after its first appearance, he told me, was still bringing him in royalties.

His last two books are, I think, much superior to his first. But his best work, he claimed, although he didn't explain why, had always remained unpublished; not only poems but an enormous autobiography of half a million words, as long, that is, as three or four ordinary novels. Some of this book I have read in typescript. Caradoc Evans used to speak of a method he employed when revising his stories, which was analagous to putting a piece of white-wood in a vice and tightening the contraption up until every inessential element, under the enormous pressure, had been squeezed right out from between the woody fibres – air, moisture, natural juices, rosin – and only the compact quintessential iron-hard timber remained. Provided one could find a vice big enough, that, it seems to me, should be the treatment for Huw's autobiography. It is full of the most glorious and astonishing stories, but the tendency of Huw's style was always inflationary, and much of the book would be more endurable and effective if it were written in a form less reminiscent of the windier Victorians.

The general objection to Huw's work is in fact this *too-muchness*. So many of the things about him were excessive. His public speeches, although staggering in their range of reference and quotation, went on far too long. He is easily the most prolific of Anglo-Welsh poets. Powys says that Huw had written more poems at fifty-five than Landor had at ninety. I would be inclined to drop Huw's age fifteen years in the comparison. Poems poured out of him. He wrote them in his weighing machine, in trains and buses and in the ordnance factory where he found a job in the Second World War. He wrote them in pencil, sometimes one poem on the back of another, and his letters had lyrics written on the blank pages. He had upstairs in his Rhondda home, he told me once, a travelling chest full of unpublished poems in manuscript. One of his later undertakings was a poem called 'Caleb of the Slag-heaps', which was to be ten thousand lines long.

A writer as prolific as this, one would be inclined to say, is bound to produce work from time to time below his highest level. But this is not the most relevant criticism of Huw's poems. Certainly he wrote far too much, but the point is that even in his weakest lyrics one comes across isolated striking lines or brilliant phrases which almost redeem the stanza if not the poem. In fact the number of successful *poems* Huw wrote is, I think, very small indeed, in spite of the fact that he was essentially a poet for whom each poem concerned some one central idea or emotion. The Welsh *cywyddwyr* sometimes construct poems by means of *dyfaliad*, which is a piling up of imagery, e.g. the golden hair of a girl might be likened to lightning, to golden lattice, to gilded ropework, etc., etc. The craftsmanship goes into the individual images embedded in the couplets rather than into the overall shape of the poem. Huw never worked like that, but I would still judge some of his poems to be better than others because they contain a greater number of these striking images, apt phrases, vivid descriptions and so on that are everywhere in his work, rather than because they have achieved a more satisfying unity as a work of art. 'The lode-star magic of their honeymoon', he writes in 'Swallow'; glow-worms are 'Cold wayside moons for ever at the full'; he sees the sea at night 'holding within its bosom every star'. Somehow in these lines, he hints at more than diurnal darkness descending upon the valleys:

> The windows darken one by one
> Upon the stellar hosts.

Using the unrhymed metre of Collins's *Ode to Evening*, he says of autumn:

> There lurks a sweet deception in the sky
> Where rooks now leisurely turn head for home
>   And swallows curve their flight,
>   Hunting some lesser wing.
>
> The crimson signal of the creeper leaf
> And the wild fever of the honey fly
>   Say: Winter will soon arrive
>   To lay this garden bare.[4]

Huw says he read Milton, Shelley, Keats, Wordsworth, 'and this last makes the greatest appeal to me'. I think the claim is borne out by his work. Some of the titles of the poems in his first volume are 'To an impetuous butterfly', 'May musings', 'Humble lines to Spring', 'To a rose tree', 'To a skylark', which give some indication of the type of subject that attracted him. He does not mention John Clare, who might well have been an influence. Huw's diction is on the whole that of the early *Golden Treasury* romantics and so it seems old-fashioned to us today. He uses inversions frequently, and words like 'maketh', 'neath', 'ne'er', 'thy', 'thee', 'yore', 'ere', and so on. Very few marks of the changes that have taken place in English poetry since *Prufrock*, published three years before the appearance of his first volumes, are to be found in his work. His stanza forms are traditional, quatrains, couplets and so on, and he was a frequent sonneteer. He was inclined to believe that what was not immediately intelligible could not be poetry. The *idea* of Dylan Thomas, the widely-acclaimed and successful young poet, appealed to him very much, because it reminded him of his own early triumphs and his brief fêting, but for Dylan's poetry he felt very little sympathy. His aim was the old one of moving us, and for him poetry should be simple, sensuous and passionate. His prime concern was with fancy, infinity and the open air, with the enigma of suffering and death, with the concept of the solitary human soul against the indifferent or hostile universe. Politics had died in him, and he is less the poet of the valley community, of its sufferings and aspirations, as Idris Davies was, than of the mountains and the moorlands which separate the valleys from one another; far more a nature poet at heart in fact, most at home in the beautiful countryside which everywhere surrounds the Welsh coal-field and so frequently makes massive invasions of loveliness into it. The words constantly in use in his poems are 'sunset', 'stars', 'winds', 'birds', 'snow', 'mountains', 'storm', 'suns', 'sea', 'dawn', 'roses', 'dew', 'flowers'. In fact, reading Huw's poetry, one is of course soon made aware of the conflicts that raged in his own soul, and the consciousness that these are in some way part of a cosmic unease; but one could cover vast areas of the poet's work without suspecting that he had lived more than half a century in mining towns in the heart of one of the most politically-conscious and industrially turbulent areas in Great Britain, and that at one time he was himself deeply involved in the struggles that convulsed the valleys communities.

As he got older his verse, or at least, since we don't know the dates of composition of his poems, his choice of verse for publication, toughened and refined itself, and his preference was for what was true rather than for what was picturesque or 'poetic'. In his first book, *Through the Upcast Shaft*, he has a poem of childhood called 'Ghosts':

Through the sorrows that I see,
    Through the tears that mar my gaze,
Cheerily will come to me,
    Ghosts of bygone days.

They will take me by the hand
    Back to days when I, with joy,
Built my castles in the sand,
    A happy, happy boy.

They will teach me then to be
    Once again the joyous child,
Laughing, romping by the sea –
    Laughing, romping wild.

Fields of hay and fields of wheat!
    How those glorious days abide!
Now I tramp the meadows sweet,
    With the ghosts for guide.

This seems to me as bogus a piece of lyricism as one could imagine. The debilitated language makes it obvious Huw didn't believe a word of it himself. Later, for his last book, he wrote, or chose, 'When Time the Sculptor Deepens', basically on the same theme, but here he forgets to be the Wordsworthian poet of ideal infancy and tells the stark truth about the poverty and misery of his childhood with moving dignity:

As Time, the sculptor, deepens
    The lines upon my face
I find my thoughts returning
    To far-off childhood days,
When clad in ragged garments
    And hunger was at hand
I combed the tidal leavings
    Of shellfish on the strand –

The strand by wild Coed Alun
    Where oft the Poor would spread
The poacher's net for salmon
    And prison risk for bread . . .
And big Wil Foundry Morfa
    And Wmffre *bach* the sweep
Now safe from water bailiffs
    In old Llanbeblig sleep!

How Need the latent quickens!
But what unhappy thrall
To be a man in thinking
When yet a schoolboy small!
And Lord it is no wonder
They voice an after rage
Who carried on young shoulders
The burdens of Old Age.

But all is not yet heartache
When in the starlight gleams
The sea by Dinas Dinlle
Whereon I sailed my dreams,
A battered bark returning
Through many a stormy night
To shores of Abermenai
And Llanddwyn's lonely light!

Too often, I think, Huw wrote down, as in the first of these two poems, what he considered he *ought* to feel and think, what was most 'poetic', judged by the Wordsworthian example, to feel and think about given circumstances and situations. But in the second poem, it seems to me, his response to his experience is direct and sincere. In his third volume, *Back in the Return* (1933), he has some highly significant lines about that compounding of blood and coal-dust which produces the familiar ink-like marks of the blue scars on the miners' hands and faces:

For blood and coaldust when they link
Make hieroglyphs of Indian ink.

That arresting couplet we might read as a sort of allegory of the poet's own life, although we should have to look deeper than his skin for the wounds out of whose rich ink Huw had written poems like 'When Time the Sculptor'.

During his last years – he died in 1961 – I saw him fairly often. Sometimes he visited my house, sometimes we met in the company of friends like Gwyn Thomas and Keidrych Rhys. Huw's health was bad by then, and even a small amount of beer was sufficient to turn him sick, stone cold and apple green. He enjoyed, I believe, the company of writers a generation or two younger than his own. His experience of life had been varied and rich and, as he was an uninhibited describer and discusser of it, he was always welcome among us on that score alone. He appreciated and thawed out in any atmosphere of goodwill and acceptance and interest in himself and his work. There were certain prickly areas in his personality, but these, with a little tact, were not difficult to circumvent, although I do remember one disastrous afternoon when this was not so. Huw, sitting with half a dozen of us in the parlour of our house, had gradually passed into one of those trance-like states which were apt to overtake him both in private company and on the platform; and with his lids down and in seeming oblivion of his surroundings, he muttered on almost incoherently about some startling mystical communication with nature which he had experienced on the Rhondda mountains in the presence of various birds and plants with outlandish names. The combination of guttural rumble, trance-like utterance and botanical Latin was too much, and I saw with horror out of the corner of my eye that two of the people present were helpless in the grip of silent and agonizing *fou rire*. When the explosion came Huw rose and left the house with scarcely another word, deeply hurt and offended. But some months afterwards, following apologies and explanations, the unforgivable was miraculously forgiven, and he later worked happily with one of the offenders in some remarkable radio programmes.

> Part mystic, part mechanic,
> Part a poet, part a panic,
>
> One part fighter, one part fustian,
> Part Agnostic, part a Christian,
> One part chance, and part designer,
> Part a book and part a miner.[5]

One part of Huw's character also was a naïve and endearing matinée idol's vanity; before a stranger to whom he was about to be introduced entered the room he would go to the mirror and ruffle up his bubble-cut curls into a discreet poetic disorder. His gestures were often theatrical, outsize; if during some story he had occasion to make the sign of the Cross, which seemed often, it was always a cross about seven feet high and five across. As well as his appearance and his manner, his sexual potency was another matter, he gave us to understand, upon which he prided himself, although I remember him once, after describing some discreditable youthful escapade in this field, turning savagely to the mirror, shaking his fist at his own image and shouting in his guttural Caernarfon accent, 'Damn you, you pluddy monkey, you!'

One could not long retain in his company the sense of awe which his reputation and the chilly grandeur of his manner and appearance might at first inspire. One sensed in him, beyond the pride and the theatricality and the egotism, something childlike and deeply hurt and betrayed which one yearned to comfort, something that hungered and thirsted for success and recognition and acceptance. Alas, very little worldly or literary success ever came Huw's way. His story was one, after a burst of interest in his early days, of the world's long neglect and of disappointment. His death in 1961 passed almost unnoticed. He received a civil list pension in the 1950s, but no prizes or honours or acclaim of any sort came to him. And yet his proud faith in his poetic destiny remained unshaken.

I have often wondered whether a figure like Huw is conceivable in any country but ours – I mean Wales, of course. Is there a comparable English or American poet, working-class, prolific, whose four books all bear the imprint of reputable London publishers and whose work appeared in such periodicals as *The Times Literary Supplement*, *Encounter* and *The Listener*, but who at the same time remained rooted in his own valleys community for the best part of sixty years, a sort of *bardd gwlad* of the coalfields, although receiving most of whatever recognition that did come his way from the critics and editors of London; who in that time worked, struggled, agitated, played chess, lectured, brought up a family of eight children and wrote his poems in the little triangle, as it were, whose corners are at the valleys townships of Merthyr Vale, Gilfach Goch and Penygraig?

Certainly in Wales we have had many Welsh-language poets of a high order – toll-gate keepers, stonemasons, station-masters – who would in England be thought of as working-class, and it is perhaps because of this powerful tradition of a peasant culture and an eisteddfodic background that men like Huw Menai, and perhaps Idris Davies and others among the Anglo-Welsh, were able to think of themselves as poets at all.

What marked him off of course from the Welsh-language writers I have referred to is his language. Apart from half a dozen *englynion* and a few stanzas in Welsh here and there, all Huw Menai's work has been done in English.[6] And the community in which he lived was not on the whole the one he wrote for or wrote about: success for him meant, I suppose, acclaim by the London or New York critics. In his own community he was at best a pet, at worst a peepshow. But Huw's loneliness and isolation all those years up there in the Rhondda Valley fortified rather than diminished his belief in himself. He is not the first

poet to seem to those about him the 'egotistical sublime'. All Huw
wanted was to be a poet, and to be recognized as one. Such absolute
dedication as his, and such triumphant faith in his poetic destiny,
seemed always to me touching, and hopeless and admirable.

IDRIS DAVIES

1905–1953

BEFORE I met Idris Davies I had the impression, from the little I had
heard about him and from the few poems of his I had read in the
usually little and often leftish magazines that he wrote for, that he was just
another half-hearted Welsh school-teacher with literary ambitions, writing his poems up there in London, querulous rather than savagely indig-
nant, imitative, self-pitying, low-powered. And from this impression of his
personality a conviction of his physical appearance began to establish
itself in my mind, and I thought of him as tallish, thin-chested, willowy,
long-necked, shouldered like a hock bottle, with a disenchanted face and
sour-looking hair. I got a very great shock the first time I saw him.

I had become by that time, in the thirties, as I have already described,
greatly interested in Welshmen like Dylan Thomas, Vernon Watkins,
Rhys Davies and Caradoc Evans who wrote in English, a category to
which, probably through Keidrych Rhys, I found out that Idris Davies
belonged, although I had already guessed that a writer bearing so un-
Saxon a name would be Welsh. But I cannot remember how the
meeting between us was arranged, or what sequence of events led up to
it. I know it took place outside the Capitol cinema in Cardiff, on a
drizzling Saturday afternoon in, I think, 1937, when Idris was still
teaching in London. He was thirty-two years of age and unmarried.

His parents lived in Rhymney, a Monmouthshire mining town, at
that time almost derelict, about thirty miles north of Cardiff where my
home was, and he used to spend part of his school holidays with them.
He frequently visited Cardiff, as we learn from his poems, and it was on
one of these trips that we first met.

The short, sturdy figure, expectant on the Capitol steps, wearing a
cloth cap, leather gloves, thick scarf and brown mac, with – our sign of
mutual recognition – a white rose in the buttonhole, was utterly unlike

anything I had imagined Idris to be. General Picton, the Welsh officer who was Wellington's second-in-command at Waterloo, held that for him the ideal infantryman was what many would regard, I suppose, as the typical Welshman, or Silurian — dark, tough, stocky, thick-necked and about five feet two inches in height. As soon as I set eyes on Idris Davies this saying came to my mind. He was, perhaps, a bit taller than five feet two, but otherwise he answered very closely to Picton's specification: he belonged physically to the dark and bright-eyed aborigines of these islands, to that obscure and inextinguishable race that went down before the fair-haired Celts, and are still to be found in their triumphant thousands in the valleys of South Wales, in the pits, in the Big Seats, in the male voice choirs, behind the scrums — short, erect, thick-set, corpulent in middle age or idleness, the hair black and the eyes flashing. Idris's shoulders were massive, his head large and his face broad. Two deep incisions ran vertically down his pallid cheeks to the line of his jaw. His straight black hair, always oiled and well barbered, was dense and springing, brushed back from his broad forehead and cut down almost to the bone at the back. One of his peculiarities was his devotion to a pair of aged wire spectacles, twisted and askew, and inexpertly repaired with beads of wet-looking solder which one's fingers itched to touch; one pebble of these remarkable eyepieces was often so closely pressed to the eyeball as to flatten it, while the other stood away far out in advance in a position from which no possible benefit could result.

Later on during the afternoon of that meeting, the first of many such, we went into a café where Idris sat opposite me, pulling contentedly at his Woodbine, holding his cigarette *inside* the cup of his hand after the manner of young colliers — a hand mutilated in an accident when he had been working in the pit. We spoke of Wales, politics, poetry, hardly at all about school. One of the things I liked about him that afternoon was his serene and easy manner. He seemed to have no violent prejudices, no touchiness or irascibility in his character, none of those hidden conflicts that produce unexpected sulks or explosions. The passion in him, so clearly discernible in his poetry, showed itself not at all in his ordinary behaviour, or perhaps only in a certain occasional cockiness, a sudden hostile plucking back of his pallid face in challenge as he listened to an unacceptable opinion and regarded one dubiously from behind his old-fashioned glasses. But in spite of this, the impression I carried away from our first meeting was one of accommodation and sweetness of temper, and these were indeed enduring elements in Idris's character.

Much of the story of his inner life and his outward circumstances is to be found in the ballad-like quatrains of his long autobiographical poem 'I was born in Rhymney'. His family had come from rural Cardiganshire in the last century to work in the Monmouthshire coalfield, and Idris's Welsh-speaking father was a miner. The poet's childhood would appear to have been that of any lively and sensitive boy brought up in a working-class home in the mining valleys, the sort of life described in prose by Jack Jones, Rhys Davies, Gwyn Thomas and others. State education in Wales has been carried on everywhere, until recently, in the English language, without regard to the language of the homes from which the pupils in the schools came. All Idris's formal education, in elementary school – he did not attend a grammar school – training college and university was English in language and content, and it is interesting to notice that nearly all the poets mentioned in his own poems are writers of English – Shakespeare, Spenser, Milton, Marlowe, Blake, Coleridge, Shelley, Yeats, Goldsmith, Keats, Joyce, Webster, Donne, Scott, Wordsworth, Lawrence. Only two Welsh-language poets, I believe, are referred to at all by him, namely Robert Williams Parry and Saunders Lewis, one of the founders of the Welsh Nationalist Party. Later, when he came back to teach in Wales, and even before that, he educated himself in Welsh; he learned again to speak the language and he would recite, or rather declaim, long passages of modern Welsh-language poetry. He also wrote one or two poems in Welsh himself, but this awareness of the literature of his own country had arrived too late in his development, I believe, to have had much influence on his own poetry in the English language. It is obvious from his work that he became a deeply patriotic Welshman, as it is that he had read Housman and Whitman, but very little evidence exists in it that he in fact knew anything much about the Welsh language or Welsh literature.[1]

His childhood home in Rhymney was bilingual, as was probably his nonconformist chapel. However much he might as a man rebel against the inadequacy of the religion in which he had been brought up, the chapel and its memories inevitably haunt his work from beginning to end; and I would guess that the Bible, and the social gospel widely preached from the pulpits of Wales in his youth, were more fundamental to his socialism than *Das Kapital* or the *Communist Manifesto*. Nonconformity is the inescapable Jesuitism of the Welsh.

When you were young, Dai, when you were young!
The Saturday mornings of childhood

With childish dreams and adventures
Among the black tips by the river,
And the rough grass and the nettles
Behind the colliery yard, the stone-throwing
Battles between the ragged boys,
The fascination of the railway cutting
On dusty summer afternoons,
And the winter night and its street-lamps
And the first pranks of love,
And the deep warm sleep
In grandmother's chapel pew
On stodgy Sunday evenings,
And the buttercup-field you sometimes noticed
Behind the farthest street, the magical field
That only the heart could see,
The heart and rarely the boyish eye,
And the pride you had in your father's
Loins and shoulders when he bent
Between the tub and the fire,
And the days you counted, counted, counted,
Before you should work in the mine.
You never, never cursed your luck
Or desired to see another town or valley,
Or know any other men and women
Than those of the streets around
The street where you were born.
Your world was narrow and magical
And dear and dirty and brave
When you were young, Dai, when you were young!
      (from 'Tonypandy', *Tonypandy and Other Poems*, 1945)

At fourteen Idris left school to work underground, although there appears to have been little economic necessity, as in Huw Menai's case, for him to have done so. He says, it's true, in 'I was born in Rhymney', which appears in the same volume as the quotation above, that he went 'Unwillingly . . . / To crawl in moleskin trousers / Beneath the rocks of Gwent'; but lines in the above passage suggest a different attitude, and the impression I received from him in conversation was that he quitted school readily enough because he felt − foolishly, he admitted − that a miner's life was more manly, and carried more prestige, and was in every way superior to the life of a school-teacher, or a clerk, or a shopkeeper. A grammar school boy could not be compared, it seemed to him then,

with a collier boy, who was paid wages, and was his own master every
night of the week, and did a job that hourly demonstrated his
toughness, strength and courage.

The General Strike, during which almost the entire working
population of Great Britain downed tools, took place in 1926. This
strike, in its general aspect, collapsed within nine days, but the miners,
always a spearhead then in the struggles of the working class, stuck it
out alone for nearly seven months after their fellow trade unionists had
capitulated and gone back to work. When they in turn surrendered and
went, beaten, into the pits again, Idris did not go with them. After seven
years in the mines he undertook during that lengthy and bitter stop-
page what he called 'the long and lonely / Self-tuition game', and
finally entered Loughborough College and Nottingham University to
train as a teacher. In 1928 at the end of his training he was appointed to
the staff of an elementary school in Hoxton in the East End of London.

He became a great lover of London, of Hampstead Heath, of Epping
Forest and especially of the Charing Cross Road area with its second-
hand bookshops. And he got to know many Welshmen then living in
the capital, including Aneirin Talfan Davies, Keidrych Rhys and Dylan
Thomas, whom he used to meet on Friday evenings. A Welsh saw has it
that the best Welshman is the Welshman away from home, and I think
Idris Davies's Welshness, his interest in Wales and his consciousness of
the whole heritage of his homeland, as distinct from his concern with
the struggles and the sufferings of the Welsh miners in the largely
anglicized valleys, were much deepened and enriched by his contact
with other Welsh exiles, many of them intensely patriotic and Welsh-
speaking; and also with cultivated English people too during this time.
His friend, David Raymond, tells a characteristic story of him.[2]
Raymond, Dylan and Idris were one night in the public bar of Henekys
in Holborn with T. W. Earp, then art critic to the *Daily Telegraph*. 'You
Welsh haven't got any culture', Tommy Earp said during an argument,
being no doubt intentionally provocative. 'You don't appreciate or even
recognize your own artists.' Idris's reaction was sudden and startling. He
jumped to his feet and began to recite Shakespeare aloud. After every
passage he turned to the people sitting around the tables with their
pints and asked in a fierce voice: 'Do you know who wrote that?' The
people addressed could only stare at him dumbly. After declaiming five
or six passages he turned to Tommy Earp and said: 'You see, nobody
answers. So what price English culture? Do you claim there isn't any
because your own English don't recognize or appreciate their supreme

artist?' T. W. Earp, David Raymond tells us, only grinned. Really he was very fond of Idris.

With the coming of the Second World War, Idris was evacuated from London with his school, first to Hertfordshire and then to two places in his native Wales, first to rural Llandysul in Cardiganshire, and then to the industrial Rhondda Valley. His stay in Wales certainly strengthened and possibly even evoked a desire to leave London for good and to settle down in his native country. In common, perhaps, with most Welsh-speaking Welshmen, his attitude upon many issues became gradually very near to that of the Welsh Nationalists. I do not think that his conversion was sudden, or that in looking at questions from a specifically Welsh angle he abandoned his deeply-rooted Socialism, that Socialism of brotherhood rather than of electrification. But being a poet he felt, I think, a certain aridity and a lack of romance in the left-wing politics of his time. When the war ended he secured, after many unsuccessful attempts, a teaching job in his native county of Monmouthshire. In 1953 he died of cancer at his mother's home in Rhymney. He was nine years older than Dylan Thomas, who was to die a few months later in the same year. He was unmarried.

When I met Idris Davies in 1937 he had not then published a volume of poems, although his work had of course appeared in several magazines, including Keidrych Rhys's *Wales*. His first book was *Gwalia Deserta*, published by Dent in 1938, in a series which also included Dylan Thomas's *Twenty-five Poems*.

The book is a sequence of lyrics, untitled, but numbered, largely on a single theme, namely the Depression, the industrial and social devastation of the mining valleys of South Wales in the twenties and thirties of the twentieth century. The economic blizzard which overwhelmed Britain and Western Europe between the two world wars hit South Wales with particular ferocity, since the economy of the area was based almost entirely upon the two heavy industries of coal and steel. When these declined, the unemployment figures in the valleys rose to be amongst the highest in Britain; in Merthyr Tydfil, for example, in 1934 56 per cent of the employable population were out of work. Through the closures of the pits and the steel works countless decent, hard-working families suffered great hardship and humiliation; savings were spent and debts incurred; the valleys lost thousands of their most adventurous and energetic families in the mass emigrations into England in search of work; it was the time of the hunger marchers, of the dejected groups at street corners, of the heartbreak of the singing

miners in the gutters of the West End, of the broken boots, the handed-
on clothing, the scratching for coal on the refuse tips of the collieries.
And it was this appalling industrial and social calamity that Idris Davies
made the chief theme of *Gwalia Deserta*.

He appears to have been, at the beginning of his writing, frequently
under the influence of a poet whose name was high in critical regard in
the twenties and thirties – A. E. Housman. One of the things Idris did
in his early poems was to give the short-lined, hymn-like quatrains, and
the rural disillusionment of the Shropshire Lad, an industrial twist:

> He is digging in the dark,
>   Jude who would the poet be,
> And dreaming of the distant isles
> And the summer on the sea.
>
> Not for always shall he grope
>   In the galleries of grime –
> 'Tis sure he shall be shouldered,
>   And need nor pick nor rhyme.

Idris outgrew the influence of Housman, and not all the poems even in
Gwalia Deserta derive from an admiration for him. A much antho-
logized piece, and one selected for a broadcast reading by Dylan
Thomas, is 'O what can you give me?':

> O what can you give me?
> Say the sad bells of Rhymney.
>
> Is there hope for the future?
> Cry the brown bells of Merthyr.
>
> Who made the mineowner?
> Say the black bells of Rhondda.
>
> And who robbed the miner?
> Cry the grim bells of Blaina.
>
> They will plunder willy-nilly,
> Say the bells of Caerphilly.
>
> They have fangs, they have teeth!
> Shout the loud bells of Neath.

To the south, things are sullen,
Say the pink bells of Brecon.

Even God is uneasy,
Say the moist bells of Swansea.

Put the vandals in court!
Cry the bells of Newport.

All would be well if – if – if –
Say the green bells of Cardiff.

Why so worried, sisters, why?
Sing the silver bells of Wye.

Exactly half the pieces in *Gwalia Deserta* are written not in rhymed and metrical stanzas, but in free verse, a form upon which in time Idris placed a stamp at least sufficiently personal and characteristic to be parodied. And some of the more persistent and striking features of the book, the nostalgia, the humour, the pervading sense of grimness, come through with greater clarity in these stark free verse sections than in the Housman-like lyrics:

O dreary township in the hills!
The damp streets under the mountain,
Ragged children on broken pavements,
Young men sitting on cemetery walls,
Young girls dreaming of London;
Old men remembering by fading fires,
Remembering Gladstone and Victoria and Mafeking;
Grey mothers sighing by the windows,
Half-listening to Jerkin's speckled cockerel crowing on the tip;
A funeral cortège creeping to the bleakest ridge
And the melancholy echoes of the chaunted hymns.
Yet sometimes in the night there is beauty
When the lights in the valley brag to the stars,
Or the moon of the moorland smiles on desolation.

A grim picture, but a true one, not at all too dark to convey the squalor that that shabby and despairing period spread over the face of South Wales. The poet has been forced to use 'grey' here to denote drabness, instead of his almost universal 'brown' for this purpose. 'Cortège' and 'chaunt' – especially 'chaunt' – seem a bit out of place in this grimy catalogue. The use of the superlative ('bleakest') is common in Idris Davies's work, sometimes, I suspect, for no better reason than that the metre demands another syllable. Much of the writing throughout this first volume, one must concede, is thin in texture and lacking in intensity; there is a home-spun air about a good many of the lyrics, and in the sound of them the steady menace of doggerel. The book has such faults, but, on the other hand, much of it is passionately felt and sincere, and I don't think it deserved the critical mauling it got in some quarters in 1938. Perhaps so much of the writing fails because Yeats was right and passive suffering is not a theme for poetry.

Idris Davies's work came very obviously out of his compassion for the plight of the people he had been brought up among and had loved, and his indignation at what he saw as the world's indifference to them, or its betrayal. Although, as far as I know, he was never a bitter and dedicated political agitator like Huw Menai, and never, like him, sacked and victimized, he identifies himself much more closely in his poetry than the older poet with the people of the valleys, with their sufferings and their aspirations. And this results in a strange reversal of expectation. Idris's poetry, the work of a school-teacher absent from South Wales during much of the Depression, is yet nearer to the political oratory of the valleys, to those passionate, biased, jeering speeches of the hillsides, of the street corners and the waste patches, that found their brilliant culmination in the fiery eloquence of Nye Bevan, than it is to the egocentric Wordsworthian musings of Huw Menai. Idris is seldom a nature poet, not the slave, as he says, 'of moonlit streams, / And midnight moors, and cold black pines, / And long blue ridges in the West'. His characters are 'Dai and Glyn and Emrys', the young colliers, and Maria, the girl working in the pop shop, and Dan the grocer, and Mrs Evans fach; and the settings of his poems are located on the beds of the valleys themselves, or on the tips, in the rows of houses, the pubs, the chapels, the Italian shop, the welfare institute, rather than, as in Huw Menai's verse, in the unspoilt scenery of the surrounding mountains; although of course he is by no means indifferent to this:

> Now in these mountain grasses beneath a winter sky
> I watch the valleys lighted, I hear the curlew cry,
> I hear the sorrowful echoes borne from the Severn Sea,
> And the dirge of desolation, the sigh of history.

O mountain grasses ignorant of man and all his pain,
Sing in this freezing twilight, murmur to me again
Of the prehistoric aeons, the landscapes pure and bare,
The centuries of silence, the unpolluted air.

O northern winds, my lovers, roar around me where I stand,
A naked creature lonely in a brown and barren land,
And scatter from my memory the weeds of human lore
And make me as cold, as careless, as a wave on a desolate shore.

('One February Evening', *Tonypandy and Other Poems*)

But this type of poem is, perhaps regrettably, relatively unusual, as uncharacteristic as the desire for indifference and numb insensitivity expressed in the last line. For two of the poet's four volumes of poetry deal entirely with events in the valleys that brought hardship and suffering to them, namely the great Depression and the General Strike. It was during his seven years as a collier, surely, that there was implanted and developed in him his love for the mining community, whose boyhood beginnings we have seen him describe; it was then he began to achieve that complete identification of himself with the people of the valleys, with the poor, the exploited and the oppressed, which is one of the dominant themes of his poetry:

O that my passion would fuse
The valleys I love to flame,
The valleys of decent homes
Threatened by shadows of shame.

O valleys that gave me birth,
And comradeship and song,
Before I go back to the earth
May my eyes see the end of this wrong.

From these broken hills of my home,
Haunts of my boyhood and youth,
I want to shout of the shadows that pass
In the sunshine and splendour of truth.

This poem appears in *The Angry Summer*, Idris's second volume of poetry. The book concerns the General Strike of 1926 and the long miners' strike which followed its collapse, and was published in 1943. Here the poet's radical idealism and his passion for social righteousness find their most complete and vehement expression. Once when I discussed the fiercely partisan poetry of the volume with a friend of a different background and a more privileged upbringing, he remarked: 'Yes, but there's another side to that question'. For Idris Davies there was not. He was a striker, and unemployed, and he knew. He saw himself poetically as the dedicated champion of the miner, not only the heroic miner, as he says, lauded for a time by the newspapers for his gallantry in rescuing his comrades from death by fire, flood or entombment; but equally the stubborn miner on strike or locked out, and the bitter and agitating miner, reviled and screamed at, and threatened and derided by a press, and by smugly secure English communities, who know nothing of the realities of the miners' lives. Much 'communist' verse was written in the thirties by the public-school Marxists, sincere, gifted and sensitive English poets of middle-class origin like Auden, Day Lewis and Spender, whose consciences, to their credit, were uneasy at the privilege and security of their own class in the face of the poverty, stagnation and calamitous human wastage they saw all around them in the Britain of that time. The fact that these poets had used an industrial and political vocabulary no doubt made it easier for Idris in *Gwalia Deserta* and *The Angry Summer* to write in the way he did, although I don't think that their influence upon him was direct, or at all discernible in a line-by-line examination. And one of the things that marks him off from them is the fact that he was not in any way privileged, and that he and his family were personally and inescapably involved in the social disaster which had befallen the community of which he was part.

By 1943, when *The Angry Summer* appeared, the sufferings and aspirations of 1926 were largely forgotten in the horrors of the Second World War. But to Idris Davies they were still alive, and as poignant as they had been twenty years previously. 'We shall remember 1926 until our blood is dry', said Dai and Shinkin, in *Gwalia Deserta*, standing at the kerb in Charing Cross Road. And so it was with the poet himself. *The Angry Summer* he once described to me as his *magnum opus*, and so I believe it to be. It is an account, unlike *Gwalia Deserta*, of an experience the poet lived through from day to day, and it was an experience which appeared to him not as passive suffering but as a bitter and attritious struggle against a ruthless and powerful enemy. The book has a passion, a unity, a richly varied coherence, not seen in so marked a degree in any of his other volumes. *Gwalia Deserta*, written more or less to the same pattern of numbered and untitled pieces, some of them lyrics and some free verse, is really a sort of preliminary sketch for it. For the poet himself *The*

Angry Summer was less a book of fifty separate poems than one long poem on 1926 divided up into sections.[3] There is deep feeling in many of these, especially in poems like 'These men went into the gloom', and 'The telephones are ringing', in which the poet expresses his passionate anger and scorn at the final betrayal of the miners' cause, on what came to be known in the coalfields as Black Friday:

> The telephones are ringing
> And treachery's in the air.
> The sleek one,
> The expert at compromise
> Is bowing in Whitehall.
> And lackey to fox to parrot cries:
> 'The nation must be saved.'
> What is the nation, gentlemen,
> Who are the nation, my lords?
> The sleek one,
> The expert at compromise,
> Is chattering in Whitehall.
> The men who have made this nation,
> Who have made her gross in wealth,
> The men who have given their flesh and blood
> From century to century,
> They do not scream and panic,
> They do not cringe and whine,
> They do not shudder in the hour of crisis.
> It is the robber and the gambler and the parasite
> Who yell when the hour of reckoning comes.
> But the sleek one,
> The expert at compromise,
> Is signing in Whitehall.
> The buying and selling is over,
> The treachery sealed, and called
> A national triumph;
> And this Friday goes down to history
> Yellow, and edged with black.

But one of the admirable qualities of the *The Angry Summer* is that it is not by any means all bitterness and savage indignation. The poet, while never wavering for a moment in his conviction of the righteousness of the miners' cause, yet manages to see all around the great struggle; he could see it from the viewpoint of the small shop-keeper, to whom it meant ruin; from the vicar's viewpoint, the parents', the penny concert organizer's, even the pigeon fancier's. So that what we have in the book is a great theme with variations and interludes, sometimes grimly comic, sometimes tender, sometimes wry or satirical. Here is one of these interspersed pieces which shows that the poet was aware, in spite of his desperate seriousness and involvement, of the funny side of the great strike:

> In the little Italian shop
> Where they sell coloured gassy pop,
> Listen to Emlyn tell his mate
> How to organize the State,
> How to end the troublous days
> And lead the world to wiser ways.
> Danny bach Dwl is eager, too,
> To put an end to ballyhoo;
> And Nipper Evans would put things right
> In this nation overnight.
> One would make things brisk and hot,
> Another kill the whole damn lot . . .
> And on and on the chatter flows
> Until Maria yawns and goes
> To pull the blinds and shut the shop
> So full of coloured gassy pop.

Idris Davies's third volume, *Tonypandy*, is his most diverse and varied work. The poems included in it were written over a considerable period, but had been rejected when *Gwalia Deserta* and *The Angry Summer* were being compiled because they fell outside the experiences which gave these two volumes their unity. *Tonypandy* does not claim to be anything other than a collection of miscellaneous poems, and the fact that the individual poems have titles and not, as heretofore, numbers, indicates that they do not derive from a single overwhelming impulse. The verse in *Tonypandy* is both simple and very obscure, austere and flowery, solemn and humorous, lyrical and declamatory. The book contains songs, satirical character sketches and poems describing various parts of Great Britain and Ireland visited by the poet. The colliers and the mining community are not ignored of course, but here, from behind the ex-miner who was their champion and passionate advocate, there steps out another Idris Davies, in some ways a rather surprising figure, a poet who delights in fine language, odd imaginings and highly coloured imagery:

SONNET

I tossed my golden anchor to the sea
To tease the twisted tides of salty joy,
And then my heart pursued the mystery
Of sea-born kings that did the moon annoy
Before the horn of summer caught the tune
Born in the shell of grief. The velvet bone
Of sea-weed forests melted in the noon
And every frond bent down to clasp the stone.
Sea-bottom surge, be gentle with my bread
For in my bread there sleeps another god
Whose hands are clean, whose heart is strong and red.
The idols of old Sabbaths loved the rod
And smiled to see our blood on window panes
And danced upon the dead in thistled lanes.

This poem was first published in *Wales* in 1937. In a letter thanking me
for a review of *Tonypandy*, the poet rebuked me for singling out for
special praise this particular sonnet. 'The only really obscure poem in
the book', he wrote, 'is the sonnet which I never really liked and which
I am very sorry I ever included in this volume. It was a typical piece of
"1930-ish" verse. Tripe of the first order'.

I find this comment interesting and revealing. Most of Idris Davies's
poetry is texturally austere and no doubt the subjects of his verse often
call for this particular quality. Someone has said that the bareness of his
verse matches the bareness of the colliery tips amongst which he was
brought up. But there was in him also, fiercely suppressed in *Gwalia
Deserta* and *The Angry Summer*, a lover of style, and fancy, and gorgeous
language, who makes an appearance, sometimes fitful, in such poems as
'Sonnet', 'Defiance', 'Interlude', 'Ruin', 'Renaissance' and perhaps
'William Morris', which Yeats said he would like to have set to music.

DEFIANCE

I showed my teeth to the London moon
And said, 'You shall not charm tonight.
I shall not be the slave of moonlit streams,
And midnight moors, and cold black pines,
And long blue ridges in the West.
There is a splendour must be left unsaid –
You shall not touch my heart tonight.
There is a magic that I know too well,

A loveliness beyond all sighing and all art,
And I will be no neophyte this hour.
Die, moon, you ravisher of boys!
There are goats and peacocks on the misty lawns,
And bearded musicians on the lake,
And smitten daughters at the harbour quay,
And dark, game women on the Holborn kerb,
And spoils enough for you tonight.
Die, moon, you vixen of the South!'
And I drew the mediaeval curtain
Sharp across the glass, and killed the moon.

Such poems have elements of fancy and a concern for language lacking in most of Idris Davies's poetry. In general, I think, Idris was inclined to believe that passion alone would make the poem, that if the pity was powerfully enough experienced the poetry would follow. He was distrustful of too great a concern with technique where his feelings were really involved, and I think that perhaps he so often wrote in free verse for this reason; namely that released from the necessity of rhyming and counting feet he could say with exactitude what he wished to. Metrically the most complicated poem he ever undertook, the 'Sonnet', he thought least of, as we have seen. His major defect as a poet is, I think, his fluency, his insufficient concern with words and language. Poetically he was a divided personality; a split seemed to run right through his work. On the one side was the profound, sacrosanct feeling, the cherished passion, on the other the despised and suspect gift of language. Hardly ever, unfortunately, did these two meet in a single poem. Yeats was one of his poetic heroes;[4] he felt and responded to the passion in Yeats's verse, but I question whether he recognized the technical mastery of it, or the cunning with which this mastery is concealed. My own admiration for Hopkins he found completely mystifying. For him Hopkins's patent absorption with technical matters meant that he was not a man of any profound feeling, in fact a sort of sissyish freak whose metrical doodling occasionally produced fairly pleasing verbal patterns. I do not think this rather un-Welsh and puritanical attitude towards language and the poet's craft had anything at all to do, as some might suppose, with the calvinistic puritanism in which he was brought up. The puritanism of the Welsh has never extended to language. The Welsh preachers Idris had listened to in his youth would be, in their eloquence, language-conscious men; and many of the greatest Welsh-language poets, word-, language- and technique-conscious to the point of obsession, some of them, have been nurtured in an almost identical religious faith. He cultivated plainness and rejected ornament and decoration because he wished his social passion to be presented in its unadorned purity, free, direct, untrammelled by art or consideration. If he could have bodied forth his deepest feelings of love, compassion and indignation without using words at all he would have done so. And if 'there is a splendour must be left unsaid', it must be so because matters more urgent than natural splendour have to be dealt with and accorded their primacy and their expression.

The poet's last volume, *Selected Poems*, was published a fortnight before his death in 1953. During his lifetime Idris Davies never became well-known as a poet, not even here in Wales, his home country. The only national figures I ever heard him mention as having shown any interest at all in him or his work were Dr Thomas Jones, CH, one-time secretary to the Cabinet, and Nye Bevan. Dr Jones was himself a native of Rhymney, and Nye the member of Parliament of a neighbouring constituency. One reason for this indifference was Idris's complete inability to strike an attitude, to pose, to dramatize himself and his affairs. He was always so natural, so completely without glamour or flamboyance, so unassuming, that he never caught the public imagination as, say, Dylan Thomas and Caradoc Evans had done. He was no myth-maker and was never *news*; and if ever a case presented itself of the style being the man, that case was Idris Davies's. His verse is generally simple, direct, wholesome, unpretentious, without adornment, and so was its author. His gaiety and his complete lack of envy, and his endearing guilelessness brought him the affection of many friends; but he cultivated always the people he liked rather than the people he could use. I don't think I have ever received so powerfully from any other man the sense that Idris gave of being completely uncalculating and completely uncorrupted.

Sometimes he was a bit cagey in the presence of people he thought were trying to do him down on account of his rather – for an *English* poet of that period – unusual background.[5] And when his applications for teaching jobs in Wales were treated with indifference and coldness, or ignored altogether, he could write to me in bitterness, 'I have learnt, perhaps too late, that it's not what one does that matters but whom one knows . . . I should have grasped that long ago when I read Schopenhauer on the "web of Maya"'. For one so frank and guileless and so completely innocent of selfish foresight this was a bitter lesson. But his dominant mood nevertheless was one of cheerfulness and serenity. He was a lover of late nights, endless talk, laughter, cafés, gaiety, freedom and unhindered tramping about. But his Bohemianism – if that is the word – included a profound regard for soap and water and fresh linen. There was in fact always a rather scrubbed, wholesome look about him, clean and polished like that shine commonly seen on the pallid skins of colliers fresh from the varnish of a soapy bath. He liked simple pleasures, simple jokes, simple natures, simple relationships and what he thought was simple poetry. The effect of his directness upon myself was often to make me feel as complicated and involved as a Celtic capital. He could extract endless enjoyment from, say, a bus ride to Cardiff's Tiger Bay, and a simple meal in a dubious dockland café at the end of it. One evening in the early days of his dreadful last illness, he and I, wandering about together in Bute Street in the Cardiff Docks, met and chatted with for some time a group of Shoni Winwns men, the Breton onion-sellers who annually visit South Wales with their onion strings and their carrying poles. Idris treasured this encounter and when he became too weak, later, to move far from his bed, he often referred to it with pleasure and recalled the strange lingo involving English, French, Welsh and Breton in which our exchanges of goodwill were carried on.

A few weeks before his death, when he was very ill, I took him out for a ride in my car. My wife and his fiancée were with us. We all knew, except Idris himself, that he had only a very short time to live. On the high mountain road running across the bleak moorland near his home we stopped the car. At that altitude the strong breeze was tonic and Idris thought he felt strong enough to walk a little. My wife and I sat in the car while he and Morfydd went slowly down the empty road ahead of us. Seen thus from behind, in this bleak and deserted landscape of his poems, the once powerful and sturdy figure seemed to have shrunk to nothing, the clothes hung loose upon it, it looked frail and uncertain, like the body of an enfeebled old man. After a short distance the walk became too much for him and he was glad to turn back. Holding on to Morfydd's arm he slowly made his return up the road to the car, and gratefully entered it. This was the saddest thing I saw during our friendship.

In a letter after his death, T. S. Eliot his publisher said this of him:

Idris Davies was very modest about his work, unsure as to which were really his best poems. The *Selected Poems*, of course, I selected out of a good many . . . my own impression of his poems remains the same: that they are the best poetic document I know about a particular epoch in a particular place, and I think that they really have a claim to permanence. Whether a volume of his complete works is worth while I rather doubt. He was a fluent writer, and I think that what he has to say is very well worth saying indeed and is best said in a limited number of poems . . . There is great integrity, I think, about his work, and his subject-matter is something that he knew from A to Z. If all poets knew their proper material as he did, there would be less futile verses in the world.

He seemed to me always to be one of the meek and the merciful and the pure in heart.

DYLAN THOMAS

1914–1953

THE first work over the name of Dylan Thomas I ever saw was a poem, 'No Man Believes', which I read in the *Adelphi*, in September 1933, in the reference room of the Cardiff Central Library. I was at that time a school-teacher in the slum district near the centre of the city which I have already described, and my midday break I often spent reading the library's fine selection of contemporary periodicals, which included the *Criterion*, *This Quarter* and, of course, *The Adelphi*, to which about that time I was myself contributing poems and reviews. Early the next year, in the same magazine and in the same surroundings, I read my second Dylan Thomas poem, 'The Woman Speaks'.

These two pieces seemed to me so extraordinary, so strange, so new, so packed with poetic energy, so rich in promise, that my interest and admiration were aroused to the extent that I felt impelled to do what I had never done before and have never done since − I wrote to the editor expressing my sense of wonder and delight at this strange and beautiful work. Sir Richard Rees passed on my letter to Dylan, and in March 1934 I received from him my first communication written, rather like that letter of his own Mrs Amabel Owen in 'The Holy Six', 'in a backward hand', with the words 'lying back giddy':

5 Cwmdonkin Drive
Uplands
Swansea

Thank you for your appreciation of my two poems in the *Adelphi*. The 'Woman Speaks' but the young man writes, and your doubt as to my sex was quite complimentary, proving (or was it merely my uncommon name?) that I do not employ too masculine a pen.

You ask me to tell you about myself, but my life is so uneventful it is not worth recording. I am a writer of poems and stories (a story of mine is appearing in the *Adelphi* quite soon), who is trying – quite vainly – to dispute Murry's contention that the object in which the artist experiences the joy of losing himself, is no longer a recognised exchange for bread-and-butter, shelter, light, and warmth. On the economic level, I have no function.

At the moment I am attempting to form an anthology of English poems and stories written by contemporary Welshmen. So far I have decided nothing definite; but if, sometime in the near future, you wish to contribute to this anthology, I should be delighted to see some of your work. What is this 'Tiger Bay?'[1] Prose or poetry?

If you are ever in Swansea, do call up here; I shall be very pleased to see you. And if you have half an hour to spare, then I hope you'll send me along a letter.

Dylan Thomas.

It is perhaps easier to understand the tremendous impact of the early work of Dylan Thomas upon a person of my temperament and background if we recall what the poetic climate of the early and middle thirties was. The arriving poets were of course Auden, Spender and Day Lewis and their followers, writers who, to their credit, were passionately concerned with events at home and abroad, with the Spanish Civil War, with the rise of Fascism, with the state of Britain, with the sort of desperate poverty and unemployment I saw around me every day in my work, and with the stagnation of the great industrial areas, including the Welsh coalfields. They seemed to hate what I hated, poverty, war, cynical exploitation and mismanagement, and to desire, as I did, fraternity, justice and peace. And yet for their poetry I felt no great sympathy. Although much of it seems in retrospect quite romantic, at the time it often appeared, to me at least, excessively hard, unemotional, cerebral, the product of head rather than of heart; and also to be strangely divorced from and irrelevant to the actual situation it was concerned with, which I knew from first-hand experience.

But it was the work of these young poets, nevertheless, that I saw praised and quoted in the journals I most enjoyed and respected. So that when I first read Dylan Thomas's poetry in one of them, as I have described, the effect was overwhelming. His work seemed, although quite unconcerned with social, political and industrial problems, warm, romantic, non-intellectual, appealing to something in us below the level of consciousness, beneath our education and our culture, something primitive, elemental.

I was at that time a passionate admirer of the work of D. H. Lawrence, and I felt that Dylan Thomas, whoever he or she might be, provided in some ways a similar type of 'new thrill'. I say 'he or she', because in 1934 Dylan, then aged nineteen, was quite unknown, even in his native Wales, outside the small circle of his artistic friends in Swansea. The ancient Welsh tales, the *Mabinogion*, had been translated into English in my home town of Merthyr Tydfil by Lady Charlotte Guest, and part of this translation, as I mentioned earlier, I had read as a class-book in the grammar school there. But I had forgotten the obscure character named Dylan in the story of 'Math son of Mathonwy'; otherwise I would have guessed, before I wrote to Richard Rees, that a person bearing this name would be certainly male and probably Welsh. I knew very few writers then, and I was ignorant too of the hazards of meeting a poet whose work I had admired; so, after the exchange of two or three further letters, I accepted Dylan's invitation and one Saturday undertook the forty-odd mile drive from Cardiff to Swansea where Dylan was then living with his father and mother.

Mr John Malcolm Brinnin quotes in his book the surprise of a friend of Dylan in America confronted by the baggy, bulbous figure of the middle-ageing poet whom she had not seen for ten years. 'Oh, Dylan – the last time I saw you you were an *angel*'.[2]

In 1934, when I first saw him, there was something rather angelic about Dylan's appearance, angelic and tremendously endearing. He was very slim and rather small – above medium height for Wales, he claimed – five feet six and a half! The proportions of the bony structure of his head were not unlike those of the young Swinburne, i.e. all the development was in the brow and, although the lips were very full, the chin was meagre. His blob of a nose he seemed to feel required explanation, and he told me early in our friendship that it had acquired its strange, rather lumpy conformation as a result of an accident, a similar accident apparently to that which had befallen the infant Shandy in a different part of his anatomy. This explanation seemed to me on a par with the romantic reason given by d'Annunzio for his baldness, and I received it with a scepticism which I hope was well concealed; I felt duly rebuked when I heard Dylan's mother many years later independently confirm some of the story, at least, in an interview.

Dylan had fair, wavy hair roughly parted in the middle and pushed back from his broad forehead, and his large wide-open brown eyes were clear and lustrous. His complexion was pale, slightly pink, almost girlish, but his whole figure gave the impression of some inner toughness, so that one could not think of him as delicate, much less fragile. At our first meeting he was wearing a black polo-necked sweater and a pair of shabby grey trousers, the sort of intellectual mufti of the thirties.

I mentioned Swinburne above. Dylan himself thought he resembled the Emily Brontë of that portrait of the three sisters said to have been painted by their brother Branwell, and in the prominence and lustre of the girl's rather staring eyes there is undoubtedly some likeness to his own. To me, although the gaiety is lacking in the picture, his face resembled much more closely that of Hazlitt in his early self-portrait. The best likeness of Dylan himself ever painted seems to me the portrait by Alfred Janes, at least of Dylan young. The disproportionate elongation of the two Augustus Johns, although no doubt 'poetic', leaves out the fun of the face and the possibility of its ever degenerating into the podgy wreck it became later. How were the painters of the last years to suggest that the head before them had conceived 'Fern Hill' and 'Poem in October'?

In *Portrait of the Artist as a Young Dog* Dylan describes, with his customary self-deflation, the room in his parents' house where his early writing was done – the bedroom with the hot-water tank in the corner and pictures of the poets torn from his father's Christmas *Bookman* around the walls. But our first afternoon together we spent in the suburban parlour of 5 Cwmdonkin Drive, which seemed to contribute certain features to 'Especially when the October wind' outside, 'The wordy shapes of women, and the rows / Of the star-gestured children in the park'; inside, the wagging clock behind the pot of ferns on the mantelpiece. I greatly admired this poem the first time I read it, and thought the first stanza magnificent; but even then I felt that each succeeding stanza was rather a slight dilution than an intensification of the poetic effect, an experience I had later with certain other of Dylan's poems. Two words intrigued me in it in a special way; after a time I began to wonder whether 'rows' in the second stanza rhymed with 'crows' or with 'cows'. And the word 'sticks' in stanza one. In Llanstephan, which Dylan had known since childhood, there is a very well-known grove of trees below the castle called the Sticks, mentioned by Dylan in 'A Visit to Grandpa's' (*Portrait of the Artist as a Young Dog*), and I have often wondered whether he remembered this when he wanted in the poem a striking and unusual word to use instead of woods, copse or grove.

Dylan's conversation I found to be self-disparaging, iconoclastic, quick-witted, delightful. He imitated for me the talk of the naïve and Welshy Swansea art students discussing one another – ''E's not 'alf a good shader, aye'; and he told me he was to speak to the local literary group on 'Obscenity in Literature', for which address he had invented all the quotations and examples himself. But even more than by his actual conversation I was struck by his extreme awareness, his sensitiveness and response to every subtle change of mood and direction in our talk. I had never then met anyone with comparable gifts who possessed comparable charm, and I soon felt strongly that warm, sympathetic flow of which several of Dylan's friends have written or spoken. He appeared at will to be able to lap his friends in a gay and loving atmosphere. We talked mostly about poetry and prose – about short stories, that is, which seemed to interest Dylan very much indeed. And, after that conversational probing in which new acquaintances have to indulge, we found, I believe to the satisfaction of both of us, that our families had their origins in the same Llanstephan area of Carmarthenshire, and that several people still living in the village were known to the two of us. I did not know then, but I discovered later, that the graves of Dylan's people were alongside those of my own relatives in the burial ground of Capel Newydd, Llanybri, on the hill behind Llanstephan.

I had seen then only Dylan's poems, but that first afternoon he showed me some of his stories and he seemed anxious to know what I thought of them. I brought back to Cardiff with me, after one of our early meetings, typescript copies of, among others, 'The Mouse and the Woman', 'The Visitor' and 'The Enemies', the stories in fact which were later to appear in *The Map of Love*. Reading in 1952 the 'Author's Prologue' to the *Collected Poems*, I remembered vividly one of our meetings in Carmarthen town in 1935 when we discussed the phrase 'a woe in its beak' which Dylan had used in 'The Enemies', one of his earliest stories. It appeared again, slightly altered, in lines forty-two and forty-three of the second part of that astonishing *tour de force* that, almost twenty years later, opened his *Collected Poems*.

I was enchanted with these stories at the time; they seemed new, vital, strange, the reverse side of the obverse poetry. And the pastel drawings he had to show me too – destroyed, later, in the air-raids on London – fantastic, highly-coloured pictures full of starlight and milk and grotesque human or subhuman figures which might have served as illustrations for the stranger, dottier passages of, say, 'The Horse's Ha' or 'Prologue to an Adventure'. Poems, stories and pictures all obviously came out of the same strange highly coloured and haunted world and I marvelled at the fecundity, the vigour and the consistency of this imagination, and at the warmth and sweetness of the character which went with it.

One further thing Dylan showed me – a volume of verse by a very attractive young woman whose name was new to me, but whom Dylan appeared to know well and whose photograph he showed me – Miss Pamela Hansford Johnson. Her book was the first of a projected series to be published by the *Sunday Referee*, in whose poetry column Dylan had appeared several times. The second volume of the series was the black bombshell known to us now as *Eighteen Poems*.

In 'The Scholars' W. B. Yeats appears to write down very sharply those who 'have no strange friend', and I felt after meeting Dylan that I now no longer qualified for the Yeatsian strictures. I did not know it at the time, but my first meeting with Dylan took place during what Professor Ralph Maud calls 'that amazing burst of creativity in the two years prior to *Eighteen Poems* (1934)', when he did so much striking work in poetry and prose, when he in fact wrote in one form or another nearly half his published poems.³ Some of the things I learnt about him that first afternoon which impressed me very much I have already mentioned, as that he was to have a book of poems published before very long. Others were that he hoped to go to London soon to make a living as a writer; that he had high hopes of his anthology of work by Welshmen writing in English; that Sir Richard Rees had returned a poem to him as being too good for the *Adelphi* and with the advice that he should submit it forthwith to the *Criterion* – surely an act of unparalleled editorial abnegation. I had enjoyed my first meeting with Dylan immensely, feeling we had a bond in such things as our Welsh backgrounds, our approval in general of the work appearing in the *Adelphi* and the *Criterion*, and in our admiration for Lawrence, Hopkins, Joyce, Yeats and Wyndham Lewis. The atmosphere of Dylan's home I sensed to be very similar to that of my own parents', or at least the differences between them were not sufficiently marked to be observed or felt in one visit.

Although Dylan told me in an early letter that he was not really unemployed, since he had never been employed, this was not true because after leaving Swansea Grammar School he worked for eighteen months as a reporter on a local newspaper, the *South Wales Daily Post*. Later he spoke freely about this period of his life and described how he had once to report a case of suicide in which a man had cut his throat sitting on the seat of the outside jakes. I do not think it need surprise us, knowing his school record, that Dylan did not go on to a university. I doubt whether he had sufficient exam-passing stamina – he certainly had not the interest – to get himself through the necessary matriculation which was at that time normally required for entrance to most universities.

Dylan's parents I had found extremely cordial and hospitable. His father in particular seemed gratified that at least one compatriot, even one as insignificant as myself, had hailed from the outside world the talent of his son, and had taken the trouble to drive down to Swansea to meet him. He did not speak very much, but he conveyed his satisfaction by his smiles of welcome and goodwill, and by his readiness to listen to what must have seemed to him a good deal of callow nonsense. From beginning to end – I saw him for the last time when Dylan took me across to the Pelican, the house he occupied in Laugharne, shortly before his death – I found this strange and sickly man invariably cordial and pleasant and deeply interested in whatever Dylan and I had to say. Dylan sometimes privately made sharp or jeering remarks about his father's restlessness and perpetual dissatisfaction, but his profoundest feelings about him are surely expressed in his poetry.

One of the first things that struck me about Mrs Thomas was that, no doubt under pressure from Dylan himself, she pronounced his name *Dillun,* or even *Dill'n,* in the manner, I learnt later, of the poet's Swansea and English friends. Welsh speakers normally pronounce the word *Dull-an,* with the accent of course on the first syllable, and I found at first the anglicized pronunciation grating and repellent, like hearing a Frenchman called *Jeen.* Mrs Thomas seemed a much less complicated person than her husband, the frustrated poet, the disappointed academic, the atheistical nephew of the celebrated preacher.[4] She was motherly and kind in a simple direct fashion, perhaps a little snobbish; her pride in Dylan was to the end unclouded. It seemed to me the pride of a mother in a good son rather than in a famous one. Sometimes her naïveté embarrassed him. Once I remember him, recently returned from one of his early visits to London, recounting in her presence the names of some of the famous poets and writers he had met, people like T. S. Eliot, Stephen Spender, Roy Campbell, Wyndham Lewis. 'And Mr —', added his mother with great pride, naming a literary politician better known then perhaps than any of those he had mentioned. Dylan showed extreme annoyance. 'Oh, he doesn't count', he said testily. 'He's nobody'. I sympathized with him deeply. How could anyone be so insensitive as even to think of, much less mention before a new and *Criterion*-reading friend, a pedestrian, moneymaking scribbler of the lowbrow class of Mr —, when the discussion was about such glamorous figures as T. S. Eliot, Stephen Spender and so on. Mothers could be quite insupportable.

The Welsh language, at the end of the nineteenth and the beginning of the twentieth century, was associated in the minds of many Welsh-men with a peasant background from which they wished to dissociate themselves, rather than with a splendid and ancient literature and a proud and independent way of life. To what extent this was the attitude of Dylan's parents I do not know. Both of them were Welsh-speaking, but I believe that like many Welsh people in suburbia they had become more used to speaking English. I have often wondered what would have happened if this were not so, if Dylan's father, instead of becoming an English teacher, had become a teacher of Welsh as, with his intensely Welsh Carmarthenshire background, he might easily have done. The language of the Thomas home in Swansea would then almost certainly have been Welsh, and Dylan might have turned out to be a Welsh-language poet. And with his passion for words, his copious language, his endless patience, his welcoming of metrical disciplines, what a superb *cynganeddwr* he would have been. But no international reputation for him then, no triumphant American visits and no packed poetry readings, no vast gramophone record and book sales, no Dylan Thomas industry. Only a few National Eisteddfod Chairs and Crowns in some suburban parlour, and a Welsh D.Litt. at sixty.

Dylan never seems in fact to have got beyond the greetings stage of the Welsh language, and of Welsh poetry he seemed to know nothing. I never heard him refer to any aspect of *cerdd dafod*, and the only Welsh-language poet I ever heard him mention was Crwys, the Rev. Crwys Williams, at one time the Arch-druid. But this mention had nothing to do with literature; it arose through talk about the Williams family who lived in Swansea, some members of which Dylan knew slightly. Several English critics have from time to time credited Dylan with a know-ledge of Welsh metrics, but I feel sure that the few traces of *cynghanedd* in his work appear there by accident,[5] or as a result of the influence of Hopkins, whose knowledge of this involved study was considerable. We know from his public readings that Dylan's acquaintance with English and American poetry was extensive, but it seems to me that no evidence exists to show that Welsh poetry could mean anything at all to him. But one feature of classical Welsh metrics he did consciously employ in his poetry, as Professor Maud and others have shown us. This is the counting of syllables per line instead of feet. In 1939 I wrote an article in *Life and Letters To-day* on 'Hopkins and Welsh Prosody', in which I mentioned this fact about *cerdd dafod*. I sometimes wonder if Dylan got his idea of basing his lines on a count of syllables, rather than on a count of feet, from it. I know he was a reader of and a contributor to the magazine at the time. Counting syllables was in itself of course nothing new to him; he had been doing it pretty strictly in *Eighteen Poems*. But there the iambic foot was nearly always the rhythmic basis of his line in a way it was not when in his later work a count of syllables replaced a count of accents. Dylan's reason for this substitution was almost certainly, I should say, his desire to break away from that heavy regular iambic beat which characterized so much of *Eighteen Poems* and *Twenty-five Poems*, and which appeared at the time to be obsessive.

Dylan's need for some strict metrical discipline reveals itself, I think, in such undertakings as the rhyme-scheme of his 'Author's Prologue' to the *Collected Poems*, in the diamond and wine-glass shapes and the internal rhyming of *Deaths and Entrances*. I have sometimes wished he had absorbed, as Hopkins did, a thorough knowledge of the *cynganeddion* and used it in his English verse; I wish that, instead of distrusting this knowledge, he had acquired it and experimented with it, adapting *cynghanedd* to traditional English metres in the way the late T. Gwynn Jones, one of the greatest of Welsh poets, skilfully grafted it upon a variation of Welsh-language blank verse. Dylan, it seems to me, is the only modern poet writing in English with the natural equipment to have undertaken the discipline.

After our first meeting I continued to see Dylan, sometimes in Swansea, sometimes in London, or Aberystwyth, or Llanstephan or Laugharne. I read poems by him in the *Listener*, the *Criterion* and Geoffrey Grigson's *New Verse*. Some of these he gave me in typescript. One, 'Jack of Christ', was a poem of about twenty stanzas of varying lengths which I printed in the *Western Mail* in 1960 when I was looking

after the paper's poetry section. This, I believe, is the only occasion the
poem has appeared in print:[6]

> For lack of faith I fell upon the desert
> Where eagles tenanted the single palm;
> Where was no God I heard His windy visit,
> And saw the spider weave Him on her loom.
> And where God was His holy house was sculptured
> A frozen lie upon the rising land.

I think Dylan was very early conscious of the uniqueness and
greatness of his gift. He had read carefully, there in his Swansea home,
and measured himself against the young poets (most of them older than
himself) appearing in the highbrow literary magazines of the early
thirties, and he knew in his heart he had nothing to fear by comparison
with any of them. But he was young, and this confidence in the
superiority of his own powers was subject to misgivings and required
reassurance. Known poets he did not really fear, but what about
someone *unknown*, another like himself working in the obscurity of a
provincial or suburban home? He questioned me about this and asked if
I thought it possible, in the circumstances of the time, for a good poet
to be entirely overlooked, to remain undiscovered and unpublished;
did I think that there could be anyone of any importance writing
poetry of whom the literary world was ignorant, as it had been ignorant
of the existence of Hopkins? I said I hardly thought this possible for a
lyric poet, but what about a poet engaged upon very lengthy works for
which it might be difficult to find room in the literary periodicals, and
which publishers might be reluctant to take on? Dylan agreed this
might be a possibility. He seemed strangely reassured by my answer. It
was clear that the belief in his own unchallengeable pre-eminence
was of enormous importance to him at that early period of his poetic
life.

I read poem after poem in those days with ever-increasing wonder
and admiration. Although I felt so great an affection for their author as a
person, I do not believe that my liking for him in any way contributed
to this admiration, or influenced at all my judgment of his work. Judgment indeed was hardly involved in this strange and overwhelming
experience. The effect of these poems was like an enchantment, going
far beyond the usual pleasure which one expects from poetry. I knew
with absolute certainty that this *was* poetry. And I know that this sense
of excitement, indeed of ecstasy, with which I first read such poems as

'Light breaks where no sun shines', cannot be discounted in any final
assessment I might try to make of this work.

One question greatly intrigued me then and still does. How was it
that Dylan, a schoolboy, provincial, inexperienced, had come to write in
that particular way, to evolve at so early an age a style of such power and
startling originality? The politically-conscious poets of the time used
the vocabulary of an advanced industrial society; they brought in
references to science, inventions, factories, machinery, Marx and Freud,
the class war and psycho-analysis. Regarded as the representative poets
of the age, they captured the poetry-reading public. But Dylan's themes
in contrast were almost never political and his vocabulary was basic,
old-fashioned in a sense. Not old-fashioned like Huw Menai's, with
'ne'er', and 'yore', and ''neath', but with words like 'milk', 'blood',
'finger', 'bone', 'honey', 'shells' and so on predominating over 'neural',
and 'strata', and 'process'. The poets under whose influence Idris Davies
and Huw Menai began to write were easily discernible – Housman in
the one case and the *Golden Treasury* romantics in the other. But Dylan's
'influences', whatever they were, did not reveal themselves at all in his
first book. It was not until many years later that he began to show that
at some time or another he had been reading Hopkins and Yeats. At
twenty he seemed fully-equipped, entirely original, completely mature
stylistically and indebted to no one. His own account of the influences
behind his work and the writers he had imitated tells us, I should think,
precisely nothing – the list includes Sir Thomas Browne, Blake,
Baroness Orczy, Marlowe, *Chums*, the Bible and 'Eskimo Nell'. This is
surely one of the unsolved mysteries of Dylan's poetry, how and why
this change came about in him from the schoolboy poet of sixteen plus,
contributing poems, light verse and parodies to the Swansea Grammar
School magazine, to the fully-formed poet of *Eighteen Poems*, which
was written, together with a great amount of other material, and
published before the next three years were out.

Not many months after our first meeting in Swansea, Dylan left home
for London to try to earn some sort of living as a writer, or literary
journalist. This was in November 1934. Through Geoffrey Grigson, an
early admirer, he got some reviewing to do for the *Morning Post*, and he
also reviewed for *The Adelphi*, as I shall show.

I suppose Dylan's parents, not having had the expense of keeping
him at a university, were subsidizing him in these early days. But

whatever the economics of his position, I feel sure that payment for his lodgings was no very heavy drain upon his finances. When I mentioned in a letter to him that I hoped to be spending a holiday in London he sent me detailed instructions of how to reach the 'ancient baroque architecture of [his] residence'. He lived in fact in a huge, empty, resounding, barn-like villa, entirely without floor coverings and almost without furniture. The landlady, who appeared to be a drug addict, wandered indifferently about the house with her hair down her back and a buff-coloured cigarette drooping from her mouth. Sharing these rooms with him at the time were two Swansea friends, Mervyn Levy the painter and Alfred Janes, whose portrait of the poet in the National Museum of Wales, at Cardiff, gives so admirable an impression of him.

But deplorable as this place was considered as lodgings, it was in some ways congenial, a sort of meeting place where young writers and painters dropped in to talk. I remember very well one afternoon sitting with half a dozen others in a semicircle on the living-room floor – there were no chairs – listening to Dylan, perched on top of a chest of drawers, reading aloud the typescript of a review he had just completed for *The Adelphi*.[7] The editor had sent him five or six slim volumes of poetry to write about, and Dylan had treated the review very maliciously, but very wittily, in the form of a tour round a zoo. He conducted the reader through a fantastic menagerie, the cages of which were the volumes of poetry, each containing some absurd, mangy or misshapen freak, and ending his tour and his review with the words, 'And this, ladies and gentlemen, is the wogga-wogga bird'. But amusing and fundamentally perceptive as this performance was, and much as we laughed at the devastating accuracy of the analyses, we protested that young poets could not publicly be treated with ridicule in this way, and, finally, Dylan agreed. I never saw the review in question in print.

Dylan, it was obvious, even after a short time in London, was becoming well-known and popular; not well-known yet of course to the general public, or even to the provincial readers of poetry, but to the serious writers and painters of the metropolis and to their hangers-on and to the artistic and literary dead-beats who inhabited pre-war Bohemia. The first relative increase in his fame, I suppose, occurred after the publication of *Eighteen Poems*, late in 1934. I was in London with him soon after his book appeared – he presented me with a signed copy – and it was a delight to me to witness the excitement and enthusiasm with which the book, and its author, were received. I did not feel altogether happy, however, as time went on, with the prodigal manner in which Dylan seemed to be prepared to bestow his friendship. He was friendly with everyone, irrespective of talent, character, charm or any other attraction, and I could not help feeling that more discrimination and reserve might have benefited him. But a less expansive Dylan would have been a fundamentally different Dylan, more fortunate perhaps, but less fascinating and strange.

I have tried to say what the effect of individual poems in this first volume was upon me. In time the books about Dylan and his work began to appear, and several of these I read, some with irritation, some with astonishment, some with a sense of deepened understanding of Dylan's poetry. One of these last was Professor Olson's *Dylan Thomas*; but the book also undertakes a task which, although no doubt inevitable, for me at least, must always be entirely unrewarding.[8] The professor, I believe, credits Dylan with knowledge he never possessed, and he does this in an attempt to make literal sense of poems that need no such paraphrase. For me, the best of Dylan's early poems are pure sensation, they have in fact achieved the condition of music; what I experienced when I first read 'Light breaks where no sun shines' seemed to me an almost identical emotion to that aroused by the high strings in the first movement of *Eine kleine Nachtmusik* – sort of transport of ecstasy. I believe this thrill, this pure sensation, to represent the highest – not the only – value of lyric poetry, and those who are able to provide it I regard as the greatest lyric poets. Professor Olson gives a very ingenious paraphrase of 'I see the boys of summer'. The odd thing is that it is the professor's paraphrase which sounds incoherent, disrupted and obscure, and the poem, intellectually impenetrable, which possesses radiance, wholeness and harmony. And I cannot help feeling a little cheered when Professor Olson thinks stanza four of the poem describes 'one aspect of death' and another interpreter says it 'suggests the act of birth'.

If I were asked in the excitement of my first encounter with this poem what its meaning was, my answer would have been something like that of William Morris questioned, after a public meeting, on his interpretation of Marx's theory of surplus value. 'I don't know what Marx meant by his theory of surplus value', Morris is reputed to have answered, 'and I'm damned if I want to know'.

One thing that is bound to strike a Welshman reading some of Dylan's English and American critics is their credulity and ignorance where the poet's homeland is concerned. How far Dylan himself was responsible for the bizarre image of Wales entertained by them is another matter. His own knowledge and understanding of the country, particularly in his early days, were by no means full; brought up in suburban and English-speaking Swansea, he knew very little about the mining valleys, the north, or the cultural life of Welsh Wales. But his marvellous comic invention was often capable of supplying to some extent at least his deficiencies of knowledge and experience. I once heard him describe to a ring of middle-class English Bohemians, the daily stripping and bathing of Welsh miners before the kitchen fire, an act which I doubt if Dylan had ever witnessed. His description transformed what was then a commonplace and decorous domestic necessity into a sort of unbridled sexual rout embodying all that was most goatish in the characters of Caradoc Evans, together with the more wayward antics of the Wragby gamekeeper.

Professor Tedlock's admirable symposium[9] has many examples of what I mean. Francis Scarfe, in 'Dylan Thomas: A Pioneer', traces the biblical references in *Twenty-five Poems* to 'memories of hot-gospelling and the diabolical grimace of the Welsh Bethel'. 'Hot-gospelling' and 'diabolical grimace', as ideas associated with the decorous Swansea nonconformity of Dylan's childhood, are so completely absurd that one wonders what prompted Mr Scarfe to think of them.[10] Susanne Roussillat tells us that in the thirties deacons in Wales 'had the right of discussing or condemning your private life' – a right claimed, I can assure Miss Roussillat, not only by deacons, not only in the thirties, and not only in Wales. Karl Shapiro writes of 'primitive fertility cults still extant in Wales'. I have wondered a good deal what this can mean. Perhaps Mr Shapiro has heard of the Horn of Plenty, presented to the Chief Bard (a nonconformist minister) by a respectable local matron during the Eisteddfod! Professor Elder Olson, a really fine critic as I have said before, claims that 'consciously or unconsciously, [Dylan] is in the tradition of the great Welsh enigmatic poets of the fourteenth century'. The great Welsh poets of the fourteenth century are, I suppose, Dafydd ap Gwilym, Llywelyn Goch ap Meurig Hen, Iolo Goch and Gruffudd Gryg. Why has Professor Olson chosen to describe them as 'enigmatic', as though enigma was their outstanding quality? And in what sense is Dylan in their 'tradition'? Surely this idea deserves more to convince us of its validity than the dozen lines or so the professor gives to it.

I have often wished, as I suggested before, that Dylan *had* known more about Welsh Wales and cared more about Welsh literary tradition.

Might not this have given him a conception of the poet other than the highly romantic one which seemed to obsess him? He early abandoned the attempt to *look* like a poet, but the idea of the wild and petted man apart seemed to remain with him for a long time, perhaps until his death, the man from whom ordinary responsibility and participation (what we see in the lives of Yeats and Hopkins and Eliot, for example) cannot be expected, who possesses nothing, no religion, no politics, no community, no thought, nothing, only that one gift which marks him off from the majority of his fellow men. I think it is more difficult for a Welsh-language poet to see himself in this way, as a man cut off, because poetry is much more a part of everyday life in Welsh Wales than it is in England – and it was to England, or rather London, that Dylan always looked. I do not wish to give the impression, as some Welsh writers have done, that every quarryman, miner, roadman and farm labourer in Wales is dedicated to poetry either as reader or writer or both. But it does seem to be true that one would be much more likely to find poetry lovers among the people I have listed in Wales than in England. I remember the story of what happened when three Welsh patriots, a school-teacher, a university lecturer and a minister of religion, set fire by way of protest before the Second World War to buildings belonging to the RAF bombing school in Llŷn, Caernarfonshire.[11] They were arrested and taken to the local police station where they passed the time awaiting their appearance in court by reciting modern Welsh-language poetry to one another. When the memory of one of them failed in the quotation of a famous sonnet, the policeman in charge of the three was able to prompt him correctly. This proves nothing of course, but on the basis of it one would be inclined to bet that the number of Williams Parry-quoting cops in rural Wales in 1936 was considerably higher than the number of Eliot-quoters in the same situation in England. Another incident occurs to me which illustrates what I have been trying to describe about the way poetry is part of community life in Welsh Wales. After an address I once delivered to the Welsh Academy on the emergence of the Anglo-Welsh, I was tackled by one of the most famous of Welsh-language poets who asked me what community I thought I, and those like me, i.e. Anglo-Welsh writers, were writing for. I said I wrote for whoever would read me, and that every poet, in Wordsworth's words, must anyway create the audience by which he is to be enjoyed. This reply seemed to puzzle him. The ideas of poetry and community were indissolubly united in his mind. It was obvious that he knew who his own audience was, i.e.

the Welsh-speaking community of whose background and standards he was acutely aware, and that he was conscious as a poet of writing for this community; that he had not in fact to create a body of readers because one existed for him already. This question of the poet and his community I find interesting, and I think it important. I sometimes wonder if the powerful self-destructive impulse in Dylan's life was not somehow mixed up with it, with his sense of being cut off, with having rejected one community and not having found another to take its place. One agonizes over many explanations when one sees sweet life being poured down the drain.

Dylan's charm and friendliness did not seem to someone as withdrawn as myself, as I have already suggested, an unmixed blessing in the Bohemia in which he thought proper as a poet to live. Watching his progress, early in his career, from one admiring group to another, I felt that, like his own 'ram rod', he was in real danger of 'dying of welcome'.

There were, I think, three principal reasons for his widespread popularity, apart from his characteristically Welsh desire to please. The first was the warmth and sensitivity of his nature, the loving charm which I have already tried to describe. The second was the fact that he possessed remarkable powers of conversation, and could be warm-hearted friend, perceptive critic, *raconteur* and buffoon as the need arose. He was certainly the best conversationalist I had then met; not perhaps the best talker, but the one whose wit and imagination and quickness to take a point most completely enchanted his listeners, and whose brilliance and ability to listen with absorbed interest stimulated and did not silence them.

The third reason for Dylan's popularity was that he seemed to have no unacceptable convictions, no strongly-held principles of any sort. In all the variations of his environment he seemed a chameleon figure, always the complete conformist. There was neither in himself nor in his work any stumbling-block, no 'sword' in the New Testament sense, to separate him from those around him. I listened to him applaud in one company opinions which he would deride in another. I felt there must no doubt be a certain amount of accommodation in our social behaviour, but Dylan's changes of front I heard at first with amazement and dismay. One of the heroes of the nonconformist pantheon is the man who stands alone, the Daniel figure who dares to do and to utter what he thinks right though the heavens fall. Measured by this sort of standard Dylan seemed to have no courage at all, to be entirely accommodating and compliant. A more charitable view would have seen him playing at that time a heroic part in a war of conquest. He, very young, very inexperienced, a provincial outsider, was engaged single-handed in the subjugation of sophisticated, sceptical and prejudiced literary London. His weapons, apart from a poetic talent superior to that of almost any person he came in contact with, were charm, warmth, friendliness, tact. I should not, I know now, have heard his changes of front with so much astonishment and impatience. But the young are intolerant and demand perfection of those they love and admire. Anyway Dylan had the balm for that sort of irritation too. Five minutes alone with him again and his warmth and sympathy made one feel that all he had said apropos of some controversy, pro and contra, was of no importance at all, and that all he cared about ultimately was the sweetness of personal relations. Perhaps this was really so.

Dylan in those early days in London lived, as I have suggested, a very conventional life, conventional that is of course by the standards of Bohemia, not of Cwmdonkin Drive and the Swansea Uplands. He was never the man to drop a brick. Aware and sensitive, he quickly learnt the taboos of his new Bohemian milieu; and he seems to have decided, as is well known by now, to play a role familiar and acceptable to it, that of the roaring boy, or rather the roaring poet. It would be utterly absurd to suggest that this was a part uncongenial to him; the thoroughness and success with which he played it proved that his self-casting was very close to nature. But I cannot help feeling that there was an element of deliberation and defensive acting in his behaviour at first. I thought his drinking and irresponsibility belonged to a phase which, when he had established himself, he could abandon. What I did not realize was that Dylan for some, to me, inscrutable reason had early determined to ride the runaway horse, to become the cut-off poet, rootless and uncommitted.[12] 'Very few eyes', says Keats, 'can see the mystery of a man's life'. Mine are certainly not among those that saw and understood the mystery of Dylan's.

I read somewhere a wise saying of Goethe, 'Beware of the thing you desire in youth, because in middle life you will get it'. If it is true that Dylan aimed at creating this myth about himself of irresponsibility and dissipation, he might be said to have achieved it, almost literally, with a vengeance.

Particularly in his early days as a writer, as I have suggested, Dylan seemed very interested indeed in short stories, both as reader and writer, and two of the authors for whom he expressed great admiration were T. F. Powys and Caradoc Evans – 'The great Caradoc Evans' one of the characters in *Portrait of the Artist as a Young Dog* calls him.

A certain dreamlike quality, as others have observed, was apt to exist in one's relations with Dylan, and I cannot be quite sure when our trip to Aberystwyth to meet Caradoc took place. All I know with certainty, for a reason which will emerge presently, is that it happened during or before 1936.[13] Dylan left the arrangements of the visit to me and I set out from Cardiff in my car and picked him up in Swansea and then we proceeded together north to Aberystwyth. He seems to have had a weakness for wearing clothes – shirts, trousers, suits – belonging to other people, and on this occasion we made a permanent swop of our pork-pie hats.

It was on this trip too, during a discussion of methods of writing, that he told me he never made notes of any sort for use in his poems and stories, that all his writing was done with the pencil in his hand and the exercise book open before him. Note-taking, he thought, was part of the trade of the novelist rather than of the poet – his stories, I take it, he regarded then as an extension almost of his poetry. I have never heard of the existence of any notebooks of Dylan's like those Hopkins kept for jotting down lines, words, images and ideas, so it seems probable that he observed this rather austere practice throughout his life. This, I suppose, constitutes the surrealist element in his work, this dependence upon what was 'given'.

I recall very little of what was said at our visit to Caradoc, although I found many years later that both Caradoc and his wife remembered the actual meeting very well. What I do recall very vividly is the Aberystwyth hotel bedroom where we spent the night. Dylan lay smoking cigarettes on the bed while I told him a story. It was new to him, and he was enthralled by it, because the matter, the substance, of what I was saying was such, he immediately and instinctively recognized, as would supply the material for one of his own short stories – the poetic-fantastic type he was writing then. The story was the true one, well-known in Wales, about Dr William Price, the druidical Chartist of Llantrisant, Glamorgan, the nudist mountain chanter and wearer of hieratical coms, who at eighty-four burned the body of his little illegitimate son Jesus Christ on the hilltop. (The prosecution of Dr Price for this act made legal history; his acquittal legalized cremation.) Dylan was eager to know everything I could tell him about the eccentric doctor and his strange theories.

When he got off the bed he found a pattern of holes spreading in the sheets which in his absorption he had burnt with his cigarette ends, and he began a Lucky Jim-like manoeuvring to try to conceal them. The story which eventually resulted from all this was of course very different from the one I had told Dylan. It was called 'The Burning Baby', first published in *Contemporary Poetry and Prose* in 1936.

Dylan's short stories were published in four separate books, *viz. The Map of Love* (1939), *Portrait of the Artist as a Young Dog* (1940), *A Prospect of the Sea* (1955) and the American *Adventures in the Skin Trade* (1955), which, as well as the fragment of a novel of that name, contains twenty of Dylan's stories. The thirty or three dozen stories of his that we have can be roughly divided into two groups: the early, more 'poetic' and fantastic *Map of Love* type, and the humorous autobiographical work to be found chiefly in the *Portrait of the Artist as a Young Dog*. Stories like 'The Visitor' and 'The Enemies' in *The Map of Love* seemed to me at my first encounter with them to achieve something new and strange. I was fascinated by their romantic and mysterious atmosphere and the brilliance of their phrasing. A story like 'The Dress' seemed to me then, and still does, very remarkable indeed; considered as the work of a boy of nineteen it is staggering.

Dylan recognized, I think, that the modern short story of writers like D. H. Lawrence, H. E. Bates and Liam O'Flaherty, has in some ways stronger affinities with the poem than with, say, the novel which, as a work of prose narrative, it might be supposed to resemble more closely; that its impulse is in fact lyrical. Between his early stories and his early poems there are marked resemblances. We see in both the same pre-occupation with language. In *Eighteen Poems* and the prose of *The Map of Love* we find the same themes of sex and death, childhood, adolescence, the flesh. We can recognize ideas and images used in both stories and poems – the tossed-up ball, the triangular winds, the fingered hair, the kissing poles, the multiplying grains of sand. We see the similarity of the vocabulary often, the appearance in both prose and verse of such images as the weather-cock and the dolphined sea, and the scarecrow, and the words 'wind', 'sea', 'milk', 'stars', 'heart', 'wax', 'files', 'candle', 'oiled', 'tick-ing', 'globes', some of them used frequently. We see the same tendency to obscurity and in many stories the same almost total lack of humour.

All the prose in *The Map of Love* I did not admire very much. The title story I found shapeless and diffuse. The version of 'The Mouse and the Woman' he showed me at one of our early meetings I thought excellent, and I recall being greatly moved by the strange beauty of some of the sections; section thirteen was one in particular. But for publication he very much enlarged the story and made it to me almost unreadable. 'The Orchards', I remember, another story of this rather inflated poetic type, gave him a good deal of trouble to complete. He showed me the script up to the point where Marlais the poet, at that time called Peter, had written two words, 'sea' and 'fire', on a clean page. Dylan there was at a standstill, in that unhappy situation of young writers who have plenty to say but nothing to say it about. 'I don't know what the devil to do with him now', he said. In such an impasse he could even fall back on describing the pencil he was using, 'the tower of wood and lead' and the 'half-moon of his thumbnail rising and setting behind the leaden spire'. But I believe stories of this type became more and more difficult for him to write, and I doubt if he attempted them after about 1938, at least not in prose. Perhaps 'A Winter's Tale' and 'Ballad of the Long-legged Bait' are such stories in verse; just as 'The Hunchback in the Park' is a *Portrait of the Artist as a Young Dog* type of situation similarly treated.

Dylan very early urged me to write short stories, and in 1937 my first collection, *The Blue Bed*, appeared.[14] In Llanstephan in, I think it was, the summer of 1938, I mentioned to Caitlin Thomas that I had started to write a second volume, a series of short stories about childhood, or at least about what was once known as 'enfance'. She seemed very surprised and told me that Dylan had already started doing exactly the same thing. His were the autobiographical stories which in 1940 appeared as *Portrait of the Artist as a Young Dog*. My own stories were collected into *The Water Music* and published in 1944.

Dylan's first three books, *Eighteen Poems*, *Twenty-five Poems* and *The Map of Love* were almost as laughless as chess. But there were experiences and passages in his own life — humorous, bathetic, bizarre — which could not well be treated in his type of poetry or in the highly-charged poetic style of his early stories. To those who knew him personally his abundant and imaginative humour was one of his most endearing qualities. It was a rich experience to be involved with him in some misadventure and to hear him describe afterwards to his friends what he claimed to have happened, to watch the whole commonplace event growing in vivid detail, fantasy and general dottiness under the play of his strange humour. But it was not until the appearance of *Portrait of the Artist as a Young Dog* that this vital and creative side of his personality found a place in his writing.

This book, *Portrait of the Artist as a Young Dog*, contained many features new to his work. It was unobscure, conventionally punctuated, written in short paragraphs of plain English. In it Dylan made his first personal appearance, and his act was largely a comic one. And the introduction of humour to his work was perhaps the first of the steps which were in the next few years to transform the obscure highbrow young poet into the famous writer whose death was news in two continents.

From about 1938 the cleavage between Dylan's poetry and his prose seemed to become more marked, although the same basic material might still be used in both story and poem. The farm called Gorsehill in 'The Peaches' and the unnamed farm in 'A Prospect of the Sea' are both surely the Fern Hill of the poem. But in the prose we have the humour, the fears, the embarrassments, the farce even of one of the poet's visits to the Llangain farm, while in the poem we have a distillation, a marvellous quintessence, of many such visits; out of his memories he creates a paean of childhood and innocency unaffected by the devastating realization of time.

'When we came to Llanstephan village at the top of the hill', Dylan wrote in *Portrait of the Artist as a Young Dog*, '[my grandfather] left the cart by the Edwinsford Arms . . . We went to look at the churchyard and the sea, and sat in the wood called the Sticks, and stood on the concert platform in the middle of the wood where visitors sang on summer nights . . .'

I had spent my school holidays since childhood in Llanstephan, largely because my father's family had come from the next parish of Llanybri. Dylan, when I first knew him, stayed at Blaencwm, from which several of his letters to various people are addressed. Blaencwm is a cluster of houses just off the Carmarthen–Llanstephan road where his uncle, David Rees, the husband of his mother's sister, had converted two small cottages into one. Farther along the road is the Fern Hill of the famous poem, and a few miles from Llanstephan, across the estuary of the Tâf, is Laugharne.

The first time Dylan and I visited the ancient township together we walked from Llanstephan, which stands at the mouth of the Towy, over the great headland, called Parc yr Arglwydd (The Lord's Park) and came down on to the picturesque and deserted flats at the mouth of the next river to pour itself into Carmarthen Bay, namely the Tâf. In this beautiful and romantic stretch of country wild life abounded and Dylan mentions and describes in the poems he was to write later some of the creatures living there, the herons, the hawks, the owls and the dabs in the river.

A small empty stone house with a bell in its roof stood beside the Tâf on the Llanstephan side, and anyone wishing to cross over to Laugharne, which could be seen on the opposite bank, was expected to ring the bell and thus bring the ferryman over the tidal estuary in his boat.[15] I cannot remember if this was Dylan's first visit ever to Laugharne. It was almost certainly his first for many years, as his obvious unfamiliarity with his surroundings showed.

This ferry across to Laugharne is no longer in use. In the thirties the ferryman was Jack Roberts, a well-known character in the Laugharne, Llanybri, Llanstephan area. As he rowed Dylan and me across the wide river mouth we could see before us upon the red cliff that 'patch / Work ark', that 'seashaken house / On a breakneck of rocks', the Boat House, where Dylan was later to live, off and on, for many years. Jack Roberts, ferryman and fisherman, and his remarkable family occupied the house next door, standing a little lower down on the cliff, at the water's edge.

We landed, explored the township and had tea at Brown's, surely his first visit to an hotel he has since made known on both sides of the Atlantic. We went through the graveyard and into the ancient parish church of St Martin. It is in that graveyard, under the simplest of wooden crosses, that Dylan now lies buried.

Perhaps it was from people like Victor Neuberg, of the *Sunday Referee*, who published his early poems, and who was once the associate of Aleister Crowley, that Dylan had got his ideas of demonism. Anyway in that dim old parish church of Laugharne, with its history of honourable association with Welsh religion and education, he wanted me to say that I could feel an atmosphere of evil around us, that I could sense oozing from the sombre walls, almost, the wickedness of the thousands who through the centuries had worshipped in it, especially of those satanic rectors who, while pretending to worship Christ, in their hearts celebrated the Black Mass.

I didn't believe a word of this, and neither did Dylan. He might be interested in strange ideas like 'Crowlianity' and strange behaviour like that of the druidical Dr Price, for the purpose of his stories, but there was very little of the crank or eccentric about him himself. As a dresser, as eater, husband, citizen, he was pretty normal in his ideas, *l'homme moyen sensuel* rather than the social pioneer or the conscious liver of the experimental life.

I always associate with this visit to Laugharne, the word 'huddled'. I used the word in ordinary conversation with Dylan that afternoon. He stopped and began repeating it over to himself, remarking on its strangeness, savouring it as though it were as outlandish as 'Chimborazo' or 'Cotopaxi' and not an ordinary English vocable in common use. This was not the first indication I had had that Dylan was not just interested in words but was obsessed by them. St John's 'In the beginning was the word' was a favourite quotation of his and it also became a line in one of his poems.

I sometimes think that this absorption with words partly accounts for the difficulty of some of his poetry. What is it that makes a poet alter a word, or several words, in a poem? How does he know which words to alter and how does he know when he has got the right ones? What tells him when to stop altering? For Dylan the words had to be *right* (whatever that means), and in achieving this the meaning for the reader might recede further and further with each emendation. Also I think that words or phrases which seemed to him potent and beautiful used to arise spontaneously in his mind and then, when he was writing a poem, these were unloaded, as it were, a glittering mass, on to the theme. Another reason for his obscurity was his lack of a sense of community and another, perhaps, his sense of the ordinariness of his themes in a literary world where the words 'intellectuals and artists' were often heard – as though these two groups were identical in their composition, their aims and their gifts.

As successive volumes of Dylan's poetry appeared, the critics of course compared them one with another and claimed to detect changes in technique, subject matter, vocabulary and so on. A growing and welcome clarity was a feature discernible to some. But Professor Maud's discoveries invalidate a good deal of this type of criticism. What I myself see in Dylan's poetry isn't anything like a gradual progression from obscurity to clearer communication. I think he wrote clear and unclear poetry at most stages of his career. What I see in all his work is a sincere, almost an agonized, attempt to make, to construct, to build up poems out of words and phrases. Mallarmé, I think it was, said that poetry isn't a matter of ideas, it's a matter of words, and I think Dylan would go all the way with him in that. But the difficulty is that words themselves are in a way ideas, or they stand for ideas. As part of language they are in some mysterious manner intimately mixed up with the entire human situation. And some of Dylan's famous obscurity arises, I think, from this sort of confusion. The words he uses are usually marvellous, but too often they are the wrong ones to convey the ideas he wants them to convey. Sometimes the words, the lines of poetry – just the words making up the phrase or the line – are so terrific that the ideas they represent don't matter. Even if we knew what the ideas behind the words were we wouldn't enjoy the poems any more – at least that is my experience and conviction. One of his finest and most obscure poems, 'Light breaks where no sun shines', probably expresses something pretty trite and commonplace, in prose terms, about the foetus and the pre-natal state, I would guess, but the actual words and phrases and lines of the poem are so filled with poetic energy that they arouse the identical feelings in one that follow the reading of some great and intelligible poem by, say, Hopkins, or Dafydd ap Gwilym, or Whitman.

I myself divide all Dylan's poems into two groups, a simple division of successes and failures. In the success group I place some poems that are completely or almost completely clear and intelligible like 'Fern Hill', 'Lament', 'In my Craft or Sullen Art', 'Do not go gentle into that good night', 'The Hunchback in the Park', 'Poem in October', 'After the funeral', 'And death shall have no dominion', 'Especially when the October wind', 'This bread I break' and 'The force that through the green fuse'. With these relatively clear poems I would place others I don't really understand properly, but which yet give me the sort of pleasure or even the physical sensation I have come to associate with fine poetry, the beard-bristling of Housman or the unwarmable iciness of Emily Dickinson. These would include 'I see the boys of summer', 'If I were tickled by the rub of love', 'Light breaks where no sun shines', 'Ears in the turret hear', 'A Refusal to Mourn the Death by Fire', 'Over Sir John's Hill'. All the poems I have named, sixteen or seventeen, plus another five or six, I would regard as the best of Dylan Thomas. All the rest to me are failures of one sort or another, although again I believe that some of these might turn out to be genuine poems when we know more about them, say the 'Ballad of the Long-legged Bait' and 'A Winter's Tale'. Because one of the difficulties in dealing with Dylan Thomas's poems is that we very often don't know what they mean. Later on, when I say I don't think Dylan is really a religious poet, I must be understood to mean of course that I believe this on the evidence of those poems which are clear to me. Perhaps when the meaning of some at the moment quite impenetrable poems has been laid bare I might be convinced that he was after all more a religious poet than he seems at the moment. Or a political poet. Or a patriotic poet.

Dylan occupied three different houses in Laugharne. Shortly after his marriage he moved into a small terraced cottage called 'Eros'. (I do not think that Dylan was at all responsible for this rather unusual name.) Then he rented 'Sea View', a much larger, detached house, a tall symmetrical structure which always reminded me of some quaint seaside dwelling in a painting by Christopher Wood or Alfred Wallis. Finally, he settled with his family in the Boat House. The little town evidently suited him very well, being, like himself, Welsh, but English in speech.

The last occasion I spent any length of time with him in Laugharne was in October 1949. The BBC had commissioned me that year to do a series of interviews with authors on 'How I Write'. Richard Hughes, Elizabeth Bowen, Rhys Davies, Professor Gwyn Jones, Emyr Humphreys and Gwyn Thomas all agreed to be cross-questioned on this subject, and so did Dylan, whose interview I intended to put on first. I travelled down to Carmarthen, where I was to put up for the night, by rail, and as the train rounded the bend between Kidwelly and Ferryside in the darkness, I went to the window to watch the lights of Laugharne across the dark waters of the bay. One of those dots of illumination I supposed must be the 'singing light' by which Dylan claimed in 'In my Craft or Sullen Art' to labour at his poems, although what he told me in our discussion the next day about his methods of composition rather put a damper on the fine and romantic feelings I remembered from the previous evening.

It was lovely when I arrived in Laugharne the next morning, and almost the first person I met when I got off the bus was Dylan himself. He was carrying a chair from the Boat House up to his 'studio', a converted garage higher up the cliff, so that I could have something to sit on while we worked at our interview. He was wearing an old brown soft hat, a leather jacket and light check trousers, very baggy, not unlike an old-fashioned comedian's. His shirt was of cream Welsh flannel, striped, and with the collar attached. He had become fat by then, particularly around the middle. His hair, once almost golden, was now much darker, although it was still ringletted and fairly thick. His teeth, which he tried to conceal in smiling, were not good, his nose had become enormous, his face bloated and pale. He looked comical, and lovely, and terrible; but, fallen angel or not, none of the old enchantment, for me, had deserted him, nor any of the charm of his 'tumble-down tongue'. In no time at all, it seemed to me, we were back on the old footing of warmth and intimacy and pleasure.

Around the walls of his garage 'studio' overlooking the estuary were reproductions of modern paintings by Rouault, Picasso, Rousseau and others, and a photograph of an imperious and magnificently-bearded Whitman – like God the Father in majesty, according to Dylan. Through the branches of a fig tree growing outside across the window, I could see on the opposite bank of the wide river the farm-house where my grandfather had been born, and close by was Pentywyn, the birthplace, according to Dylan, of *his* grandfather. This I learnt later from Dylan's mother was not true, although a relative of his had at one time occupied the farm. The statement was in fact merely another of those charming and rather childlike attempts of his at saying what would please and be of interest, and create a bond between himself and his listener.

During our discussion Dylan explained that his method of work was to potter about in the morning, to write in the afternoons and to visit Brown's Hotel at night, a sequence which, although confirmed by Caitlin, rather contradicts 'In my Craft or Sullen Art'. (Supposing, that is, the 'singing light' to be some sort of humming house-light. One critic thinks it is the moon, but that too makes him a night writer.) I had sent on beforehand the questions I intended to ask, and he showed me the answers he had begun to prepare. To me they seemed brilliant, both revealing and marvellously expressed, and I told him how absolutely splendid they appeared to me. The only thing wrong with them from the point of view of my commission was that as material for a radio programme intended for the general listener they were rather too involved and concentrated; there seemed to be enough material in one answer, duly treated, to last the whole half-hour of the broadcast, and I felt that ordinary listeners at one hearing would, for this reason, be unlikely to make head or tail of what Dylan was saying. I tried to put this point to him and with great sweetness he agreed to try again. But he never completed the task and in the end the series went on without him. He explained to me later that the cause of his non-appearance before the microphone was 'trouble with his rib'. That he intended anything beyond the obvious meaning of the phrase did not at first dawn on me. But upon reflection, when I recalled Caitlin's opposition to his revealing what she called his 'secrets' to everybody, and the resultant tension which existed at the Boat House during my visit, I began to feel that the word 'rib' was probably being used by Dylan in its picturesque biblical sense. I have since often deeply regretted my concern at that time for the entertainment of the general listener.[16]

During the war, when every journey was expected to be really necessary, I seldom met Dylan, but after 1945 I began to see him again, even if only for what he called 'our annual hour'. But apart from the difficulties imposed upon it by the conditions of the war, I think that probably other factors had by then operated upon our friendship. I don't mean there was ever any quarrel, or disagreement, or even coolness between us. Dylan was uniformly cordial and always welcoming to whatever friends I had with me when I visited him. But as time went on I was conscious of not having rejected enough, of representing too clearly for him what he always wished to put behind him – Welsh nationalism and a sort of hill farm morality, petit bourgeois narrowness and convention and so on. For my part I had a constitutional aversion to entering, even if my job had permitted it, the sort of hurricane that Dylan appeared to be creating around himself, the full devastation of which I did not realize until I read Brinnin's book. The post-war years were of course for him a time of growing fame, but I never saw the slightest sign of self-importance in him as a consequence; in spite of all the fêting and the adulation he remained remarkably modest and unassuming and friendly.

Dylan's best volume of poems is often held to be *Deaths and Entrances*, published in 1946. Ultimately poets are judged not by volumes but by individual poems, which relieves one of committing oneself to an order of merit for the volumes. Dylan wrote superb poetry at every stage of his career, and *Deaths and Entrances* contains pieces as fine as any he had ever written, 'Poem in October', 'Fern Hill' and 'In my Craft', for example. But I cannot pretend that I had watched Dylan's development as a poet until then with complete satisfaction. After the raptures of *Eighteen Poems*, *Twenty-five Poems* was something of a disappointment to me, although Rayner Heppenstall's assurance that most of the pieces in it had been written before *Eighteen Poems* did mitigate to some extent the sense of anticlimax. I had, no doubt unreasonably, expected that Dylan's poetry, while retaining its power and excitement, would become increasingly less obscure. But this did not happen, at least not to the extent I had hoped, and unlike some of his readers I find 'In country sleep' and 'In the white giant's thigh' almost as baffling as 'How soon the servant sun' or 'I see the boys of summer'.

I explain my disappointment to myself in two ways, one of which is difficult to set out without seeming to express a general disapproval I certainly do not feel. I sometimes think Dylan did not speak out more clearly, and concealed the meaning of his poems, because he was conscious of some intellectual inadequacy in them. He was not a Surrealist poet – the intricate syllabic patterns of his poems and the elaborate rhyme-schemes seem to me the antipole of Surrealist practice. But he was, I think, an 'unconscious' poet, one who relied very much on what was 'given' to him. Judged from an intellectual as opposed to an artistic-emotional standpoint, he seldom had anything to advocate at a time when opinions, attitudes, commitment, wit-writing, seemed important. He was not the poet of a community, of a party, or of a religion. His best poems are expressions of powerful emotion, and lean heavily on the evocative powers of description for their effect – he is much more, it seems to me, a descriptive poet than, as he thought himself, a narrative one. It is no use our blaming Dylan for not embracing a religious or political faith which would provide him with some intellectual structure for his verse when that first glorious uprush of lyrical poetry exhausted itself at nineteen or twenty. Or for not constructing, like W. B. Yeats, a framework, however crazy, of his own. Dylan, although intelligent and quick-witted, was not an intellectual, not deeply concerned with ideas. At its best his poetry is without politics, without religion, without philosophy, expressing, as music might do, pure sorrow, or nostalgia, or joy. His 'meddling intellect' operated in his work only at the level of a line by line concern with technique. A work outside his poetry perhaps best illustrates this. *Under Milk Wood* was originally designed to follow a fairly rigid plot, but Dylan proved incapable of sustaining a scheme worked out in advance which would have involved intellectual invention and contrivance. He preferred to rely on what came to him minute by minute and scene by scene. For this reason I find quite incredible the claims of some of his critics that towards the end of his life he intended large-scale stage productions – full-length plays presumably. Without some radical change in him I feel sure this would have been an impossibility. If Dylan had lived and continued to write, I think that what had happened earlier to his prose might have happened to his poetry, i.e. that it might have been massively invaded by his humour. There are indications of this in Mr Waldo's song in *Under Milk Wood* and in the magnificent 'Lament' in the *Collected Poems*. Dylan's gift was essentially lyrical; he was a writer of the short flight. *Under Milk Wood*, for example, is not really a play at all, with development and climax, but rather a series of short and lively scenes, the sort of thing Dylan always did admirably, the number of which could be increased or reduced without damage to the architecture of the whole. The length of the play seems quite arbitrary.

And yet Dylan from time to time appeared to feel he *ought* to believe in something or other. In one of his first letters to me he wrote: 'You are, I suppose, a good Socialist. As a Socialist myself, though a very unconventional one, I like to read good propaganda, but the most recent poems of Auden and Day Lewis seem to me to be neither good poetry nor propaganda. A good propagandist needs little intellectual appeal; and the emotional appeal in Auden wouldn't raise a corresponding emotion in a tick'.

This was in the thirties, when Bohemia was a sort of left-wing satellite. Later, when I met him in London, he was wearing the reddest red tie I had ever seen and he explained it by saying he was about to join the Young Communists. I pointed out that he had already passed the upper age limit for membership of this organization which, if I remember correctly, was then eighteen. He did not appear unduly cast down at this information, perhaps even a little relieved, and I never heard that he pursued his intention to the extent of joining the adult section of the party. His left-wing sympathies were largely, I think, an expression of personal rebelliousness, a desire, common in young writers, to be on the *anti* side. I never saw him as much of a co-operative do-er, a man of action. There was, I think, a strain of passivity in his nature.

Again before the war he expressed pacifist opinions, and he even began to gather together a symposium of anti-war statements from his friends, of whom I was one, with a view to publishing them. What happened to this project I do not know, and Dylan's pacifism I believe did not endure long. Some critics have held that he is a religious poet.[17] That he wrote a few 'religious' poems I would agree, but hardly enough, I would think, to justify the title 'religious poet', any more than, say, Lawrence's handful of poems about the First World War would suggest for him the title of War Poet. Certainly Dylan, like Stanley Spencer, uses a good deal of religious symbolism in his work, but this, it seems to me, is potent for him more because it is associated with childhood than because it concerns anything an adult would call 'religion'. He has, as far as I know, nothing to say about the great themes of religious poetry, the love of God, the sense of separation from or of oneness with Him, and we have only to compare him with Hopkins to see how small a part religion plays in his work. Memories of the Bible are frequent in his poems, but how strict a student of the book he was as an adult I do not know. I notice that he always refers to the final book of the New Testament as 'Revelations'.

The last time I saw Dylan was in Cardiff in 1953, the year of his death. He had come to speak to the students at the university college and to read *Under Milk Wood*. He seemed to me then sick, with an air of profound unhappiness, even desperation, about him. But, sick or not, he gave us splendidly of his sleeping Llareggub, beside its 'sloe-black, slow, black' sea, with its poisoners, and livers-in-tally, and wives in the wardrobe, the enchanting little Welsh Erewhon where chapels have bells and where the excessively paternal Johann Sebastian Bach is of the feminine gender.

Within a few weeks of this meeting Dylan was dead.

Brinnin's book appeared in 1956 and much of it was a revelation and a profound shock to me. Dylan's early drinking I had put down to a common sort of adolescent bravado and conformity. I thought of it as a phase which would pass with increasing age and a sense of achievement and as the attractions of bars and bar-flies diminished. What I had never suspected in him was this powerful urge towards self-destruction revealed in Brinnin's terrible words. Why did Dylan, sensitive and compassionate, behave like this – he, with the care of a family, greatly loved by a large circle of friends, highly successful as a writer and performer, one of the most famous poets of two continents? How false and terribly sentimental seemed now the picture of him as the carefree Bohemian, the picture, I suspect, that prompted much of the ballyhoo at the time of his death. Much nearer the truth was Philip Toynbee's description of him – 'a most unhappy and ill-fated man'. Another writer speaks of the 'deep psychotic wounds' from which he suffered. I believe there must be truth in this, but of their real nature, by whom, where, when and why delivered, I, at least, do not know. To me this important aspect of Dylan's life is a complete enigma.

For someone like myself who knew Dylan when he was young, and was so greatly attracted to him as he was then, a sort of necessity exists to come to terms with Brinnin's book. I feel, regretfully, that it cannot be denied that what Brinnin tells us is in substance true. But I do not accept that this book tells us the truth about Dylan. Leaving aside for a moment his poetic talent and his gifts as writer, actor and reader, I remember that after years of a quite unusual amount of praise and petting he remained natural, approachable and unspoilt; which, when one recalls the arrogance and self-importance of people without anything like his talent, is surely no small virtue in him. He was without malice, greed or pettiness. I do not think he ever hated anyone or held anyone cheaply, or tried to do anyone down. I remember also his devotion to his parents, especially his steady sympathy and concern for his sick and frustrated father.

The last letter I had from Dylan is dated 15th February 1953 – that is, it was written a few months before his death, and during the period of his life dealt with by Brinnin. This is part of what he says: 'Thanks very much for writing. So sorry not to have been able to answer at once: I've been away, in Swansea and in London. But I'm writing to Idris today. I've known him, off and on, and always, unfortunately, in little bits, for years and years; and I was terribly sorry to hear from Vernon, and from you, about his illness. I think he's a fine chap and a real poet, God bless him.' The 'Idris' Dylan speaks about is Idris Davies, at that time suffering from the disease that was to kill him within three months. The next time I visited Idris, he told me with great pleasure and pride that he had just received a letter of encouragement and good wishes from Dylan. This is a small matter, perhaps, but for me, at least, it is one that helps to get the whole picture of Dylan's later life into a more understandable focus.

And I am sure it is relevant to remember again those summers in Llanstephan and Laugharne before the war, when the legend, although growing, was only up to Dylan's shoulder. It always seemed, as Keidrych Rhys has remarked, to be sunny at that time. Sometimes Keidrych came down from Llangadog to join us, alone or with writer friends, and we went swimming at the Grafel Gwyn, the lovely sandy bay in Llanstephan. Keidrych and I went swimming, that is: Dylan sat on the rocks and wrote a poem in pencil in an exercise book and appreciated Keidrych's figure, even in youth inclining to *embonpoint*, clad in old-fashioned bathing-drawers borrowed from my landlady. Sometimes, after Dylan's marriage, my wife and I went over to Laugharne; sometimes Dylan and Caitlin came to Llanstephan, arriving once, I remember, bedraggled and exhausted, having scrambled for miles across the rocky and desolate shore between the two places instead of taking the road over the headland behind the Laugharne ferry.

'There is no such thing as the one true Dylan Thomas', Caitlin Thomas has written. But, like her, I am sure it is possible to arrive at a better truth than Brinnin's about this strangely loveable and haunted man.

VIII

CONCLUSION

A N Anglo-Welsh writer can be Welsh by blood, birth and residence, Welsh-speaking and a writer about Wales, like Emyr Humphreys, R. S. Thomas and Caradoc Evans. Or, at the other extreme, he can be Welsh by blood, but not a writer about his native land and without the understanding and knowledge of our country resulting from domicile in it and a familiarity with its language. Some of the variations in between these two extremes I attempted to cover by my definition of an Anglo-Welsh writer as a Welsh man or woman who writes about Wales in English. At no point so far have I tried to define a Welsh man or woman.

The editors of the *Dictionary of Welsh Biography*, who were of course very early forced to make up their minds on this point, say in their introduction that 'the very great majority' of the people recorded in their book were Welsh by birth or residence. With 'of Welsh descent' they would, quite rightly, it seems to me, have nothing to do; but on the other hand, non-Welsh people who have lived and worked in Wales and have affected her history – 'these men', the editors say, 'could not have been excluded'. This seems to me fair and sensible. Mr Conor Cruise O'Brien in his *Writers and Politics* defines Irishness as not being 'primarily a question of birth or blood or language; it is the condition of being involved in the Irish situation and usually of being mauled by it'. I would settle for that, *mutatis mutandis,* as a definition of Welshness also. To me, anyone can be a Welshman who chooses to be so and is prepared to take the consequences.

This question of feeling oneself to be Welsh is, I believe, one that is increasingly occupying the more serious among the younger Anglo-Welsh writers. Ezra Pound early in the twentieth century, in an attempt to restore to vigour a debilitated poetic tradition, sought to direct the eyes of the young English poets outwards, towards the literatures of Europe and Asia. This was excellent, but the first place for an Anglo-Welsh writer to look, it seems to me, is obviously backwards, so that he may know as much about the Welsh part of his country's traditions as he normally does about the Anglo. Earlier I suggested (in what now seems to me a quite inadequate fashion) some ways in which I thought Welsh tradition might influence a modern Anglo-Welsh poet. What I really meant was something much more profound and enriching than the learning of a few technical tricks, which is what certain of my words might suggest. I intended to advocate a natural and thorough-going acceptance of Welsh poetry as part of the modern Anglo-Welsh poet's equipment, a familiarity not only with the prosodic aspect of Welsh poetry, but also with the wide variety of its moods and forms, its dialogues between dead and living, its *cywyddau brud*, its gnomic poetry, its hymns, its *marwnadau*, its moralizing, its *cywyddau gofyn*,[1] its bardic controversies, its pedigree poems, its poems of praise of noble and churchman, of love, locations and nature. It is familiarity with know-ledge and experience of this sort, it seems to me, that will enrich the poetry of future Anglo-Welsh poets; from the pressure of such a tradition could arise a body of poetry of great freshness, complexity, variety and richness, which would transcend the rather thin imitations of English and American poetry which some contemporary Anglo-Welsh poets are still writing now.

A certain need for qualification I think arises here. That a writer should recognize his own roots is a fine and enriching thing, and noth-ing but good I believe can come to many Anglo-Welsh writers through greater involvement and understanding and the sort of acknowledg-ment of tradition about which I have been speaking. But no writer ought to be judged by the extent to which he does this. Nationalism can give a man a new strength of feeling, new ideas, an idealism, a fresh way of looking at the world around him. Other experiences are capable of doing the same, and I do not believe a writer ought to be given extra marks, as it were, for his commitment to a cause, or that we should repeat the old left-wing criticism of the thirties, with Welsh National-ism substituted for Marxism. Allied to the question of commitment is that of the audience of the writer, to which I have already briefly

referred. 'Whom do you think you are writing for?' is a question
thought by those Welsh critics who ask it of the Anglo–Welsh to be
particularly devastating. Yeats is held to be the great exemplar here, the
Irishman who wrote in English for his 'own race'. (Though, oddly
enough, the Yeats poem sometimes quoted in support of this, 'The
Fisherman', is really about *not* writing for his own race.) Again, it is no
doubt comforting and stimulating for an artist to be aware of his
audience, but for critical purposes the concept is worthless. When I am
experiencing the whole marvellous impact of some great art work, say
Bleak House, how can it possibly be of the least concern to me whether
Dickens knew for whom he was writing? He is at the time writing
for me. In his challenging booklet *Is there an Anglo-Welsh Literature?*
Saunders Lewis describes *Spring of Youth* by Ll. Wyn Griffith as 'a fine
thing, subtle and sensitive'. It is difficult to see how these virtues are
diminished in any way because '[Wyn Griffith's] implied audience', as
Mr Lewis says, 'is English'.[2] It seems to me that this idea of trying to
make value judgments of a work of art on a basis of the author's awareness of an audience is critically quite unrewarding.

A question I have not explored to the extent I perhaps should have
done is the important one of the relation between language and
religion as far as the Anglo–Welsh are concerned. When they have
coherent politics, and sometimes when they haven't, the Anglo–Welsh
are largely radical, that is Socialist or Nationalist. Few, as far as I know,
have retained any important connection with the religion of the
community in which so many of them were brought up, i.e. nonconformity. The question arises as to the part played by the rejection of
formal religion in the production of the Anglo–Welsh, in a country
where the chapels have been custodians of the language and of a
distinctive way of life, where the links between nonconformity and
Welshness have been, and still are, many and powerful, and where Welsh
literary and cultural movements and societies – the Cymrodorion,
Undeb Cymru Fydd, etc. – still draw their support, I would say,
overwhelmingly from chapel membership. Did those Anglo–Welsh who
lost their Welsh and their Welshness do so because they abandoned the
traditional religion of their families? Or were they constrained to reject
a whole way of life, including nonconformity, because of their
ignorance of or indifference to the language? I am not sure that general
answers can be given to these questions. When one deals with a matter
as personal as religious belief perhaps one has to examine cases
individually to arrive at correct answers.

Another interesting question I have not pursued is the difference between the earlier Anglo-Welsh writers, the poets of Raymond Garlick and the novelists of Professor Leclaire on the one hand, and the writers grouped around *Wales*, *The Welsh Review*, *Life and Letters To-day* and then *The Anglo-Welsh Review* and *Poetry Wales* on the other. The first Anglo-Welsh were of course the products of the literate classes of their time, i.e. the property owners and the clerisy, not of popular education. How Welsh were these early writers? What was their attitude to their mother country? How powerful was the influence of England upon them? Did they feel involved with Wales or was their attention directed entirely over the border? What had they in common, if anything, with the modern writers of industrialized and anglicized Wales? Something is probably to be learnt about the Anglo-Welsh of today from attempting to answer these questions and others like them.

One is frequently asked what the future of Anglo-Welsh is to be. This question has of course two distinct meanings. If the meaning is, 'How will the future regard what has already been written by Anglo-Welsh writers?' the answer is that no one can possibly tell. Literary history warns us of the folly and rashness of tipping works for 'immortality', whatever that means. (Twenty years of remembrance? Two hundred? Two thousand?) Still, I think some of the lyrics of Dylan Thomas, as I have already said, stand a good chance of survival, and 'In Parenthesis' perhaps, and some of Caradoc Evans's early stories. Gwyn Thomas's 'The Keep' might find, I would guess, a place among the performable plays of the future. Perhaps much more than this will interest unborn generations, perhaps much less, perhaps nothing. Nobody knows and nobody can know, what out of the enormous mass of serious writing produced in the English-speaking world of the first half of the twentieth century will have the ability to 'stay news'.

Sometimes the question appears to have a slightly different meaning, namely: 'Will the Anglo-Welsh "movement" continue, or will it die out?' Again so many imponderables exist in our rapidly changing world that even the most general prophecy is impossible. If the relevant part of my theory is correct, Anglo-Welsh writers ought to continue to appear around the shrinking periphery of the Welsh language. But will the use of the Welsh language continue to decline? There are signs now that it might not do so. Anglo-Welsh writers appeared in large numbers in heavily-industrialized South Wales. But is the whole of South Wales to remain an area of heavy industry? Again with the large-scale closing of pits and the shifting of the steelworks to the coastal strip there are clear signs to the contrary. What effect will the spread of education, particularly higher education, have on those who wish to become writers? And what part will nationalism, even Nationalism, play in the development of their thought and their allegiances? All these factors will I think influence what and how much will be written in English in the Wales of the future.

What I myself would welcome in Anglo-Welsh writers is, as I have said, a wider knowledge of the past and present of our country, particularly of our native literature, and a deeper sense of identity with her destiny. This would surely result ultimately in closer unity between Welsh and Anglo-Welsh, so that the two groups could recognize each other as Welshmen and not merely as antagonists. I would welcome a rejection of London or New York as the literary capital of Wales, and the appearance not only of better poets and novelists than we have already produced, but also — this we lack — critics of sensitivity and responsibility. I would like Anglo-Welsh writers to see themselves first as Welsh men and women. The only English thing about an Anglo-Welsh writer ought to be the language the writer uses.

NOTES

Notes without brackets are those of Glyn Jones and appeared in the original edition; notes in brackets are the editor's.

CH. I, LETTER TO KEIDRYCH

1. [Keidrych Rhys (1915-1987), born near Llandeilo, Carmarthenshire, began his literary career in London in 1937; he founded the literary periodical *Wales* in the same year. *Wales* was more orientated towards Modernism and the experimental than Gwyn Jones's *The Welsh Review* (founded in 1939); those published in the pages of *Wales* included Dylan Thomas, Vernon Watkins, Rhys Davies, Idris Davies and Glyn Jones. His correspondence with Keidrych Rhys in 1937–8 indicates GJ's active involvement in the early issues of the journal, including advice on selection of material for publication and help with proofing. After serving in the army during the war, Rhys returned to Wales, to Llanybri, Carmarthenshire, where he lived with his wife, the poet Lynette Roberts, to whom he was married from 1939 until 1949. In this period he set up the Druid Press, which published R. S. Thomas's first volume, *The Stones of the Field* (1946). Rhys edited several anthologies of poetry, including *Modern Welsh Poetry* (Faber, 1944), which contained work by a number of the figures associated with *Wales*, including Dylan Thomas, Alun Lewis, Lynette Roberts and GJ, as well as R. S. Thomas and Emyr Humphreys. Rhys returned to London in 1950 where he worked in journalism and public relations.]
2. [Constantine FitzGibbon, *The Life of Dylan Thomas* (London: Dent, 1965) and *Selected Letters of Dylan Thomas*, ed. Constantine FitzGibbon (London: Dent, 1966).]
3. [In his draft revisions GJ cites Raymond Garlick's *An Introduction to Anglo-Welsh Literature* (Cardiff: University of Wales Press, 1970).]
4. ['Thoughts on the Burne-Jones exhibition', *Welsh Outlook* 20/10 (1933), 281–2. The piece was published under the *nom-de-plume* 'M. G. Gower', which GJ used on a number of occasions in the early 1930s; 'Gower' was a family name on his mother's side.]
5. [On the publication of Welsh authors in *Life and Letters To-day*, see Meic Stephens, 'The Third Man: Robert Herring and *Life and Letters To-day*', *Welsh Writing in English: A Yearbook of Critical Essays*, 3 (1997), 157–69.]

CH. II, AUTOBIOGRAPHY

1. In *Presenting Welsh Poetry* (London: Faber, 1959).
2. See 'Seventy Anglo-Welsh poets', an article by Raymond Garlick in *The Welsh Anvil*, the magazine of the Guild of Graduates of the University of Wales, December 1954. [See also Raymond Garlick, *An Introduction to Anglo-Welsh Literature* (Cardiff: University of Wales Press, 1970; new edn., 1972).]
3. [Presumably GJ is referring to the fact that Slough and Coventry were economic centres to which many Welsh workers and their families emigrated, especially in the years of Depression in south Wales in the 1930s, to work in the car manufacturing industry.]
4. [Garlick, *Introduction*, 21–22.]
5. [For a discussion of 'The Hymn to the Virgin' and a full text, see Tony Conran, 'Ieuan ap Hywel Swrdwal's "The Hymn to the Virgin"', *Welsh Writing in English: A Yearbook of Critical Essays*, 1 (1995), 5–22. GJ gives a fuller discussion of the poem's use of traditional metres in Ch.VI.]
6. ['Ah me, 'tis like a vision of *Hell*, and will never leave me, that of those poor creatures broiling, or in sweat and dirt, amid their furnaces, pits and rolling mills . . . The town might be, and will be, one of the prettiest places in the world. It *is* one of the sootiest, squalidest, and ugliest; all cinders and dust mounds and soot', Thomas Carlyle to Jane Welsh Carlyle, 16 August 1850, *Collected Letters of Thomas and Jane Welsh Carlyle*, ed. Ian Campbell, Aileen Christianson and Hilary J. Smith, 26 vols. (London: Duke UP, 1997), vol. 25, p. 157.]
7. [Gwyn A. Williams, 'The Merthyr of Dic Penderyn', in Glanmor Williams (ed.), *Merthyr Politics: The Making of a Working-Class Tradition* (Cardiff: University of Wales Press, 1966), 9.]
8. See Jack Jones's autobiography, *Unfinished Journey* [London: Hamish Hamilton, 1937], which takes up the story of Merthyr in the 1880s.
9. See especially *Black Parade* [1935], although it deals with a later period. Jack Jones's picture of the town was indignantly rejected by many people in Merthyr. One councillor said to him: 'Why did you have to write a "*Black* Parade", Jack? Why didn't you write a "*White* Parade"?' I feel some sympathy with these complaints as the next paragraphs show.
10. [*Cynganeddion*: the forms of *cynghanedd*, the intricate system of alliteration and internal rhyme used in Welsh poetry.]
11. Few members of the modern Welsh middle classes seem in fact to be more than a generation or two removed from the shirt-sleeves. In the past the path away from the farm, the quarry or the pit lay in the direction of the pulpit. Almost one might say, looking around the Welsh scene, that if the Nonconformist minister, like the Catholic priest, had been celibate, we would now be without a middle class.
12. Professor David Williams, in his *The Rebecca Riots* (Cardiff: University of Wales Press, 1955), [34–5] has a splendid illustration of what we are capable of in this line. The Bala magistrates in 1838, local squires and gentry, threatened to 'strike' because a grocer had been appointed to sit on the bench with them.

13. Williams, *The Rebecca Riots* [ch. 1]. To the spiritual and social disjunction the professor adds the physical separation of absenteeism which in some areas of Wales was widespread.

14. Literally the words mean 'The People', but literalness is here inadequate to convey all that the words could stand for to a Welshman.

15. The families of the great Merthyr iron kings, for example, originated in London (Bacon), Yorkshire (Crawshay), Shropshire (Guest) and Worcestershire (Homfray).

16. [It was 1997 before the situation of 1906 was repeated, with no Tory member returned in Wales in the general election of that year, though the overwhelming majority of seats were now held not by the Liberal Party, as in 1906, but by the Labour Party, which won 34 of the 40 parliamentary seats in Wales, with Plaid Cymru winning 4 and the Liberal Democrats 2.]

17. [From 1916 to 1923 GJ attended Cyfarthfa Castle Grammar School in Merthyr, housed in the former home of the Crawshays, the local ironmasters. The school had been opened in 1913.]

18. [In 1925 GJ began teaching at Wood Street School – near what is today Cardiff's central bus station – in an area then called 'Temperance Town', a name which belied its nature. The cheap housing which had been put up in the nineteenth century on land reclaimed when the route of the River Taff was altered was by this time one of the worst slum areas in Cardiff, despite its proximity to the town centre. By now GJ's parents had moved to Cardiff, where his father was a clerk with the General Post Office; GJ lived with his parents, in Roath and then Cathays, until he married in 1935.]

19. [The episode in GJ's early story 'I was born in the Ystrad valley' (c.1935), when the protagonist visits a young boy in his home in the city slums, draws directly upon such visits.]

20. [For details of GJ's reading in this period, see the Introduction to *The Collected Stories of Glyn Jones*, ed. Tony Brown (Cardiff: University of Wales Press, 1999), pp. xxvi–xxvii.]

21. [See Richard Burnham, '*The Dublin Magazine*'s Welsh poets', *Anglo-Welsh Review*, 60 (1978), 49–63.]

22. [*Means test*: this was a system introduced by Ramsey MacDonald's National Government in November 1931, whereby unemployment benefit could be drawn as of right for only twenty-six weeks. Thereafter, the unemployed had to submit to a close examination of the family's financial means by 'the means test man', an inspector of the Local Assistance Committee. The benefit allowed was reduced if the means test revealed any household income, such as earnings by a son or daughter, which could be set against benefit.]

23. [*Urdd y Deyrnas* (The Order of the Kingdom) had been founded in the early 1920s. 'Inspired by the inter-denominational students' movement, the S[tudent] C[hristian] M[ovement], the *Urdd* became the chief focus of non-sectarian religious activity amongst the youth of Wales' (Robert Pope, *Building Jerusalem: Nonconformity, Labour and the Social Question in Wales, 1906–1939* (Cardiff: University of Wales Press, 1998) 176). It organized study groups and conferences and argued for the necessity for young

Christian believers to involve themselves in social reform. The Fellowship of Reconciliation was a pacifist Christian group which had been formed in December 1914. It had focused opposition to the churches' support for the Great War; in particular it had opposed the Military Services Act of 1916, which introduced conscription. As a result of his registering as a conscientious objector, in November 1940, GJ was dismissed from his teaching post; by then he was teaching at Allensbank School, a secondary school in the Heath area of Cardiff. An account of GJ's registration as a CO and its consequences is given in the Introduction to *The Collected Stories of Glyn Jones*, pp. xli–xliv.]

24. Between 1894 and 1897 an earlier magazine bearing this title, 'a national magazine for the English-speaking parts of Wales', had appeared monthly, edited by O. M. Edwards, the Welsh patriot, from Lincoln College, Oxford, where he was history tutor. In his first editorial he says: 'There is, undoubtedly, something like a literary awakening among English-speaking Welshmen; there is a strong desire for a literature that will be English in language but Welsh in spirit.' The dawn these modern-sounding words spoke of would appear to have been, in 1894, a false one.

25. [GJ and his family became members of Minny Street Chapel, Cathays, a congregation of the Welsh Independents. GJ remained a member of this chapel, serving later as a deacon, until the end of his life.]

26. See Matthew Arnold's *Celtic Literature*. Yeats's 'lifeless hymnal' (Vernon Watkins, 'Yeats in Dublin', *The Lamp and the Veil* (London: Faber, 1945) is very wide of the mark).

27. *Cywyddwyr*: writers of *cywyddau*, poems having seven syllables per line and rhyming accented syllable with unaccented. The poets of this anthology flourished, apparently, between 1400 and 1600.

28. [In 1931, for example, GJ attended a course of evening classes taught by Saunders Lewis, which included the study of W. J. Gruffydd's recent *Y Flodeugerdd Gymraeg* (The Welsh Anthology, 1931). GJ's notebook for the course shows him making careful notes of the various forms of *cynghanedd*. By the mid-1930s he was translating from Welsh poetry. See, for example, 'The Wind's Complaint', *Collected Poems*, ed. Meic Stephens (Cardiff: University of Wales Press, 1996), 188.]

29. *Tir Newydd* = 'New Territory', a Welsh-language 'little magazine' edited by the Welsh poet Alun Llywelyn-Williams, which appeared between 1935 and 1939. [An English translation of GJ's article was published as 'Notes on Surrealism', *New Welsh Review*, 28 (Spring 1995).]

30. Only a small number of writers, of course, encounter another possible language in adolescence. The case of Bobi Jones bears me out. Professor Jones's mother tongue was English; in his grammar school [Cathays High School, Cardiff], under a brilliant teacher [W. C. Elvet Thomas], he became deeply interested in Welsh. He has since written Welsh poetry of sufficient merit to be included in *The Oxford Book of Welsh Verse*.

CH. III, BACKGROUND

1. *Welsh Short Stories* (London: Faber, 1937), *Welsh Short Stories*, edited by Gwyn Jones (London: Penguin, 1940), *Welsh Short Stories*, edited by Gwyn Jones (Oxford: World's Classics, 1956), *Welsh Short Stories*, edited by George Ewart Evans (London: Faber, 1959).

2. Brynmor Jones gives a figure far in excess of fifty. In his *A Bibliography of Anglo-Welsh Literature, 1900–1965* [Cardiff: Wales & Monmouthshire Branch of the Library Association, 1970] he lists over 400 authors. But various factors put the vast majority of these outside the consideration of the present work. Mr Jones says in effect in his valuable introduction that Anglo-Welsh authors, for the purposes of his thesis, are those who write about Wales, so that the Welsh-based books of non-indigenous authors like Kingsley Amis, Showell Styles, A. J. Cronin, P. H. Newby, Jeremy Brooks, 'Taffrail', Rose Macaulay and very many others less well known find a place in it. Then a large number of Mr Jones's authors wrote before the First World War; many have not produced a volume, and many are the authors of work which cannot be regarded as having any connection with literature. Mr Jones's aim was, quite rightly of course for his purpose, comprehensiveness and completeness.

3. A discussion of 'interpretation' and related matters will be found in the stimulating pamphlet *Is there an Anglo-Welsh Literature?* by Saunders Lewis, published by the Cardiff Branch, Guild of Graduates of the University of Wales, Cardiff, 1939. [See also Bobi Jones, 'The Anglo-Welsh', *Dock Leaves*, 4/10 (1953), 23–8 and 'Anglo-Welsh: More definition', *Planet*, 16 (Feb.–March 1973), 11–23, and material in the bibliography at the end of this edition.]

4. [On Josef Herman's vision of Wales, see Josef Herman, *The Early Years in Scotland and Wales* (Llandybïe: Christopher Davies, 1984) and 'A Welsh mining village', *New Welsh Review*, 48 (Spring 2000), 11–13 (repr. from *Wales*, 1946); the same issue of *New Welsh Review* (9–11) contains an obituary of Herman. See also Robyn Tomos, 'Josef Herman a'i gyfoeswyr: chwilio am arwyddion arlunwyr Canol Ewrop yng Nghymru oddi ar 1940', Ivor Davies and Ceridwen Lloyd Morgan (eds.) *Darganfod Celf Cymru* (Cardiff: University of Wales Press, 1999), 140–65.]

5. [The English-language section of Yr Academi Gymreig was created in 1968, the year of publication of *The Dragon has Two Tongues*.]

CH. IV, INTRODUCTION TO SHORT STORIES AND NOVELS

1. [Publication details of the anthologies discussed are given in note 1 to Ch. III.]

2. This means that the grammar schools helped to produce not only the writers but also, as Harri Webb has pointed out, an audience to read them (*Poetry Wales*, 2/3 (1966), 35–9).

3. Of the thirty-seven authors in the four short-story anthologies, only five or six, I believe, were born with non-Welsh surnames (Rowe, Wright, Goodwin, Devereux, Heseltine). Most of the remainder have names common or very common in Wales: Daniel, Davies (2), Edwards, Evans (5), Griffith, Griffiths, Hughes (2), Humphreys, Jones (4), Lewis (2), Pryce, Pugh, Richards (2), Thomas (2) and Vaughan (3).

4. Gwyn Thomas's humorous short story, 'Wind of Innocence', in *Ring Delirium 123* [London: Gollancz, 1960], is an excellent comic demonstration of the way choice of subject-matter and method of treatment can be conditioned by background and upbringing.

5. [GJ's own short stories, of course, as well as his novel *The Island of Apples* (1965), frequently centre on the experience of children.]

6. In one of her autobiographies, Nina Hamnett describes the feud between the members of a Nonconformist chapel in an English village and a group of artists of various sorts who have taken the house next door. A situation like this, I feel, would be very unlikely to arise in Welsh Wales. Welsh-language writers and poets, whether Christian or not, would probably feel too powerfully the bond of language and background and shared tradition.

7. [In a letter to Gwyn Jones, 12 June 1942, GJ called *How Green was My Valley* 'a fake but a charming fake' (Prof. Gwyn Jones Papers, NLW II 9/2); Gwyn Jones replied, 14 June 1942: 'Richard Llewellyn has certainly pulled off a remarkable job. It's fake, as you say, but it is such a very good fake. Even in the furniture world we recognize the value of a good fake' (Glyn Jones Papers, NLW).]

8. [S. Beryl Jones, 'Dorothy Edwards as a writer of short stories', *Welsh Review*, 7/3 (Autumn 1948), 184–93.]

9. The anonymous reviewer of the 1937 Faber anthology, *Welsh Short Stories*, in *Wales*, 3 (1937), remarked that reading it 'one would not guess 26 per cent of our men unemployed, etc., etc. '. Among those who did write short stories about unemployment and depression are Alun Lewis, George Ewart Evans, Rhys Davies, William Glynne-Jones and Gwyn Thomas.

10. Joseph Keating (1871–1934), at one time worked underground. [He wrote a number of novels about industrial South Wales, including *Maurice: The Romance of a Welsh Coalmine* (1905), a volume of short stories (*Adventures in the Dark*, 1906), and an autobiography (*My Struggle for Life*, 1916). Lucien Leclaire's *General Analytical Bibliography of the Regional Novelists of the British Isles, 1800–1950* was published in Paris in 1954.]

11. Jack Jones, Richard Llewellyn, Alexander Cordell and Richard Vaughan are historical novelists in a sense different from the one I intend here. B. Dew Roberts, H. L. V. Fletcher and L. A. Knight have also written historical novels.

CH. V, THREE PROSE WRITERS

CARADOC EVANS

1. Caradoc is here at his game of literal translation from Welsh; he means his backside.
2. Caradoc Evans, 'Self-portrait', *Wales* (January 1944), 83–5.
3. See Caradoc's autobiographical novel *Nothing to Pay* (Faber, 1930). [The novel was reissued by Carcanet in 1989, with an afterword by John Harris.]
4. Oliver Sandys, *Caradoc Evans* (London: Hurst & Blackett, 1946), 155.
5. R. B. Marriott, 'Caradoc Evans', *Wales* (Summer 1945), 61–4.
6. Caradoc Evans, *The Earth Gives All and Takes All*, with an Introduction by George Green (London: Dakers, 1946). The novel *Madge Carrington and her Welsh Neighbours* (Stanley Paul, 1911) also gives an unflattering picture of Welsh people. Its author, 'Draig Glas' (Arthur Tyssilio Johnson) was said to be the author of *The Perfidious Welshman* (Stanley Paul, 1910). [John Harris's essay, 'Publishing *My People*: The book as expressive object', *New Welsh Review*, 1 (Summer 1988), 23–30, makes reference to these contemporary images of Wales.]
7. 'Self-portrait' 85.
8. Ibid.
9. Oliver Sandys, *Full and Frank* (London: Hurst & Blackett), 133–4.
10. [GJ's discussion of Caradoc Evans in an unpublished draft essay entitled 'Anglo-Welsh short story writers', probably written in the 1950s, some passages of which are echoed in *DTT*, includes the following: 'Sometimes I am tempted to think that Caradoc's truly appalling vision of life is not to be explained by the facile reasons often given for it. In his stories he is not paying back the insults and humiliations of his first thirty years. He is not taking a diabolical delight in pillorying individuals or the vices of community. Sometimes, I am almost persuaded, his best stories are less those things than a *cri-de-cœur*, an agonised cry of protest and indignation at the horror of life itself. Or they are his attempts to objectify, to make something out of, the emotions of bitterness with which the spectacle of existence on this planet have filled him.']
11. [As a boy, through into his mid-teens, GJ spent part of his summers at the farm of his 'Uncle John', actually a cousin of his father, who lived with his two unmarried sisters. The farm, Y Lan, was near Llangynog, in Welsh-speaking Carmarthenshire.]
12. 'Self-portrait' 84.
13. [Caradoc Evans, *My People*, ed. John Harris (1915; Bridgend: Seren, 1987), 111–12.]

JACK JONES

1. [GJ and his wife, Doreen (who had been brought up in Rhiwbina), settled there after their marriage in 1935 and lived in the area until 1939, when they moved to Manor Way, Cardiff. Other literary figures who lived in

Rhiwbina included the poet Alun Llewelyn-Williams, Prof. S. L. Bethell (Shakespeare scholar and Professor of English at University College, Cardiff) and Catherine Maclean, senior lecturer in the same Department, who became a literary mentor to GJ in his early years in Cardiff (see Ch. II). Construction of the 'garden village' had begun in 1913.]

2. [Jack Jones, *Unfinished Journey*, with a preface by David Lloyd George (London: Hamish Hamilton, 1937), 34–7. Further references are included in the text.]

3. [*ILP-er*: A member of the Independent Labour Party, founded by Keir Hardie in 1893. It remained in existence until 1946; the ILP was generally to the left of the Parliamentary Labour Party and, despite its links with the main body of the Labour movement, its MPs were never bound to obey the Labour Party whip. *Conchy*: a Conscientious Objector.]

4. [Jack Jones, 'Nofelau'r Cymry Seisnig', *Tir Newydd*, 8 (May 1937), 5-9.]

5. Jack Jones, *Me and Mine: Further Chapters in the Autobiography of Jack Jones* (London: Hamish Hamilton, 1946), 180–1.

6. On p. 333 of *River Out of Eden* [London: Hamish Hamilton, 1951], Jack says: 'This and what followed should have been made known as and when it happened, but for years past the town has been growing over everything and everybody so rapidly that births and deaths and marriages and family affairs generally have been swallowed up before they could be recorded.'

7. *Me and Mine*, 345–6.

GWYN THOMAS

1. [See Gwyn Jones, *Times Like These* (1935), Jack Jones, *Black Parade* (1937), Lewis Jones, *We Live* (1939), Rhys Davies, *Jubilee Blues* (1938); Idris Davies, *Gwalia Deserta* (1938) and *The Angry Summer* (1943); B. L. Coombes, *These Poor Hands* (1939); Jack Jones, *Unfinished Journey* (1937) and *Land of my Fathers: A Play* (1937).]

2. Cedric, Dylan's representative poet of the 1930s, 'will be spending the long vacation in "somewhere *really* alive. I mean, but really. Like the Rhondda Valley or something. I mean, I know I'll feel really *orientated* there . . . I mean, one's got to know the miners"'. *A Prospect of the Sea* (London: Dent, 1955).

3. [For a full list of works by Gwyn Thomas, including those published after the original edition of *DTT* and those published after Gwyn Thomas's death, see John Harris, *A Bibliographical Guide to Twenty-Four Modern Anglo-Welsh Writers* (Cardiff: University of Wales Press, 1994).]

4. H. W. J. Edwards, *The Good Patch* (London: Cape, 1938).

5. [Gwyn Thomas, *A Hatful of Humours*, ed. Brian Hammond (London: Schoolmaster Publishing, 1965), 70.]

6. [Gwyn Thomas, *All Things Betray Thee* (London: Michael Joseph, 1949), 29–30. Further references are to this edition and are given in the text.]

7. In his book *Hanes Annibynwyr Cymru* (The History of the Welsh Independents) (Swansea: Gwasg John Penry, 1966), Dr Tudur Jones, describing the protests and the activities of the Independents, the religious

denomination in which Gwyn was brought up, during the Depression, says (I translate), 'Whatever criticism can be fairly levelled at this generation of Independents, no one can accuse them of standing indifferently on one side. They shared to the full the agony of their era'. Dr Jones lists the discussions on unemployment which took place in the various assemblies of the Independents in Wales, and the deputations on the matter to Prime Ministers Ramsay Macdonald and Neville Chamberlain which they organized or took part in in 1935 and 1937.

CH. VI, INTRODUCTION TO POETRY

1. Welsh prose writers have from time to time protested against what seems to them the excessive prestige of poetry at the Eisteddfod. They point to the fact that both the major Eisteddfod awards are for a poem. Suggestions have been made that one of these, the Crown, might be awarded for a novel, a prose play or a collection of short stories.

2. [See notes 1 and 5 to Ch. II.]

3. [GJ wrote a short but technically detailed essay on Hopkins's use of Welsh traditional metres: 'Hopkins and Welsh prosody', *Life and Letters To-day* (1939), 51–4. (On the possible effect of this essay on Dylan Thomas, see the essay on Dylan Thomas in Ch. VII.) Hopkins's use of *cynghanedd* is also discussed in Anthony Conran, 'Gerard Hopkins as an Anglo-Welsh poet' in William Tydeman (ed.), *The Welsh Connection* (Llandysul: Gomer, 1986), 110–29.]

4. [See M. Wynn Thomas, '"Shaman of shifting form": Tony Conran and Welsh *barddas'*, in Nigel Jenkins (ed.), *Thirteen Ways of Looking at Tony Conran* (Cardiff: Welsh Union of Writers, 1995), 78–102.]

5. ['Trefîn' was the bardic name of Edgar Phillips, 1889–1962, who was Archdruid from 1960 to 1962. *Caniadau Trefîn* was published in 1950.]

6. 'This general interest in poetry . . . can be directly attributed to the Eisteddfod. It affected . . . not only the rural areas . . . but also the new industrial districts such as Merthyr Tydfil . . . The strict metres, the product of an aristocratic society, became (in the nineteenth century) the delight of farmers and craftsmen, coalminers and quarrymen', G. J. Williams, 'The Eisteddfod', *Welsh Review* 4/4 (Winter 1947), 259.

7. ['Gwenallt' was the bardic name of David James Jones (1899–1968). For English-language discussions of Gwenallt, see Ned Thomas, *The Welsh Extremist* (Talybont, Dyfed: Y Lolfa, 1973), ch. 4; Dyfnallt Morgan, *Gwenallt* (Writers of Wales; Cardiff: University of Wales Press, 1972); Donald Allchin and D. Densil Morgan, *Sensuous Glory: The Poetic Vision of D. Gwenallt Jones* (Norwich: Canterbury Press, 2000), which also contains translations by Patrick Thomas.]

8. See Keidrych Rhys (ed.), *Modern Welsh Poetry*, 34–5. The title of Walter Dowding's poem means 'To the old language (i. e. Welsh) and her songs'.

9. [Though see Emyr Humphreys, *Collected Poems* (Cardiff: University of Wales Press, 1999).]

10. Three of these 'elders', namely Dylan Thomas, Vernon Watkins and the present writer, were taken severely to task by some of the later generation of Anglo-Welsh writers for what seemed to them these serious deficiencies; see *Triad: Thirty Three Poems by Peter Griffith, Meic Stephens and Harri Webb* (Merthyr Tydfil: Triskel Press, 1963). [In his Introduction to the booklet, Anthony Conran writes: 'For some years now, the poetry of English-speaking Wales has had the appearance of a hangover from the great days of the Forties. Only R. S. Thomas, of recent poets, has had the guts to keep the home fires burning. But during this interregnum the situation has clarified. We are no longer satisfied with Dylan; the remnants of the school of Llaregyb are pale ghosts to us now. We had sooner have, for all his naivety, Idris Davies than Vernon Watkins or Glyn Jones. Honesty about Tonypandy or Eglwys Fach has superceded rhetoric about Poly Garters and Revivals in the Never-never land of daydreams.']

11. The Editor of *Poetry Wales* writes: 'our first commitment as our title has it, is to the craft. Our second is to the country . . . But we protest, on our contributors' behalf, that there is more sympathy for the senior literature' (i.e. Welsh-language literature) 'among us, than there was in our first heyday, twenty years ago', *Poetry Wales*, 2/1 (1966), 3. This is true, although I would regard 1946 as a second heyday. The first was unquestionably round about 1937, as I tried to show in Ch. II.

12. Gray's gusty bard would appear to have more in common with the manic twitchers described by Gerald the Welshman in Chapter XVI of *Description of Wales* than with the true poets, the officers of the princely courts with their rigidly prescribed duties. [In Thomas Gray's 'The Bard', the Welsh poet with 'Loose . . . beard and hoary hair' and 'robed in sable garb of woe, / with haggard eyes . . . ' stands on a rock 'o'er old Conway's foaming flood' and prophesies vengeance on the invading Edward I: 'Hark, how each giant-oak and desert cave / Sighs to the torrent's awful vice beneath! / O'er thee, oh king! their hundred arms they wave, / Revenge on thee in hoarser murmurs breathe; / Vocal no more, since Cambria's fatal day, / To high-born Hoel's harp or soft Llewellyn's lay'. The rest of the poem continues in a similar emotional register before the bard, in the final lines, commits suicide: '. . . headlong from the mountain's height / Deep in the roaring tide he plunged to endless night'.]

13. [Although, in recent years, the complex nature of the relations between the poets of the two traditions, and a comparison of their responses to the same historical circumstances, has begun to be examined; see, for example, M. Wynn Thomas, 'Hidden attachments: Aspects of the relationship between the two literatures of modern Wales', *Welsh Writing in English: A Yearbook of Critical Essays*, 1 (1995), 145–63, repr. in M. Wynn Thomas, *Corresponding Cultures: The Two Literatures of Wales* (Cardiff: University of Wales Press, 1999), 45–74, and the same author's discussion of Alun Lewis and Alun Llewelyn-Williams in *Internal Difference: Twentieth-Century Writing in Wales* (Cardiff: University of Wales Press, 1992), 49–67.]

14. [On R. S. Thomas, however, see Jason Walford Davies, 'Thick ambush of shadows: Allusions to Welsh literature in the work of R. S. Thomas', *Welsh Writing in English: A Yearbook of Critical Essays*, 1 (1995), 75–127.]

15. [R. Williams Parry, 'Hedd Wyn', in Alan Llwyd (ed.), *Cerddi R. Williams Parry: Y Casgliad Cyflawn 1905–1950* (Denbigh: Gwasg Gee, 1998), 59.]

16. This was pointed out by Gerald Morgan in his review of *Beirdd Benfro, Western Mail* (16 September 1961).

17. [GJ himself translated one of the most famous of *llatai* poems, Dafydd ap Gwilym's 'The Seagull', *Collected Poems of Glyn Jones*, 52–3.]

18. [For English-language discussions of Waldo Williams (1904–71), see James Nicholas, *Waldo* (Writers of Wales; Cardiff: University of Wales Press, 1975) and Ned Thomas, 'Waldo Williams and the springs of hope', *Poetry Wales*, 22/4 (1987), 66–71. Translations of the major poems will be found in Tony Conran, *The Peacemakers: Waldo Williams* (Llandysul: Gomer, 1997) which also has a substantial Introduction.]

19. Bobi Jones, the Welsh-language poet, writing critically in the magazine *Dock Leaves* about the Anglo-Welsh, says: 'But the main problem, their function as *a bulwark of civilisation* against suburban conformity, and *their relationship to the community* which has reared them and its traditions, has been only superficially dealt with', *Dock Leaves* (Spring 1953), 25–6, my italics.

20. [Harri Webb, 'Yet another Aberystwyth anthology', rev. of *Presenting Welsh Poetry*, trans. Gwyn Williams, *Wales* (November 1959), 67.]

21. Gwyn Williams also wrote *An Introduction to Welsh Poetry* (Faber, 1953) as well as *The Rent that's Due to Love* (Editions Poetry, 1950) and *The Burning Tree* (Faber, 1956), two volumes of excellent translations of Welsh poetry into English. [His translations were collected as *To Look for a Word* (Llandysul: Gomer, 1976).]

22. T. H. Jones was the author of *The Enemy in the Heart* (1957), *Songs of the Mad Prince* (1960), *The Beast at the Door* (1963) and *The Colour of Cock-crowing* (1966), all published by Hart-Davis. T. H. Jones also wrote a study of Dylan Thomas in the 'Writers and Critics' series (Edinburgh: Oliver & Boyd, 1963). [See also *The Collected Poems of T. Harri Jones*, ed. Julian Croft and Don Dale-Jones (Llandysul: Gomer, 1977).]

23. [See Alun Lewis, *Collected Stories*, ed. Cary Archard (Bridgend: Seren, 1990).]

24. [See also Roland Mathias, *Burning Brambles: Selected Poems, 1944–1979* (Llandysul: Gomer, 1983). A full bibliography will be found in John Harris, *A Bibliographical Guide to Twenty-Four Modern Anglo-Welsh Writers*. See Jeremy Hooker, 'Roland Mathias: "The strong remembered words"', *The Presence of the Past* (Bridgend: Poetry Wales Press, 1987), 141–50, and M. Wynn Thomas, '"All lenient muscles tensed": The poetry of Roland Mathias', *Poetry Wales*, 33/3 (January 1998), 21–6.]

CH. VII, THREE POETS

HUW MENAI

1. These will be found chronicled in R. Page Arnot, *South Wales Miners* (London: Allen & Unwin, 1967).
2. [The Social Democratic Federation had been founded in 1884 by H. M. Hyndman, the Marxist author of *England for All: The Text-Book of Democracy* (1881). *Justice*, founded in the same year, was the SDF journal.]
3. An Anglo-Welsh writer who really was a check-weigher was Lewis Jones (1897–1939), the Communist author of *Cwmardy* (London: Lawrence & Wishart, 1937) and *We Live* (London: Lawrence & Wishart, 1939). [For an account of Huw Menai's life and politics and an analysis of the poems, see Michael J. Dixon, 'Beyond the Slagheaps: The Marginality of Huw Menai', *Welsh Writing in English: A Yearbook of Critical Essays*, 3 (1997), 18–41.]
4. [Huw Menai, 'In a public garden', *The Simple Vision* (London: Chapman & Hall, 1945), 66.]
5. [Huw Menai, 'Back in the return', *Back in the Return and Other Poems* (London: Heinemann, 1933), 73.]
6. He also wrote *englynion* in English and attempted an English *cywydd* like Trefin's 'The Gale'. [See Huw Menai's three-part essay 'The bilingual mind', *Wales* (September 1958), 31–4; (October 1958), 8–14; (February 1959), 23–7; this was followed by a correspondence on *cynghanedd* in English between Huw Menai and Edgar Phillips (Trefin): (March 1959), 23, 26; (April 1959), 75–6; (June 1959), 51–3.]

IDRIS DAVIES

1. [In fact nine poems in Welsh by Idris Davies have survived, none of which were collected and five of which remained unpublished. Unpublished diaries also show him, in the late 1930s, studying the Welsh literary tradition. See *The Complete Poems of Idris Davies*, ed. Dafydd Johnston (Cardiff: University of Wales Press, 1944), pp. xiii–xiv, and Dafydd Johnston, 'Idris Davies a'r Gymraeg', in M. Wynn Thomas (ed.), *DiFfinio Dwy Lenyddiaeth Cymru* (Cardiff: University of Wales Press, 1995), 96–119.]
2. ['Trwbadwr y Cwm Du', *Y Cymro* (17 April 1953), 6.]
3. [On the structure of *The Angry Summer* and an argument for its essentially dramatic nature, see Tony Conran's Introduction to his edition: *The Angry Summer: A Poem of 1926* (Cardiff: University of Wales Press, 1993.]
4. In spite of Yeats's satisfaction with the idea of great wealth in the hands of a few and the rest suppliant at the gate, the chronic condition of industrial south Wales, which used to rouse in Idris frenzies of protesting indignation.
5. The excellent Penguin *Contemporary Verse* (1950) gives biographical information about the poets it includes, and this enables me to illustrate my point. Of the sixty-one poets included, more than half, I judge, went straight from their schools to Oxford or Cambridge. Of the remainder, twenty-one went to a provincial university or art school or some other

such institution, and only about four or five left school at fourteen. And not one of these, as far as I can tell, undertook, like Idris, a manual job.

DYLAN THOMAS

1. It was a poem, published over a pseudonym ['M. G. Gower'] in the *Adelphi* in April 1934. [See *Collected Poems*, 7, where the poem appears under its later title, 'Dock'.]
2. [John Malcolm Brinnin, *Dylan Thomas in America: An Intimate Journal* (London: Dent, 1956), 10.]
3. Ralph Maud, *Entrances to Dylan Thomas's Poetry* (Pittsburgh: Pittsburgh UP, 1963), 122.
4. [D. J. Thomas's uncle, William Price (1834–79) was a prominent Unitarian minister, well-known for his radical attitude to landowners on behalf of tenants. He was also a poet, whose bardic name was 'Gwilym Marles'. See Constantine FitzGibbon, *The Life of Dylan Thomas* (London: Dent, 1965), 7–9.]
5. Such things do happen. Some years ago, when music halls were commoner in London, I saw in bulbs outside one of them a – faulty – example of *cynghanedd sain* – 'Fifty Nifty Naughties'. At least, I have always assumed that the proprietor was not a student of classical Welsh poetry.
6. [The poem was published in the *Western Mail* (3 July 1960). For the text of the poem see Dylan Thomas, *The Notebook Poems 1930–1934*, ed. Ralph Maud (London: Dent, 1989), 195–9 and notes.]
7. [Compare the scene in the bohemian flat in GJ's story 'The Tower of Loss', written in the 1960s but set in the 1930s, *Collected Stories* 294-312.]
8. [Elder Olson, *The Poetry of Dylan Thomas* (Chicago: Chicago UP, 1954).]
9. E. W. Tedlock (ed.), *Dylan Thomas: The Legend and the Poet* (London: Heinemann, 1960).
10. The basis of Gwilym's sermon in 'The Peaches' I would guess to be something Dylan had heard from some revivalist on Swansea sands (e. g. Mr Matthews the 'hellfire preacher' in 'One Warm Saturday') rather than from a Welsh Nonconformist minister, like his own nice uncle David Rees, say.
11. [D. J. Williams, Saunders Lewis and Revd Lewis Valentine, imprisoned for setting fire to the bombing school at Penyberth in 1936.]
12. A rather un-Welsh writer, in fact, since the phenomenon of bohemianism, a product of large cities, hardly exists for the poets of Welsh Wales, who are salaried amateurs, not rentiers or literary hacks. It is difficult to be a dedicated bohemian if you have a steady job and live in Aberystwyth. Welsh Wales has no literary capital unless it is the *maes* [field] of the National Eisteddfod.
13. [Correspondence between the two writers, as well as other textual evidence, confirms what GJ suggests in Ch. V, that the trip to meet Caradoc Evans took place in 1934.]
14. [However, GJ had already begun to write short stories, before his meeting with Dylan Thomas; see the discussion of the relations between the two men and their writing in *Collected Stories*, xxxi–xxxiv.]

15. [Compare the ferry in GJ's story 'The Wanderer', *Collected Stories*, 110–18.]
16. [One of GJ's unpublished journals, now in the National Library of Wales, contains an account of GJ's visit to Laugharne, indicating that it took place on 15 October 1949. Much of the journal entry is incorporated directly into the *DTT* account, though in the journal GJ describes the return to the Boathouse after his discussion with Dylan about the radio talk:

At the end of two hours we went down to the cottage. Caitlin was there and Colm Garan, the 6 months (?) baby. Eiron(wy) [sic] was out. Llewellyn was away in school. The ratcatcher had been there and a workman was blocking up the holes.

There is no bannister there, but a rope.

We had a meal. Were Dylan and his wife not on good terms? [*inserted at foot of the page:* Does she resent having another baby? She was in bathing the day he was born.] She appeared to be indifferent and he very uxorious. She was at times, I thought, hostile to Dylan, and said, 'I thought you weren't going to broadcast any [?more]. And this, giving away your secrets'. The meal was copious but I had nothing to drink as only beer was available. 'We don't often have a teetotaller in this house', said Dylan.

Earlier, at the beginning of his account of their discussion of the radio talk, GJ writes in Welsh (the rest of the account of his visit being in English):

Byddwn yn teimlo yn gartrefol bob amser gyda Dylan, y mae 'fflow' rhyngom, yr ydym yn gallu chwerthin gyda'n gilydd. I'r sawl sydd ddim yn gofyn trefn, a dawn fusnes etc., y mae ef yn hawdd iawn i ddod ymlaen ag ef. Nid oes dim balchder o gwbl yn ei natur. Bob amser y byddem yn cwrdd byddwn yn syrthio dan dylanwad ei swyn.
[I always felt comfortable with Dylan, there's a 'flow' between us, we are able to laugh together. For those who don't ask order or a business sense, it is very easy to get along with him. There is no pride in his nature at all. Every time we met, I would fall under the influence of his charm.]

17. *Druid of the Broken Body*, an assessment of Dylan Thomas as a religious poet, by Aneirin Talfan Davies (London: Dent, 1964), had not appeared when these words were written.

CH. VIII, CONCLUSION

1. [*Cywyddau brud*: *cywyddau* of prophecy; *marwnadau*: elegies; *cywyddau gofyn*: *cywyddau* of asking (see p. 126).]
2. [Saunders Lewis, *Is there an Anglo-Welsh Literature?* (Cardiff: University of Wales Guild of Graduates, 1939), 11.]

BIBLIOGRAPHY

The original edition of *The Dragon has Two Tongues* had a 'Bibliographical Note' which listed the books of the six authors discussed in individual chapters plus a quite detailed account of the limited amount of material on Welsh writing in English available in 1968, almost entirely in magazines. Since then, of course, the volume of critical material has developed to a degree by which Glyn Jones felt surprised and gratified. He expressed the view that in a new edition there should be up-to-date bibliographical information, for the information of students and others coming to the English-language literature of Wales for the first time.

CARADOC EVANS

My People. London: Andrew Melrose, 1915 (short stories).
Capel Sion. London: Andrew Melrose, 1916 (short stories).
My Neighbours. London: Andrew Melrose, 1919 (short stories).
Taffy. London: Andrew Melrose, 1914 (play).
Nothing to Pay. London: Faber, 1930 (novel).
Wasps. London: Rich & Cowan, 1933 (novel).
This Way to Heaven. London: Rich & Cowan, 1934 (novel).
Pilgrims in a Foreign Land. London: Andrew Dakers, 1942 (short stories).
Morgan Bible. London: Andrew Dakers, 1943 (novel).
The Earth Gives All and Takes All. London: Andrew Dakers, 1946 (short stories).
Mother's Marvel. London: Andrew Dakers, 1949 (novel).

Editions

Fury Never Leaves Us: A Miscellany of Caradoc Evans. Ed. John Harris. Bridgend: Poetry Wales Press, 1985.
My People. Ed. and introduced by John Harris. Bridgend: Seren, 1987.
Nothing to Pay. Ed., with Afterword, by John Harris. Manchester: Carcanet, 1989.
Selected Stories. Ed. John Harris. Manchester: Carcanet, 1993.

Selected Criticism

Gramich, Katie, 'The Madwoman in the Harness-loft: Women and Madness in the Literatures of Wales', in Katie Gramich and Andrew Hiscock (eds.), *Dangerous Diversity: The Changing Faces of Wales* (Cardiff: University of Wales Press, 1998), 20–33.

Harris, John, 'Publishing *My People*: The Book as Expressive Object', *New Welsh Review*, 1 (Summer 1988), 23–30.

—— 'The Devil in Eden: Caradoc Evans and his Wales', *New Welsh Review*, 19 (Winter 1992–93), 10–18.

—— 'Novel to Play: The Trials of *Taffy*', in Sam Adams (ed.), *Seeing Wales Whole: Essays on the Literature of Wales* (Cardiff: University of Wales Press, 1998), 25–54.

Jones, Gwyn, 'A Mighty Man in Sion: Caradoc Evans (1878–1945)'. *Background to Dylan Thomas and Other Explorations* (Oxford: Oxford University Press, 1992), 72–88.

Rees, W. J., 'Inequalities: Caradoc Evans and D. J. Williams: A Problem in Literary Sociology', *Planet*, 81 (June/July 1990), 69–80.

Thomas, M. Wynn, '*My People* and the Revenge of the Novel', *New Welsh Review*, 1 (Summer 1988), 17–22.

Wiliams, Gerwyn, 'Gwerin Dau Garadog', in M. Wynn Thomas (ed.), *DiFfinio Dwy Lenyddiaeth Cymru* (Cardiff: University of Wales Press, 1995), 42–79.

Williams, Trevor, *Caradoc Evans* (Writers of Wales; Cardiff: University of Wales Press, 1970).

JACK JONES

Rhondda Roundabout. London: Faber, 1934 (novel).
Black Parade. London: Faber, 1934 (novel).
Land of my Fathers. London: French, 1937 (play).
Unfinished Journey. London: Hamish Hamilton, 1937 (autobiography).
Bidden to the Feast. London: Hamish Hamilton, 1938 (novel).
Rhondda Roundabout. London: Hamish Hamilton, 1939 (play).
The Man David. London: Hamish Hamilton, 1944 (biography).
Me and Mine. London: Hamish Hamilton, 1946 (autobiography).
Off to Philadelphia in the Morning. London: Hamish Hamilton, 1947 (novel).
Transatlantic Episode. London: French, 1947 (play).
Some Trust in Chariots. London: Hamish Hamilton, 1948 (novel).
Give me Back my Heart. London: Hamish Hamilton, 1950 (autobiography).
River out of Eden. London: Hamish Hamilton, 1951 (novel).
Lily of the Valley. London: Hamish Hamilton, 1952 (novel).
Lucky Lear. London: Hamish Hamilton, 1952 (novel).
Time and the Business. London: Hamish Hamilton, 1953 (novel).
Choral Symphony. London: Hamish Hamilton, 1955 (novel).
Come Night, End Day. London: Hamish Hamilton, 1956 (novel).

Selected Criticism

Davies, James A., 'Kinds of Relating: Gwyn Thomas (Jack Jones, Lewis Jones, Gwyn Jones) and the Welsh Industrial Novel', *Anglo-Welsh Review*, 86 (1987), 72–86.

Edwards, Keri, *Jack Jones* (Writers of Wales; Cardiff: University of Wales Press, 1974).

Hughes, Glyn Tegai, 'The Mythology of the Mining Valleys', in Sam Adams and Gwilym Rees Hughes (eds), *Triskel Two: Essays on Welsh and Anglo-Welsh Literature* (Llandybïe: Christopher Davies, 1973), 42–61.

Smith, Dai, *Aneurin Bevan and the World of South Wales* (Cardiff: University of Wales Press, 1993), Ch. 5, pp. 115–39. Jack Jones is discussed with other writers of industrial south Wales.

Williams, Raymond, 'Working-class, Proletarian, Socialist: Problems in Some Welsh Novels', in H. Gustav Klaus (ed.), *The Socialist Novel in Britain: Towards the Recovery of a Tradition* (Brighton: Harvester, 1982), 110–21.

GWYN THOMAS

The Dark Philosophers. London: Dobson, 1946 (novel).

Where did I put my Pity? London: Progress Publishing Co, 1946 (short stories).

The Alone to the Alone. London: Nicholson & Watson, 1947 (novel).

All Things Betray Thee. London: Michael Joseph, 1949 (novel).

The World Cannot Hear You. London: Gollancz, 1951 (novel).

Now Lead us Home. London: Gollancz, 1952 (novel).

A Frost on my Frolic. London: Gollancz, 1953 (novel).

The Stranger at my Side. London: Gollancz, 1954 (novel).

A Point of Order. London: Gollancz, 1956 (novel).

Gazooka and other stories. London: Gollancz, 1957.

The Love Man. London: Gollancz, 1958 (novel).

Ring Delirium 123. London: Gollancz, 1960 (short stories).

The Keep. London: Elek, 1962 (play).

A Welsh Eye. London: Hutchinson, 1964 (essays).

A Hatful of Humours. London: Schoolmaster Publishing, 1965 (articles from *The Teacher*).

The Loot. London: Cassell, 1965 (play).

A Few Selected Exits. London: Hutchinson, 1968; rpr. Seren, 1985 (autobiography).

The Lust Lobby. London: Hutchinson, 1971 (stories).

The Sky of Our Lives. London: Hutchinson, 1978 (three novellas).

Selected Short Stories. Bridgend: Poetry Wales Press, 1984; rpr. Seren, 1988.

Sorrow for Thy Sons. Intro. Dai Smith. London: Lawrence & Wishart, 1986 (novel).

The Thinker and the Thrush. Intro. Michael Parnell. London: Lawrence & Wishart, 1988 (novel).

Editions

Three Plays. Ed. Michael Parnell. Bridgend: Seren, 1990 (*The Keep, Jackie the Jumper, Loud Organs*).
Meadow Prospect Revisited. Ed. Michael Parnell. Bridgend: Seren, 1992 (stories).

Selected Criticism

Davies, James A., 'Kinds of Relating: Gwyn Thomas (Jack Jones, Lewis Jones, Gwyn Jones) and the Welsh Industrial Novel', *Anglo-Welsh Review*, 86 (1987), 72–86.
George, Philip, 'Three Rhondda Working Class Writers', *Llafur*, 3/2 (1981), 5–13.
Golightly, Victor, 'Gwyn Thomas's American "Oscar"', *New Welsh Review*, 22 (Autumn 1993), 26–31.
—— '"We, who speak for the workers": The Correspondence of Gwyn Thomas and Howard Fast', *Welsh Writing in English: A Yearbook of Critical Essays*, 6 (2000), 67–88.
Jones, Roger Stephens, 'Absurdity in the Novels of Gwyn Thomas', *Anglo-Welsh Review*, 56 (1976), 43–52.
Michael, Ian, *Gwyn Thomas* (Writers of Wales; Cardiff: University of Wales Press, 1977).
Parnell, Michael, *Laughter from the Dark: A Life of Gwyn Thomas* (London: John Murray, 1988).
Smith, Dai, 'Breaking Silence: Gwyn Thomas and the Pre-history of Welsh Working-class Fiction', in Clive Emsley and James Walvin (eds.), *Artisans, Peasants and Proletarians, 1760–1860: Essays Presented to Gwyn A. Williams*. (London: Croom Helm, 1985), 104–23.
—— 'The Darkest Philosopher', *Aneurin Bevan and the World of South Wales* (Cardiff: University of Wales Press, 1993), 140–58.
Williams, Raymond, *The Welsh Industrial Novel*, Inaugural Gwyn Jones Lecture (Cardiff: University College Cardiff Press, 1979).
—— 'Working-class, Proletarian, Socialist: Problems in Some Welsh Novels', in H. Gustav Klaus (ed.), *The Socialist Novel in Britain: Towards the Recovery of a Tradition* (Brighton: Harvester, 1982), 110–21.

HUW MENAI

Through the Upcast Shaft. London: Hodder & Stoughton, 1920 (poems).
The Passing of Guto. London: Hogarth, 1929 (poems).
Back in the Return. London: Heinemann, 1933 (poems).
The Simple Vision. London: Chapman & Hall, 1945 (poems).

Selected Criticism

Conran, Anthony, 'Huw Menai: Trapped Between Worlds', *The Cost of Strangeness: Essays on the English Poets of Wales* (Llandysul: Gomer, 1982), 77–103.

Dixon, Michael J., 'Beyond the Slagheaps: The Marginality of Huw Menai', *Welsh Writing in English: A Yearbook of Critical Essays*, 3 (1997), 18–41.

IDRIS DAVIES

Gwalia Deserta. London: Dent, 1938 (poems).
The Angry Summer: A Poem of 1926. London: Faber, 1943 (poems).
Tonypandy and Other Poems. London: Faber, 1945 (poems).
Selected Poems. London: Faber, 1953.
Fe'm Ganed i yn Rhymni/I was Born in Rhymney. Intro. R. George Thomas. Llandysul: Gomer, 1990 (prose extracts and poems, five in Welsh).

Editions

Collected Poems of Idris Davies. Ed. Islwyn Jenkins. Llandysul: Gomerian Press, 1972.
The Angry Summer: A Poem of 1926. Intro. Tony Conran. Cardiff: University of Wales Press, 1993.
The Complete Poems of Idris Davies. Ed. Dafydd Johnston. Cardiff: University of Wales Press, 1994.

Selected Criticism

Conran, Anthony, 'The Achievement of Idris Davies', *The Cost of Strangeness: Essays on the English Poets of Wales* (Llandysul: Gomer, 1982), 104–54.
—— 'Welsh Studies "come of age"' [essay-review of the *Complete Poems*], *New Welsh Review*, 29 (Autumn 1995), 9–12.
Jenkins, Islwyn, *Idris Davies* (Writers of Wales; Cardiff: University of Wales Press, 1972).
Johnston, Dafydd, 'Dwy Lenyddiaeth Cymru yn y Tridegau', in John Rowlands (ed.), *Sglefrio ar Eiriau* (Llandysul: Gomer, 1992), 51–62: compares Davies with Gwenallt.
—— 'Idris Davies a'r Gymraeg', in M. Wynn Thomas (ed.), *DiFfinio Dwy Lenyddiaeth Cymru* (Cardiff: University of Wales Press, 1995), 96–119.
Jones, Roger Stephens, 'The Angry Summer: An Essay on the Structure of Idris Davies's Poem', *Planet*, 37–8 (1977), 21–8.

See also:

Poetry Wales, 16/4 (1981): Idris Davies Special Issue. Contains fifteen previously uncollected poems and extracts from the poet's diaries and includes, among other essays, Richard Poole, 'Idris Davies: The Bitter Dreamer'; John Pikoulis, 'The Watcher on the Mountain: The Poetry of Idris Davies'; Ioan Williams, 'Two Welsh Poets: James Kitchener Davies (1902–52); Idris Davies (1905–53)'; Tony Bianchi, 'Idris Davies and the Politics of Anger'.

DYLAN THOMAS

Eighteen Poems. London: Sunday Referee and the Parton Bookshop, 1934.
Twenty-five Poems. London: Dent, 1936.
The Map of Love. London: Dent, 1939 (stories and poems).
Portrait of the Artist as a Young Dog. London: Dent, 1940 (short stories).
Deaths and Entrances. London: Dent, 1946 (poems).
Collected Poems 1934–1952. London: Dent, 1952.
The Doctor and the Devils. London: Dent, 1953 (filmscript).
Under Milk Wood. London: Dent, 1954 (play).
Quite Early One Morning. London: Dent, 1954 (broadcast material).
A Prospect of the Sea. London: Dent, 1955 (short stories).
Adventures in the Skin Trade. London: Putnam, 1955 (novel).

Editions

Poet in the Making: The Notebooks of Dylan Thomas. Ed. Ralph Maud. London: Dent, 1968.
The Poems. Ed. Daniel Jones. London: Dent, 1971.
Early Prose Writings. Ed. Walford Davies. London: Dent, 1971.
Selected Poems. Ed. Walford Davies. London: Dent, 1974. Rev. edn. Dent (Everyman), 1993.
The Collected Stories. Ed. Walford Davies. Intro. Leslie Norris. London: Dent, 1983. Rpr. Dent (Everyman), 1993.
The Collected Letters of Dylan Thomas. Ed. Paul Ferris. London: Dent, 1985. Rpr. Paladin, 1987. New edn, Dent, 2000.
Collected Poems, 1934–1953. Ed. Walford Davies and Ralph Maud. London: Dent, 1988. Rpr. Dent (Everyman), 1991.
The Notebook Poems, 1930–1934. Ed. Ralph Maud. London: Dent, 1989. Rpr. Dent (Everyman), 1990.
The Broadcasts. Ed. Ralph Maud. London: Dent, 1991.
The Film Scripts. Ed. John Ackerman. London: Dent, 1995.
Under Milk Wood: The Definitive Edition. Ed. Walford Davies and Ralph Maud. London: Dent, 1995.

Selected Criticism

Ackerman, John, *A Dylan Thomas Companion: Life, Poetry and Prose* (London: Macmillan, 1991).
Cleverdon, Douglas, *The Growth of Milk Wood* (London: Dent, 1969).

Conran, Anthony, *The Cost of Strangeness: Essays on the English Poets of Wales* (Llandysul: Gomer, 1982), 169–88.

Cox, C. B. (ed.), *Dylan Thomas: A Collection of Critical Essays* (Englewood Cliffs, NJ: Prentice-Hall, 1966).

Davies, Aneirin Talfan, *Dylan: Druid of the Broken Body* (Swansea: Christopher Davies, rev. edn. 1977).

Davies, James A., *A Reference Companion to Dylan Thomas* (Westport, CT: Greenwood, 1998), includes extensive material on the critical reception of Thomas's work.

Davies, Walford, *Dylan Thomas: New Critical Essays* (London: Dent, 1972).

—— *Dylan Thomas* (Writers of Wales; Cardiff: University of Wales Press, 1972; rev. edn. 1990).

—— *Dylan Thomas* (Milton Keynes: Open University Press, 1986).

—— 'Bright Fields, Loud Hills and the Glimpsed Good Place: R. S. Thomas and Dylan Thomas', in M. Wynn Thomas (ed.), *The Page's Drift: R. S. Thomas at Eighty* (Bridgend: Seren, 1993).

Heaney, Seamus, 'Dylan the Durable', *The Redress of Poetry* (London: Faber, 1995), 124–45.

Jones, T. Harri, *Dylan Thomas* (Edinburgh: Oliver & Boyd, 1963).

Loesche, Katherine T., 'Welsh Poetic Syntax and the Poetry of Dylan Thomas', *Transactions of the Honourable Society of the Cymmrodorion* (1979), 159–202.

Mathias, Roland, *A Ride through the Wood: Essays on Anglo-Welsh Literature* (Bridgend: Poetry Wales Press, 1985), 57–87.

Maud, Ralph, *Entrances to Dylan Thomas's Poetry* (Pittsburgh: University of Pittsburgh Press, 1963).

Moynihan, William T., *The Craft and Art of Dylan Thomas* (London: Oxford University Press, 1966).

Tedlock, E. W. (ed.), *Dylan Thomas, the Legend and the Poet* (London: Heinemann, 1960).

WELSH WRITING IN ENGLISH: A SELECTIVE BIBLIOGRAPHY

Bibliographical / Reference

Harris, John, *A Bibliographical Guide to Twenty-Four Modern Anglo-Welsh Writers* (Cardiff: University of Wales Press, 1994).

Jones, Brynmor, *A Bibliography of Anglo-Welsh Literature, 1900–1965* (Cardiff: Library Association, 1970).

Jones, Glyn and Rowlands, John, *Profiles* (Llandysul: Gomer, 1980).

Stephens, Meic (ed.), *The New Companion to the Literature of Wales* (Cardiff: University of Wales Press, 1998).

See also the annual bibliographies of critical work, compiled by John Harris, published annually in the journal *Welsh Writing in English: A Yearbook of Critical Essays* for the years from 1993 onwards.

Literary History

Burnham, Richard, '*The Dublin Magazine*'s Welsh Poets', *Anglo-Welsh Review*, 60 (1978), 49–63.

Garlick, Raymond, *An Introduction to Anglo-Welsh Literature* (Writers of Wales; 2nd edn.; Cardiff: University of Wales Press, 1972).

Johnston, Dafydd, *The Literature of Wales* (Pocket Guide; Cardiff: University of Wales Press, 1994).

Jones, Gwyn, 'The First Forty Years: Some Notes on Anglo-Welsh Literature', in Sam Adams and G. R. Hughes (eds), *Triskel One: Essays on Welsh and Anglo-Welsh Literature* (Swansea: Christopher Davies, 1971); rpr. in Gwyn Jones, *Background to Dylan Thomas* (Oxford: Oxford University Press, 1992).

Knight, Stephen, 'How Red was My Valley?: The Working Class Novel in Wales', *Planet*, 98 (1993), 83–94.

Lewis, Peter Elfed, 'Poetry in the Thirties: A View of the "First Flowering"', *Anglo-Welsh Review*, 71 (1982), 50–74.

Mathias, Roland, *Anglo-Welsh Literature: An Illustrated History* (Bridgend: Poetry Wales Press, 1986).

Discursive/Theoretical Essays on 'Anglo-Welsh' Writing

Barnie, John, 'The Anglo-Welsh Tradition', *The King of Ashes* (Llandysul: Gomer, 1989).

Conran, Tony, 'Ye Bryttish Poets: Some Observations on Anglo-Welsh poetry', *Anglo-Welsh Review*, 84 (1986), 8–18.

—— 'Modernism in Anglo-Welsh poetry', in Nigel Jenkins (ed.), *The Works: The Welsh Union of Writers' Annual* (Cardiff: Welsh Union of Writers, 1991).

—— '"Anglo-Welsh" Revisited', *Planet*, 108 (1995), 28–34.

Jones, Bobi, 'The Anglo-Welsh', *Dock Leaves* 4/10 (1953), 23–8.

—— 'Anglo-Welsh: More Definition', *Planet*, 16 (1973), 11–23.

—— 'Demise of the Anglo-Welsh?' *Poetry Wales*, 28/3 (1993), 14–18.

Lewis, Saunders, *Is There An Anglo-Welsh Literature?* (Cardiff: Guild of Graduates, 1939).

Thomas, M. Wynn, 'Hidden Attachments: Aspects of the Two Literatures of Modern Wales', *Welsh Writing in English: A Yearbook of Critical Essays*, 1 (1995), 145–63.

Thomas, R. S., 'Anglo-Welsh Literature', in Sandra Anstey (ed.) (3rd edn.), *Selected Prose* (Bridgend: Seren, 1995, 41–4); originally 'Llenyddiaeth Eingl-Cymreig', *Y Fflam* (1952).

Critical

Adams, Sam, *Seeing Wales Whole: Essays on the Literature of Wales* (Cardiff: University of Wales Press, 1998).

—— and Gwilym Rees Hughes (eds.), *Triskel One: Essays on Welsh and Anglo-Welsh Literature* (Swansea: Christopher Davies, 1971). *Triskel Two* (1973).

Bianchi, Tony, 'Aztecs in Troedrhiwgwair: Recent Fictions in Wales', in Ian A. Bell (ed.), *Peripheral Visions: Images of Nationhood in Contemporary British Fiction* (Cardiff: University of Wales Press, 1995), 44–76.

Conran, Anthony, *The Cost of Strangeness: Essays on the English Poets of Wales* (Llandysul: Gomer, 1982).

—— *Frontiers in Anglo-Welsh Poetry* (Cardiff: University of Wales Press, 1997).

Curtis, Tony (ed.), *Wales: The Imagined Nation, Essays in Cultural and National Identity* (Bridgend: Poetry Wales Press, 1986).

Gramich, Katie and Andrew Hiscock (eds.), *Dangerous Diversity: The Changing Faces of Wales* (Cardiff: University of Wales Press, 1998).

Hooker, Jeremy, *The Presence of the Past* (Bridgend: Poetry Wales Press, 1987).

Humfrey, Belinda, *Fire Green as Grass: The Creative Impulse in Anglo-Welsh Poetry and Short Story in the Twentieth Century* (Llandysul: Gomer, 1994).

Jones, Gwyn, *Background to Dylan Thomas and Other Explorations* (Oxford: Oxford University Press, 1992).

Ludwig, Hans-Werner and Fietz Lothar (eds.), *Poetry in the British Isles: Non-Metropolitan Perspectives* (Cardiff: University of Wales Press, 1985).

Mathias, Roland, *A Ride through the Wood: Essays on Anglo-Welsh Literature* (Bridgend: Poetry Wales Press, 1985).

Thomas, M. Wynn, *Internal Difference: Twentieth-Century Writing in Wales* (Cardiff: University of Wales Press, 1992).

—— (ed.), *DiFfinio Dwy Lenyddiaeth Cymru* (Cardiff: University of Wales Press, 1995).

—— *Corresponding Cultures: The Two Literatures of Wales* (Cardiff: University of Wales Press, 1999).

Tydeman, William (ed.), *The Welsh Connection* (Llandysul: Gomer, 1988).

Literary/Critical Journals

Wales (1st ser. 1937–9; 2nd ser. 1943–9; 3rd ser. 1958–9).

The Welsh Review (1st ser. 1939; 2nd ser. 1944–8).

Life and Letters To-day. The monthly numbers of *Life and Letters To-day* between 1938 and 1950 contain work about and by many Anglo-Welsh writers, including Alun Lewis, Keidrych Rhys, Dylan Thomas, Idris Davies, Geraint Goodwin, Gwyn Jones, Margiad Evans, George Ewart Evans, Con Morgan, Brenda Chamberlain and Vernon Watkins. Several numbers during these years (March 1940, 1943, 1946, 1947, September 1948) are 'Welsh' numbers.

Dock Leaves (1949–57; became *The Anglo-Welsh Review* in 1957).

The Anglo-Welsh Review (1957–88).

Poetry Wales (1965–).

Planet (1970–80 and 1985–).

The New Welsh Review (1988–).

Welsh Writing in English: A Yearbook of Critical Essays (1995–).

INDEX